ADVENTURES IN CARD PLAY

Here is a bridge book with a difference – a book that begins where most others leave off. It springs from a combination of two rare talents.

Géza Ottlik – Hungarian bridge writer turned novelist – who nowadays writes about bridge only as a form of relaxation, has an unmatched genius for discovering and analysing strange and fascinating aspects of advanced play that have been overlooked by other writers.

Hugh Kelsey – Scottish novelist turned bridge writer – a grand master of bridge whose books have been acclaimed throughout the world, is renowned especially for skilful high-level analysis and the ability to express complex ideas in simple prose.

The result of this collaboration is a remarkable book of unusual power. The reader who embarks on these 'adventures' must expect to face a stern intellectual challenge. His imagination will be stimulated, however, and his aesthetic sense cultivated in such a way that he may be able to take an almost lyrical delight in the contemplation of the structural beauty of certain combinations of cards.

When *Adventures in Card Play* was published originally it received a remarkable press. Here is a selection of some of the many enthusiastic notices:

'Will undoubtedly take its place among the classics on play and defence.'   – R.A. Priday, *Sunday Telegraph*

'Exciting and original'   – Eric Bowtell, *Oxford Times*

'A most remarkable book'
     – E.P.C. Cotter, *Financial Times*

Also by Hugh Kelsey

DOUBLE SQUEEZES
STRIP-SQUEEZES
SIMPLE SQUEEZES
IMPROVE YOUR PARTNER'S DEFENCE
SHARPEN YOUR BRIDGE TECHNIQUE
WINNING CARD PLAY
SLAM BIDDING
LOGICAL BRIDGE PLAY
TEST YOUR DEFENSIVE PLAY
TEST YOUR PAIRS PLAY
TEST YOUR FINESSING
TEST YOUR TRUMP CONTROL
TEST YOUR COMMUNICATIONS
TEST YOUR CARD-READING
TEST YOUR TIMING
TEST YOUR PERCENTAGES
TEST YOUR ELIMINATION PLAY
TEST YOUR SAFETY PLAY
INSTANT GUIDE TO BRIDGE
START BRIDGE THE EASY WAY
MASTER PERCENTAGES IN BRIDGE
MASTER FINESSING
MASTER SLAM BIDDING
MASTER SIGNALS
MASTER DOUBLES (with Ron Klinger)
BRIDGE ODDS FOR PRACTICAL PLAYERS
(with Michael Glauert)
IMPROVE YOUR OPENING LEADS (with John Matheson)

ADVENTURES IN CARD PLAY

Géza Ottlik and Hugh Kelsey

LONDON
VICTOR GOLLANCZ LTD
in association with Peter Crawley
1989

First published in Great Britain April 1979
in association with Peter Crawley
by Victor Gollancz Ltd
14 Henrietta Street, London WC2E 8QJ
This edition first published October 1983
Second impression September 1986
Third impression September 1989

British Library Cataloguing in Publication Data
Ottlik, Géza
  Adventures in card play.
  1. Contract bridge.
  I. Title   II. Kelsey, H.W.
  795.4153   GV1282.3
  ISBN 0–575–03365–7

Printed in Great Britain by
WBC Print Ltd, Bristol

Contents

	Acknowledgments	*page* 6
	Preface	7
1	Changing Your Tack	9
2	Finesses to Take – and to Avoid	28
3	Entry Squeezes	49
4	Caught in the Backwash	63
5	Shifting Threats	81
6	Tricks With Trumps	105
7	Elopement for All	122
8	The Fiercer Trump Squeezes	141
9	Entry-Shifting Without Trumps	164
10	Non-Material Squeezes	178
11	Non-Material Finesses	200
12	Non-Material Throw-Ins	213
13	Adjusting the Hand Pattern	226
14	Non-Material Dummy Reversals	241
15	It's a Knockout	253
16	The Entry Squeeze Revisited	269

Acknowledgments

The authors are grateful to Edgar Kaplan and Jeff Rubens for permission to use material from Géza Ottlik's articles first published in *The Bridge World*.

Preface

Are you an experienced player with a fair grasp of advanced techniques? If so, you may find both profit and pleasure in joining our expedition. We are starting out on a voyage of discovery, the object of which is to demonstrate that bridge is by no means 'played out'. In an attempt to penetrate the mysteries that surround our game we shall be following unfamiliar paths of card play, crossing uncharted seas and exploring unknown shores.

Our purpose is not so much to instruct as to learn. By the very act of setting down on paper ideas that we do not fully understand we hope to shed some light in dark corners and perhaps to advance the frontiers of knowledge a little.

Those who come along with us will need to be tough, resilient and hard-working. There is no room for passengers on this trip. You will need to have all your wits about you to cope with the trials and dangers that lie ahead, and there may be times when you will wish you had stayed at home. If you have a taste for adventure, however, we can promise that the journey will be worth while.

I

Changing Your Tack

As every schoolboy knows, the shortest distance between two points is a straight line. The proposition is fine in theory but of dubious practical value, for the schoolboy soon discovers that any attempt to move in a straight line is apt to end painfully in a hacked shin or bleeding nose. For thousands of years sailors have recognized that the only way of making progress against a head wind is to plot a zigzag course. And it is much the same in the play of the cards. Although you are heading towards a fixed point, the fulfilment or the defeat of the contract, you have to do a lot of tacking to take advantage of changing winds, and at times you may have to haul hard about to avoid foundering on an unsuspected reef or shoal.

What do you do, for instance, if declarer plays a diamond?

Well, in general, you will either follow suit, discard or ruff. Of course, you may face your hand and claim the rest or, exceptionally, hurl your cards along with the ashtray and anything else that comes to hand at your partner's head. More probably you will suppress your violent impulses, and you may even, of all things, single out and play the right card to the trick.

Yes, but what do you do in particular on a late September day of unusual splendour, having arrived at this little lake-side resort, looked in vain for your friend's yacht all along the waterfront, returned to the hotel and found yourself in no time at a bridge table in a team-of-four tournament, if declarer leads a diamond from dummy?

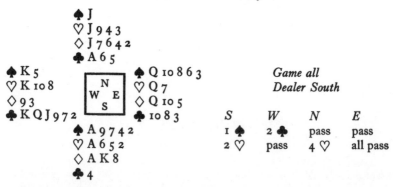

```
                    ♠ J
                    ♡ J 9 4 3
                    ◇ J 7 6 4 2
                    ♣ A 6 5
♠ K 5                                   ♠ Q 10 8 6 3        Game all
♡ K 10 8          ┌─────┐              ♡ Q 7              Dealer South
◇ 9 3             │  N  │              ◇ Q 10 5
♣ K Q J 9 7 2     │W   E│              ♣ 10 8 3
                  │  S  │                               S      W      N      E
                  └─────┘                               1 ♠    2 ♣    pass   pass
                    ♠ A 9 7 4 2                         2 ♡    pass   4 ♡    all pass
                    ♡ A 6 5 2
                    ◇ A K 8
                    ♣ 4
```

You were East, and partner had led the king of clubs to the ace. Declarer ruffed a club, cashed ace and king of diamonds, and led a low heart to the eight, nine and queen. You had to think for quite a while about the possible distributions, and you decided finally on a spade shift – queen, ace, five.

Now, as the cards lie, declarer is home if he plays the heart ace and concedes a diamond. But there is danger in this course, for if the defence can draw a third trump after taking the diamond, declarer is sunk. So he led his diamond to your queen. That was what you hoped for; you returned a spade for dummy to ruff. At this point if declarer cashes the heart ace, ruffs a spade and leads an established diamond, partner will ruff and dummy's remaining diamond will be stranded. Should declarer play a diamond at once you can ruff with your 'worthless' trump. And if he tries club ruff, spade, partner will find the counter – heart king, club. So you are ready for whatever line declarer chooses.

But declarer – a competent foreign player – didn't lead anything but sank into a long meditation. You sat back, satisfied, your defence settled. Somebody, a hand at the yard, had told you that the *Cormorant*, your friend's yawl and one of the few unadulterated good things of life, sailed off with a fine morning breeze for a cruise round the big lake and can't be expected back before Monday – three days hence. You should have sent a cable last night. Only, last night you didn't dream of coming down this morning. You may try a phone call before dinner to a mutual friend, a yachtsman berthed not too far away. Or you may catch the *Cormorant* up by rail. . . .

Declarer stirred, fidgeted, ill at ease, but didn't lead anything. You returned from the cockpit of the *Cormorant* and your nostalgic memories of tacking about, beating to windward or sailing majestically before the wind under a blazing blue full-summer sky and, having nothing better to do, you reconsidered the position at the table.

Obviously declarer does not have the ten of hearts. If he now plays a diamond from the table, you ruff. . . . Oh, what is that? He will over-ruff with the ace and, heavens! Partner will be fixed. He dare not ruff a spade lead with his king, for declarer will pitch the club from dummy . . . and if he lets the table ruff, declarer will escape with a club ruff and another spade lead towards dummy's bare jack of trumps.

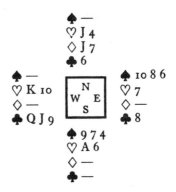

♠ —
♡ J 4
◇ J 7
♣ 6

♠ —   ♠ 10 8 6
♡ K 10   ♡ 7
◇ —   ◇ —
♣ Q J 9 ♣ 8

♠ 9 7 4
♡ A 6
◇ —
♣ —

Have you no defence, then? Yes, you have. You won't ruff the diamond lead after all (although this was the original purpose of your spade attack); you will throw your club. If South discards, West will ruff with the ten of hearts and return a club, and your seven of hearts will knock out declarer's ace. Phew! A lucky escape! If declarer had led a diamond without delay you would have played your trump. . . . But since he planned his play on alternate tacks, he presumed that you were aware all the time of *your* alternative defence, the club discard.

Were you on the wrong course in attacking dummy's trump entries? Not at all. Any other defence yields the contract easily. But you had to veer, to alter your bearing suddenly when the rocks ahead became visible. You beat the declarer's *coup en passant* by means of an 'uppercut', a device belonging to the same family of card plays. The defence isn't very hard to spot even if you don't call it anything (or call it a thingummyjig), but it helps to fix it in your memory if you can give it a proper name.

Declarer actually continued: club ruff, spade. West ruffed with the king of hearts and returned a club. South ruffed with the ace and led another spade, but partner's ten of hearts forced out dummy's jack and promoted the setting trick for your seven of hearts.

It was brought home to you how easy it is to overlook an alternate tack as declarer when you played this three no trump hand a little later.

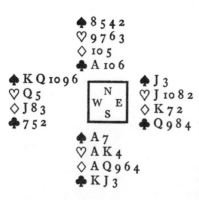

♠ 8 5 4 2
♡ 9 7 6 3
◇ 10 5
♣ A 10 6

♠ K Q 10 9 6
♡ Q 5
◇ J 8 3
♣ 7 5 2

♠ J 3
♡ J 10 8 2
◇ K 7 2
♣ Q 9 8 4

♠ A 7
♡ A K 4
◇ A Q 9 6 4
♣ K J 3

West led the king of spades, East played the jack, and you held up your ace until the second round. You had to hope for an even diamond split and the king with East. Needing two entries in dummy for your 'avoidance play', you led the club jack. This could work in two ways: either a cover by West or a win by East gives you the entries you need. But East thought for a while and then ducked. An excellent gambit, presenting you with a club trick while denying you two extra diamond tricks!

What on earth could you do now? Three rounds of hearts, putting East in? If he returns a diamond, one entry suffices for the avoidance play. If he shifts to clubs, that gives you the extra entry as well, but his long club sets up for the fifth defensive trick (East can hardly hold five clubs, for then he would have taken his queen and returned the suit). It seems you are reduced to playing for both diamond honours onside; you can take a deep finesse and subsequently end-play East. . . .

But wait a minute. It must surely be better to cash the ace of diamonds before crossing to dummy: then the one entry suffices for your avoidance play. Well, ace of diamonds! East drops the king – he must, with or without the jack! And now you see the idea: fortunately, you took the precaution of unblocking the ten of diamonds from dummy, and after cashing your heart and club winners you lead a spade to throw West in. Eventually he must lead a diamond, giving you nine tricks.

Your original analysis was inaccurate, but fortunately you managed to steer yourself away from the obsession with the repeated avoidance play in time. It was correct to run the jack of clubs at trick three, of course. But when the jack wins, you have to change your tack and cash the ace of diamonds. If East plays a low card, you cross to the ace of clubs and try a single-lead avoidance. If East jettisons the king of diamonds, the throw-in will work whenever West's shape is 5–2–3–3, and also when it is 5–1–3–4 or 5–0–3–5 with the diamond jack.

'Wear' your defence

Seeing your game in yachting terms, you may recall instances where the defence had to turn away from its natural course, wear, quite to the opposite direction.

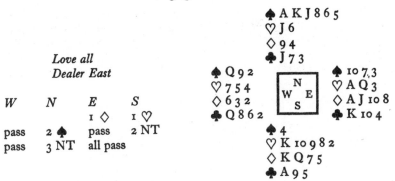

Love all
Dealer East

W	N	E	S
		1 ◇	1 ♡
pass	2 ♠	pass	2 NT
pass	3 NT	all pass	

Against this impertinent contract partner hit on the club lead: two, three, ten, five. Your club king was allowed to hold the second trick, and you had to consider your next move. A red suit shift did not seem promising: partner could hardly have a diamond honour since he did not lead your suit, nor were his hearts likely to be as good as 10 x x. But before continuing with a 'safe' club you took a moment to count your impending discard-troubles. On dummy's last spade you would be forced to let go either your third heart, in which case declarer would lead a heart, or the diamond jack, in which case he would lead a diamond.

Was there anything else to try? What about a spade switch at trick three? Why, that must defeat the contract if South has a singleton spade! Declarer will be unable to cash the ace of clubs before running the spades, which will leave you with an extra 'idle' card – the four of clubs – to throw on the last spade. Thus, in the end-position below you are able to keep two diamonds and three hearts, which is one card too many for declarer to deal with no matter how he himself discards.

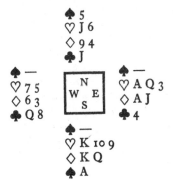

You either set up a long heart or end-play South according to his choice of play, because you have been able to retain an exit card in diamonds.

With this spade lead you managed to elude a sort of squeeze. It is not exactly a material squeeze. If you permit the declarer to cash the club ace before running the spades, you are not squeezed out of a winner, but you are forced to give up the 'elbow-room' of the five-card end-position with disastrous consequences.

Again, you may find the right defence if

[13]

you have never heard of 'non-material' or strategic squeezes, elbow-room, playing space or margin, but the sharp turn-about, switching from your natural defensive course to a deliberate concession of both lead and tempo, is surely easier to spot if you have familiar names for the concepts at issue.

This deal reminds you of another three no trump hand played in 1937. How would you defend in the East seat?

South opened two no trumps and North raised to three.

West led the queen of spades and the king held the first trick. When the hand was played, the declarer won the spade continuation and led the diamond four to the seven, eight and deuce! Richard L. Frey justly praised the clever defensive hold-up.

However, today's declarer may duck the second and also the third round of spades . . . and make his contract. By the time South wins the fourth spade you have been forced to part with two hearts. A hold-up in diamonds won't help you now. After the eight of diamonds, South plays the ace of hearts and the three top clubs (you can't afford to unblock), then cashes the king of diamonds and throws you in with the club for a 'stepping-stone' end-play.

```
                      ♠ 7 5
                      ♡ 9 4 2
                      ◇ A Q 10 9 8
                      ♣ 8 7 4
♠ Q J 10 8 2                        ♠ K 9
♡ Q J 8 3          ┌─────────┐      ♡ K 7 6
◇ 7 3             │    N    │      ◇ J 6 5 2
♣ 10 5            │  W   E  │      ♣ J 9 3 2
                  │    S    │
                  └─────────┘
                      ♠ A 6 4 3
                      ♡ A 10 5
                      ◇ K 4
                      ♣ A K Q 6
```

What if you shift to a heart at some stage instead of playing four rounds of spades? No use. South holds up his ace and a similar end-play develops. Declarer can always make his contract if you insist on the 'natural' defence of attacking the majors.

Mind you, West can beat him by hauling about and leading a diamond at trick three. When the eight of diamonds wins, South's best shot is to play the ace and king of clubs (preventing a later unblock by East) and cash the ace of spades. If East discards a small heart, South overtakes the king of diamonds with dummy's ace and leads a heart, and it doesn't matter what East does. If he plays the king, he is given the trick; if he plays low, the ace wins; and either way he will be end-played as before. East must therefore drop the king of hearts under the ace of spades. Then declarer is helpless.

But is it really good defence for East to continue spades at trick two? West is unlikely to be able to see the position so clearly and will probably plug away at his spades. East does better to shift to diamonds at trick two – an even earlier turn off course – especially as today's declarer may have the jack of hearts instead of the ten. That holding doesn't permit East the luxury of throwing away the heart king if the play develops as in the last paragraph, for declarer can then switch *his* course to end-play West.

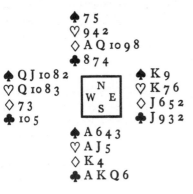

♠ 7 5
♡ 9 4 2
♢ A Q 10 9 8
♣ 8 7 4

♠ Q J 10 8 2   ♠ K 9
♡ Q 10 8 3   ♡ K 7 6
♢ 7 3   ♢ J 6 5 2
♣ 10 5   ♣ J 9 3 2

♠ A 6 4 3
♡ A J 5
♢ K 4
♣ A K Q 6

The diamond switch at trick two represents an early turn-about, but is it early enough? Alas, it is already too late! After the opening lead of a spade (or a heart), declarer is home if he has the jack of hearts.

The diamond shift is won by the eight, two clubs are cashed and the five of hearts is led. West plays the ten, and East can make his own arrangements: (a) If he plays small, declarer wins the diamond ace and leads a heart from the table to catch him in the familiar dilemma. (b) If East overtakes with the king and continues hearts, declarer ducks and East is again stripped of his major suit cards, while if East returns any other suit, West will be end-played in hearts.

The only way to defeat the contract in the above layout is to start immediately on the backward-tempo tack by leading a diamond. There is a yachting analogy in setting a course away from your destination to avoid a dangerous coast, or perhaps to 'fetch a trade wind'. However, it is of academic interest only, for it is hardly possible for West to find the killing diamond lead, even if he has radar on board.

There is a better chance of spotting this kind of defence at trick two, when you have more information and a sight of dummy. Stay in the East seat for the next hand.

♠ 8 7 4 3
♡ A Q J 10 6
♢ 4 2
♣ 10 5

Love all
Dealer South

♠ K J 9 6 2   ♠ Q
♡ 8 3   ♡ K 9 7 4
♢ 5   ♢ Q J 10 9 7 3
♣ A 8 6 4 3   ♣ 7 2

♠ A 10 5
♡ 5 2
♢ A K 8 6
♣ K Q J 9

S	W	N	E
1 ◊	1 ♠	2 ♡	pass
3 NT	all pass		

West leads the six of spades and your queen wins the first trick. Now a prompt switch to a low heart will bring about the declarer's downfall. West has to co-operate by denying dummy a club entry and by leading his second heart when in with the ace of clubs. Any other return at trick two gives South an easy time. He knocks out the ace of clubs and takes a heart finesse. You must hold off, and eventually you have to concede two further heart tricks when you are thrown in with a diamond.

A case for similar treatment:

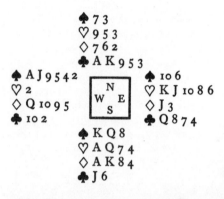

♠ 7 3
♡ 9 5 3
◇ 7 6 2
♣ A K 9 5 3

♠ A J 9 5 4 2
♡ 2
◇ Q 10 9 5
♣ 10 2

♠ 10 6
♡ K J 10 8 6
◇ J 3
♣ Q 8 7 4

♠ K Q 8
♡ A Q 7 4
◇ A K 8 4
♣ J 6

South opens one heart, West makes a weak jump overcall of two spades, and South eventually plays in three no trumps.

West leads the five of spades to your ten. Declarer takes his time, but finally plays the eight, giving you your chance. Do you see it?

It takes an immediate shift to a low club to defeat the contract. Partner can lead a second club when in with the ace of spades, thus holding declarer to eight tricks. If you return anything else at trick two, the contract will be made. On a diamond switch, for instance, South will win, knock out the ace of spades, win the diamond return, lead the jack of clubs and let it ride. You will have to hold off, and South will then cash his spade winner to force a heart discard from you. A club to the king will be followed by a heart finesse, and you will be thrown in on the third round of hearts to concede two further club tricks to dummy.

An abrupt defensive veer-around is needed on the next hand – you have to sacrifice a natural trick in one suit in order to gain three in another.

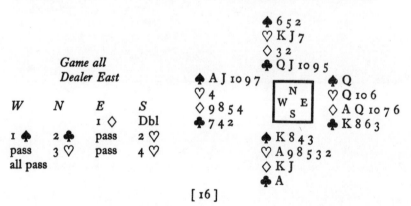

♠ 6 5 2
♡ K J 7
◇ 3 2
♣ Q J 10 9 5

Game all
Dealer East

♠ A J 10 9 7
♡ 4
◇ 9 8 5 4
♣ 7 4 2

♠ Q
♡ Q 10 6
◇ A Q 10 7 6
♣ K 8 6 3

W	N	E	S
		1 ◇	Dbl
1 ♠	2 ♣	pass	2 ♡
pass	3 ♡	pass	4 ♡
all pass			

♠ K 8 4 3
♡ A 9 8 5 3 2
◇ K J
♣ A

West leads the nine of diamonds to your ace. Clearly you need spade tricks to defeat the contract, and at trick two you switch to the queen of spades on which South plays the three and West the seven. Now you have to reconsider your defence. It will not do to sit back and wait, expecting to score a trump and a further spade trick. If partner has the ace of spades, declarer will have the rest of the top cards and his pattern is likely to be 4–6–2–1. So you change your tack at trick three by leading the six of hearts! This surrenders your trump trick, but it destroys the threat of dummy's clubs and restricts declarer to eight tricks.

If you lead a club or a diamond at trick three, South will cash his minor suit winners and throw you in by means of a first-round trump finesse. Whatever you return will give him the extra entry he needs to set up the clubs, and he will make his contract.

Shifting Tack in Planning

You reach six hearts against silent opposition, and the opening lead of the queen of diamonds is not particularly welcome.

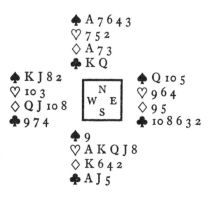

♠ A 7 6 4 3
♡ 7 5 2
◇ A 7 3
♣ K Q

♠ K J 8 2
♡ 10 3
◇ Q J 10 8
♣ 9 7 4

♠ Q 10 5
♡ 9 6 4
◇ 9 5
♣ 10 8 6 3 2

♠ 9
♡ A K Q J 8
◇ K 6 4 2
♣ A J 5

Setting up spades looks a poor chance now. Even if trumps behave, you can ruff only two spades and must concede a spade trick; then another diamond will nail you down in dummy and you will be unable to reach your ace of clubs. So you look for an alternative tack – a ruff in dummy. What about diamond ace, diamond to king, three clubs, pitching the diamond, heart ace and king? Then you can negotiate a diamond ruff if the suit breaks 3–3 or if East has no more than two trumps.

Looking more closely at the trump spots, you see that you may succeed when East has three trumps if he hodls 6 4 3, 9 4 3 or 10 4 3, but you must not touch the trump suit before attempting your first ruff with the heart seven. If this is over-ruffed, draw one trump and ruff the fourth diamond with the heart five. Is this worth trying?

Well, your 'table presence' tells you no. You sense that West has led from length in diamonds, in which case he is not likely to have three or four hearts, and the probability of success when *East* has three hearts is too slender. Yet you seem to have little choice. Or have you? What about a ruffing squeeze if West holds five spades and four diamonds . . .?

Oh, forget about squeezes, spot-cards, percentages. *Relax.* Let your relaxed concentration work for you without tetanizing it by an all-out mental effort, for it has to steer you back to the spade-establishing tack.

The simple solution is to rely on 3–2 trumps and 4–3 spades, ruffing *three* spades in hand. You win the first trick with the king of diamonds and draw two rounds of trumps. Then spade ace, spade ruff, club queen, spade ruff. When the spades behave you are home. Club king, spade ruff, club ace, pitching a diamond, and you claim twelve tricks. By setting up a trump trick for the defence, you were able to ruff out the spades *in tempo* so as to make your club ace as well.

Why was it so hard to see? Well, the 100 honours in trumps acted as a red herring, didn't they? with A K x x x in hearts you would hardly have a problem.

As for your famous table presence, you remember this six-spade hand.

```
♠ Q 9 7
♡ 10 5
◇ A 7 6 5 2          North-South game
♣ 8 4 3              Dealer South

   N
 W   E
   S                 S        W      N      E
                     1 ♣      3 ♡    pass   pass
♠ A J 10 8 4         3 ♠      pass   4 ◇    pass
♡ A                  5 ◇      pass   5 ♠    pass
◇ K 8 3              6 ◇      pass   pass   6 ♡
♣ A K Q 5            6 ♠      all pass
```

You won the opening lead of the ten of clubs and, sensing tension around the table, you felt a slight but distinct urge to bang out the trump ace in the expectation of dropping West's stiff king ('How pleasant to meet you, Sire'). There is nothing like a subtle table presence. Nevertheless, your team-mates might not understand if, after all . . .

So you went on to think out a plan to deal with all likely distributions. You saw that you might be able to get rid of your diamond loser if West had the doubleton spade king, seven hearts and two cards in each minor suit. Spade ace, heart ace, club king, diamond king, diamond to ace, heart ruff, club queen! Well, well . . . no good. West would discard and, although you could throw him in with a trump, one ruff and discard would not be enough to give you the contract.

But this line would succeed if West had a 2–7–1–3 shape, as shown in the following diagram.

Oh, come on, now! East would hardly save against six diamonds with a 3–3–4–3 hand and two trump tricks. Could your table presence have gone askew? No, it didn't. It told you merely that your opponents were not altogether displeased with your contract. You couldn't help sensing their optimistic expectations, but that didn't have to mean the king of spades offside, let alone blank.

You therefore hauled about to plan for the king of spades on-

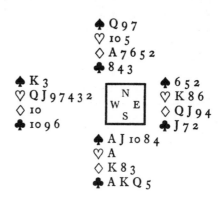

side, which was what the declarer in the other room would do anyway. You could bank on a friendly diamond split, but it would not be possible to set up the suit since you needed the ace as an entry for the trump finesse. The contract could not be made if East had king doubleton in spades. That would give West three spades and a singleton club, and there would be no way to avoid a club loser or a club ruff. You could succeed if East had K x x in trumps, however. After two rounds of trumps you could test the clubs and ruff a club in dummy.

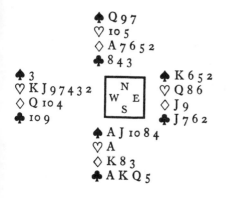

What about K x x x with East? Again there would be no difficulty, provided that you took the precaution of cashing the ace of hearts before crossing to dummy. Heart ace, diamond to ace, spade seven run, spade nine. If West shows out on the second trump, ruff a heart and test the clubs, either ruffing the fourth club and exiting in diamonds, or, if East is 4–3–3–3, conceding the third diamond to him for an end-play.

But, of course, East turned out to have all five trumps. That was the source of his optimism, in fact.

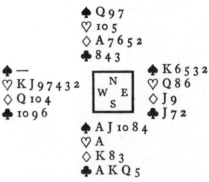

You simply stopped playing trumps when West showed out on the first round. After ruffing a heart, you cashed your club winners and the king of diamonds. If East's pattern had been 5-2-2-4 you could have ruffed a club, finessed in spades, and exited with a diamond. But when the clubs proved to be 3-3 you were undismayed. That was why you had not continued with a second round of spades: you needed dummy's queen and nine for a spectacular ending.

```
              ♠ Q 9
              ♡ —
              ◇ 7 6 5
              ♣ —
♠ —                        ♠ K 6 5 3
♡ K J 9 7       N          ♡ Q
◇ Q          W     E       ◇ —
♣ —             S          ♣ —
              ♠ A J 10
              ♡ —
              ◇ 8
              ♣ 5
```

You exited with the eight of diamonds, and whether East ruffed or threw his heart he could not make another trick. In practice he elected to discard the heart. West then had to lead a heart into the triple void, and when you ruffed on the table with the nine of spades East's king was smothered to death.

Smother play is not a technique that is met with every day, and for that reason it can be hard to spot the danger in defence.

```
              ♠ A J 7
              ♡ A Q 3
              ◇ Q 10 4
              ♣ K J 9 2
♠ K 10 5                   ♠ Q 8 6 4 2
♡ J 7 6 4       N          ♡ K 10
◇ 9 8 5      W     E       ◇ A 6 2
♣ Q 5 3         S          ♣ A 6 4
              ♠ 9 3
              ♡ 9 8 5 2
              ◇ K J 7 3
              ♣ 10 8 7
```

Match-point pairs
Game all
Dealer East

W	N	E	S
		1 ♠	pass
pass	Dbl	pass	2 ♡
pass	2 NT	pass	pass
Dbl	pass	pass	3 ◇
pass	3 ♡	pass	pass
Dbl	all pass		

West doubled two no trumps to ask for a spade lead. In practice there is no way to defeat this contract, and perhaps South should have left his partner there. Still, it didn't much matter for he managed to bring home the nine-trick contract too. . . .

Against three hearts West led the five of spades (yes, the ten would have worked better) to your queen. You shifted to the two of diamonds – partner might have a doubleton, or the king. No, South won with the jack and led the club ten, three, *nine*, ace. You played the ace and another diamond. South won with the king, played the club eight to the queen and king, the club two back to the seven, a spade to the jack, the spade ace for a diamond discard, the heart ace, the three of hearts to your king . . . and in the diagram position you had to smother partner's 'sure' trump trick on your spade return.

How frustrating! South cleverly managed all his finesses with just two entries. The club seven with West would have sufficed to kill the whole pretty manoeuvre. But perhaps you have already noticed that you missed an

```
              ♠ —
              ♡ Q
              ◇ —
              ♣ J
  ♠ —        ┌──────┐      ♠ 8 6
  ♡ J 7      │  N   │      ♡ —
  ◇ —        │ W  E │      ◇ —
  ♣ —        │  S   │      ♣ —
              └──────┘
              ♠ —
              ♡ 9 8
              ◇ —
              ♣ —
```

opportunity. You were careful not to help declarer with a spade return. Yet a spade continuation at trick two, another spade after winning the club ace, and still another spade when in with the diamond ace would have defeated the contract. Since you will have to make a triple-void lead eventually, you should plan to do so when West still has a loser to discard rather than at a time of declarer's choosing.

This winning defence sails throughout on an independent tack – in opposite direction, as it were, to any natural defensive aim such as setting up tricks, establishing suits, preparing ruffs, attacking entries, etc. The instant spade return into dummy's tenace wouldn't normally seem a sound or promising play. You have to see the entire course to appreciate the necessity for this 'veering'.

You may have an instinctive awareness of the danger ahead without being able to give it a name. If you could identify it in your mind as a smother-play menace, you might more easily be able to 'lay a course' for the counter-smother defence of the repeated spade attack.

Tacking on unknown waters

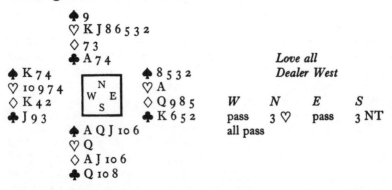

```
              ♠ 9
              ♡ K J 8 6 5 3 2
              ◇ 7 3
              ♣ A 7 4                      Love all
♠ K 7 4              ♠ 8 5 3 2             Dealer West
♡ 10 9 7 4    ┌─────┐  ♡ A
◇ K 4 2    W  │  N  │ E ◇ Q 9 8 5    W     N     E     S
♣ J 9 3       │  S  │  ♣ K 6 5 2     pass  3 ♡   pass  3 NT
              └─────┘                all pass
              ♠ A Q J 10 6
              ♡ Q
              ◇ A J 10 6
              ♣ Q 10 8
```

West leads the three of clubs and a disappointing dummy goes down; partner had promised a near-solid suit with his three-heart bid. East wins the king of clubs and switches to the nine of diamonds. The jack fetches the king, and West returns the jack of clubs to your queen. You lead the queen of hearts, planning to switch to spades when this wins, but East unexpectedly takes the ace of hearts and returns the eight of diamonds to your ten.

To defend like this East must have started with either four hearts or the ace singleton. He is obviously 4–4 in the minor suits and can hardly have a singleton spade since West did not lead the suit. His pattern must be 4–1–4–4, then, and the defenders have succeeded in breaking up your entries. So you cash the ace of diamonds and think about ways of squeezing East. Club to the ace, heart king, club discard from East, spade ten discard from hand! (A diamond discard and spade continuation won't do; if West has the king, he will return the heart ten and make a fifth trick). Now the heart jack. If East pitches the diamond queen, you throw the spade six, discard another spade on the fourth heart, and the forced spade return sees you home. East must therefore part with a spade on the jack of hearts.

Now it is easy if East has the king of spades. You throw the six of spades from hand, take a spade finesse, and throw East in with the diamond to force a spade return. Unfortunately, there is no guarantee that East has the king of spades.

```
              ♠ 9
              ♡ J 8 6 5
              ◇ —
              ♣ —
♠ 7 4 2              ♠ K 8 5 3
♡ 10 9    ┌─────┐  ♡ —
◇ —    W  │  N  │ E ◇ Q
♣ —       │  S  │  ♣ —
          └─────┘
              ♠ A Q J 6
              ♡ —
              ◇ 6
              ♣ —
```

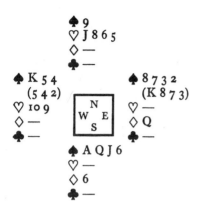

♠ 9
♡ J 8 6 5
◇ —
♣ —

♠ K 5 4
(5 4 2)
♡ 10 9
◇ —
♣ —

♠ 8 7 3 2
(K 8 7 3)
♡ —
◇ Q
♣ —

♠ A Q J 6
♡ —
◇ 6
♣ —

Another possibility is that East may have the eight and seven of spades, in which case you should be able to squeeze him no matter who holds the king. When East throws a spade on the jack of hearts you discard the *jack* of spades from hand. On the next heart, conceded to West, East crumbles under the pressure. When he parts with a further spade you throw your diamond, and West cannot defeat you no matter which card he returns.

Well, it looks very pretty yet you are not satisfied – a showy ending but a weakish chance. Can't you squeeze East anyway, whatever his spades may be? Heart king, club from East, spade ten from hand; all right so far. Heart jack, spade from East. Now if you discard your diamond you threaten to take four spade tricks. Oh, but your hand will be squeezed – in one suit – on the next heart lead.

Whether you discard the six of spades or the jack, you will be unable to prevent the defenders from making a spade trick.

What about a low heart instead of the jack on the previous trick? If East discards a spade, you can pitch the diamond and West will be end-played. But, of course, East will throw his diamond on the low heart and you will be one-suit-squeezed in the same way.

So, stepping backwards by still another trick, you see at last the simple

♠ 9
♡ 8 6 5
◇ —
♣ —

♠ K 7 4
♡ 10
◇ —
♣ —

♠ 8 5 3
♡ —
◇ Q
♣ —

♠ A Q J 6
♡ —
◇ —
♣ —

solution. After the ace of clubs you'll lead a low heart, not an honour, from dummy. Then you can discard your diamond, keeping your spade suit intact for the end-play. And that is essential, for this particular throw-in needs all the elbow-room, playing margin or manoeuvring space that you can give it.

Well, was it a waste of time and effort racking your brains over that unusual potential squeeze against spot-cards in an untouched suit? Not really, for you may be dealt any day (or at least any century) a hand like the following one.

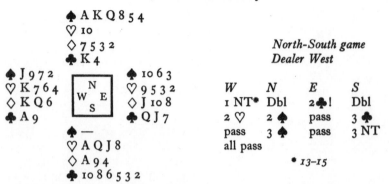

♠ A K Q 8 5 4
♡ 10
◇ 7 5 3 2
♣ K 4

North-South game
Dealer West

♠ J 9 7 2		♠ 10 6 3
♡ K 7 6 4	N	♡ 9 5 3 2
◇ K Q 6	W E	◇ J 10 8
♣ A 9	S	♣ Q J 7

W	N	E	S
1 NT*	Dbl	2♣!	Dbl
2 ♡	2 ♠	pass	3 ♣
pass	3 ♠	pass	3 NT
all pass			

* *13–15*

♠ —
♡ A Q J 8
◇ A 9 4
♣ 10 8 6 5 3 2

West attacks with the king of diamonds and continues the suit to knock out your ace. He plays the ace on your club lead and returns the nine of clubs to dummy's king. You cash the long diamond and two spade honours, pitching clubs from hand, which leaves this rather hopeless-looking position:

A small spade won't do this time since East has kept his spades. His ten would win, and the club queen followed by a heart would put you two down.

If East had the king of hearts, you would have a choice of two ways of making the contract – by a squeeze, or by a finesse and throw-in.

On the bidding, of course, the king of hearts is marked in the West hand. How-

♠ A 8 5 4
♡ 10
◇ —
♣ —

♠ J 9		♠ 10
♡ K 7 6	N	♡ 9 5 3
◇ —	W E	◇ —
♣ —	S	♣ Q

♠ —
♡ A Q J 8
◇ —
♣ 10

ever, if East has the nine of hearts, you will still be able to squeeze him. Play the ace of spades, discarding the jack of hearts (not the club) from your hand. The next spade lead forces a heart discard from East, you throw your club, and West is powerless to defeat you whether he returns the king of hearts or a small one.

Squeezes in one suit are known to you mainly in the form of throw-in menaces, as in this situation.

At no trumps South needs two more tricks. The play of the spade ace squeezes East, who has to concede a heart trick no matter how he discards

In practical play you may need to do some preparation.

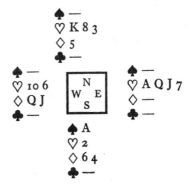

♠ —
♡ K 8 3
♢ 5
♣ —

♠ —
♡ 10 6
♢ Q J
♣ —

♠ —
♡ A Q J 7
♢ —
♣ —

♠ A
♡ 2
♢ 6 4
♣ —

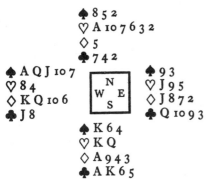

♠ 8 5 2
♡ A 10 7 6 3 2
♢ 5
♣ 7 4 2

♠ A Q J 10 7
♡ 8 4
♢ K Q 10 6
♣ J 8

♠ 9 3
♡ J 9 5
♢ J 8 7 2
♣ Q 10 9 3

♠ K 6 4
♡ K Q
♢ A 9 4 3
♣ A K 6 5

West opens one spade, South bids two no trumps and eventually, through a transfer bid, becomes declarer in four hearts.

When West leads the king of diamonds, South should hold up his ace for one round in order to 'rectify the count'.

Subsequently, in the process of drawing trumps, declarer should ruff two diamonds (not one diamond and one club) in dummy to strip West of his outside winners. The ace and king of clubs come next, and when a club is ruffed with the last trump on the table, West is squeezed in spades – either South's king or dummy's eight must make a trick.

You have already seen that there is a suicide-squeeze variant of the one-suit squeeze. It may be quite simple in form; nevertheless it can be deadly if you do not spot the danger in time.

You play six no trumps on the lead of the king of diamonds. Don't hold up mechanically, thinking that it can't possibly hurt. It can and it will. Try the play.

You will have no safe discard on dummy's last club, and you will go down with the king of spades on-side. The correct play is the ace of diamonds at trick one. You cannot afford to give up any elbow-room, for the extra idle card is needed to avert the self-squeeze in spades.

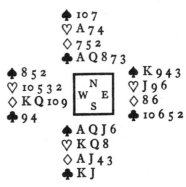

♠ 10 7
♡ A 7 4
♢ 7 5 2
♣ A Q 8 7 3

♠ 8 5 2
♡ 10 5 3 2
♢ K Q 10 9
♣ 9 4

♠ K 9 4 3
♡ J 9 6
♢ 8 6
♣ 10 6 5 2

♠ A Q J 6
♡ K Q 8
♢ A J 4 3
♣ K J

The next hand introduces a complication.

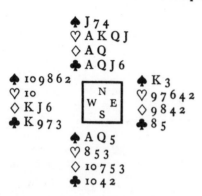

♠ J 7 4
♡ A K Q J
◇ A Q
♣ A Q J 6

♠ 10 9 8 6 2
♡ 10
◇ K J 6
♣ K 9 7 3

♠ K 3
♡ 9 7 6 4 2
◇ 9 8 4 2
♣ 8 5

♠ A Q 5
♡ 8 5 3
◇ 10 7 5 3
♣ 10 4 2

Sitting South, you respond one diamond to North's big club. West comes in with one spade, North bids two spades, and you show your modest values with a jump 'o three no trumps.

Partner has touching confidence in your dummy play, and the next thing you know you are playing seven no trumps on the lead of the ten of spades.

Now try to make it. Even with all four hands on view it's not too easy. We shall leave you to wrestle with the problem for a while, and when we return to it later you will see how much easier it is when you can put a name to the technique required.

Why all this preoccupation with names? What on earth is the point of giving fancy labels to things that you can probably tell apart anyway? Has it any reason, purpose or importance?

Yes, you believe it has. In the first place it enables you not only to talk or write about a thing more fluently but also to *think* about it with greater clarity. Secondly, you will even be able to feel a thing, to sense it, more directly if you can associate it with a name. This is a great help to your concentration, which works partly at the subconscious, intuitive level.

In practical play what happens is that you carry out a rapid mental check of the techniques at your disposal to see which of them should be applied to the case in hand. You have a built-in computer, working at electronic velocity, which scans the repertoire of your accumulated bridge knowledge and selects the play that is most appropriate for the occasion. But it can produce only such knowledge as has previously been fed into the machine. Now this is where correct nomenclature can help. The naming is a way of tabulating knowledge, of putting things in proper order on the memory tapes of your bridge computer where they will be available for both deliberate and intuitive use in the future.

In a three no trump contract, for example, declarer's mind may ask: (a) Will it do to establish high-card tricks? Computer answers: No! (b) Can I set up a long suit? No! (c) A straightforward squeeze? No! (d) A throw-in? No! (e) A one-suit squeeze? Yes! Yes! Yes! But the final affirmative will be possible only if the technique (and the name) of the one-suit squeeze has previously been programmed into the computer.

In fact there is no such thing as something known that has no name.

Certain eminent scholars would have us believe that the only important function of language is that relating to inter-human communication. But you, bridge-player, know that language begins long before its social aspect comes into play . . . as a private, individual code system. The first thing you do when you discover something new is to give it a name. When you learn, for instance, that you can sometimes make an extra trick by leading towards the ace-queen and playing the queen, you may call it 'encompass', 'cul-de-sac', 'hem-in', 'shoo-shoo' or 'bow-bow'. You will certainly call it something because you need a private designation to facilitate its mental handling. Indeed, you could not recognize or even remember a thing once met if you had no secret name for it well before being informed of what your neighbours call it. And it is not until you learn that they call it a 'finesse' that the subsequent function of language begins to operate – the one concerned with human co-operation.

2

Finesses to Take – and to Avoid

Language, the uses of; co-operation, human. Your yachtsman friend could tell you a thing or two about these scholarly themes, only it might not be the kind of tale you would like to hear. Anyway, you lost the bridge tournament and found him instead, located his boat and got aboard the next afternoon. And, as the exceptional Indian summer continued, you were allowed to indulge in complete idleness and almost complete silence for days on end.

Silence? Well, Alec was always a taciturn lad. 'Hello,' he said, 'you'll come in handy.' His mate had had to leave abruptly. 'No crew?' you asked. He mumbled something as you thudded down into the dinghy, ending: 'Take an oar.' You had known Alec a long time, and the paramount advantage of his company was that speech was hardly necessary. His mumbling about the missing crew meant reassurance and could be interpreted as: 'Don't panic. You won't have to scrub the decks. I'm perfectly capable of managing the *Cormorant* single-handed, as you well know.' Okay, skipper, you thought. Sailing alone in a similar vessel, Alec had fallen foul of authority somewhere on the south-eastern shores of the Adriatic and had been held for some years as a political prisoner in a dilapidated fortress. Silent before, he was even less talkative after his release, but he did once confide that it was by thinking out bridge problems that he had preserved his sanity during those years of solitary confinement.

'We'd better turn in,' he said after dinner.

'Man, I can't fall asleep so early.'

'You can. We're sailing at sunrise.'

'Why the rush?'

'This place is fouled, you see.'

'Fouled?' You looked at him dumbfounded.

'Not the anchorage. The family.'

'I see.'

'Or would you . . .?'

'Heavens, no!'

'Then good-night.'

The threat had been that his two handsome, clever and utterly unbearable teenaged nephews might pay a visit next morning. Thus you slipped away at dawn, just as the sun was beginning to climb in still cool splendour above the horizon.

Alec's experiences during the dark years of his imprisonment were not a suitable topic for conversation on a sunny morning. NON NUMERO HORAS NISI SERENAS, said the sundial. So, under the pellucid September sky you fell back on recollections of those long summer forenoons and longer afternoons spent at your great-aunt Clara's country place.

'You remember Aunt Clara?'

'Sure, *and* Aunt Alice,' said Alec.

Aunt Clara was just short of eighty when you were twelve. She was a little old darling and a marvellous card-player who took it upon herself to initiate you into the mysteries of bridge. The fact of the matter was that they needed a fourth from time to time, and a twelve-year-old boy was better than no one at all. Still, you have reason to be grateful to her. The clarity of her mind was unimpaired by age and she taught you to appreciate the crystal-clear and softly sparkling quality of the game.

'Always take your finesses,' she said. 'Look here, this is a major tenace. You can make one more trick with the missing king onside, see?'

'Oh, not necessarily,' put in great-aunt Alice. Being a mere youngster of seventy-two, she was instantly rebuked by Clara.

'Don't confuse the boy, you silly little thing!'

'But I remember a hand . . .'

'Later. At the moment we are dealing with finesses.'

Well, the modest finesse may be one of the most elementary plays in the game, yet, as you learned in time from Aunt Clara, it embodies a fundamental principle of card-play that is shared by many more advanced techniques. It profits from the enforced 'premature commitment' of the opponent who has to play ahead of your high cards.

♠ A J 8 4
♡ 7 5 4
◇ Q 10
♣ J 6 5 2

```
   N
W     E
   S
```

Take your finesses? All right, but when and which ones?

With a part-score of 30, you play in a contract of three spades. West leads the king of hearts and is allowed to keep the first trick. You win the heart continuation as East follows low-high.

♠ Q 10 9 7 6
♡ A 6 2
◇ A J 4
♣ A 9

Obviously the correct play now is to finesse first in spades and later in diamonds. You will succeed in making nine tricks unless you are unlucky enough to find both finesses wrong.

Fine. But next time you have no part-score and you bid on to game. How should you play in four spades after winning the second heart? It doesn't take a genius to spot the correct line, but it's easy enough to go wrong unless you realize that this is a new day, another contract, a different problem.

In four spades the position of the spade king is irrelevant; it is only the diamond king that matters. If the diamond finesse is wrong, you will have four losers even if the trump finesse is right. But if the diamond finesse is right, you can make ten tricks with the trump king offside provided that you don't attempt the trump finesse. Play the queen of spades to dummy's ace and return the queen of diamonds. When the king appears, win with the ace, play the four of diamonds to the ten, return to hand with the ace of clubs, and discard dummy's heart on the jack of diamonds. After ruffing your heart, you are happy to concede a trump and a club trick.

Sometimes the problem is not which suit to finesse but which card. West deals and opens one spade, playing five-card majors.

The bidding continues:

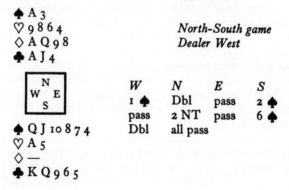

♠ A 3
♡ 9 8 6 4   *North-South game*
◇ A Q 9 8   *Dealer West*
♣ A J 4

W	N	E	S
1 ♠	Dbl	pass	2 ♠
pass	2 NT	pass	6 ♠
Dbl	all pass		

♠ Q J 10 8 7 4
♡ A 5
◇ —
♣ K Q 9 6 5

You believed that West had made another of his idiotic first-round psyches, but you have to think again when he doubles and leads the king of hearts to your ace.

It is tempting to cross to the ace of spades and discard your heart loser on the ace of diamonds, but that will not do if West has all five missing trumps, as seems likely. Nor can you afford to run the queen of spades at trick two; you have to risk everything on a deep finesse of the eight of spades.

When West plays low and East shows out, you are practically home. A spade to the ace, the diamond ace for a heart discard; careful now, the *jack* of clubs to your king, and the queen of spades to force out the king. You can ruff the heart return, draw the remaining trumps and play a club to the ace, picking up the rest of the tricks even if West started with a singleton club. The full hand:

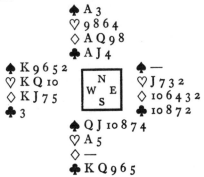

```
                    ♠ A 3
                    ♡ 9 8 6 4
                    ◊ A Q 9 8
                    ♣ A J 4
   ♠ K 9 6 5 2                    ♠ —
   ♡ K Q 10         N             ♡ J 7 3 2
   ◊ K J 7 5    W       E         ◊ 10 6 4 3 2
   ♣ 3              S             ♣ 10 8 7 2
                    ♠ Q J 10 8 7 4
                    ♡ A 5
                    ◊ —
                    ♣ K Q 9 6 5
```

Still in the field of 'regular' finesses, there are some that may be termed insurance finesses. As a young player you were often envious of the 'table presence' of the great experts, which apparently enabled them to smell out the location of every key card and the distribution of each suit. It took some time to master the knack, but eventually you found yourself making the 'right guesses' as in this six no trump hand.

```
                                 ♠ Q 8 4
                                 ♡ 5 3
    North-South game             ◊ K 8 3
    Dealer East                  ♣ A K 10 7 5
                      ♠ J 5                    ♠ K 9 7 6 3 2
 W    N    E    S     ♡ Q J 10 9 6 4    N      ♡ 7 2
           pass 1 ◊   ◊ J 9 7 4    W       E   ◊ 5
 2 ♡  3 ♣  pass 4 ♣   ♣ 4              S       ♣ J 8 6 2
 pass 4 ◊  pass 6 NT                  ♠ A 10
 all pass                             ♡ A K 8
                                      ◊ A Q 10 6 2
                                      ♣ Q 9 3
```

In the open room on the last board of the match you became declarer in six no trumps. West led the queen of hearts to your ace. You cashed the ace of diamonds, played a club to dummy's ace, and returned a club for a finesse of your nine. Subsequently, you were able to establish a long diamond as your twelfth trick.

The players assembled from the other room, including the one who had gone down in the same contract. 'I see,' he remarked bitterly, 'that you picked up the club suit with some nonchalance.'

Well, there was nothing nonchalant about your finesse, of course; it was a matter of insurance. In the first place you took account of East's silence. With seven spades he would no doubt have opened with a pre-emptive bid. West was therefore marked with at least two spades along with his six hearts, plus the diamond and the club which you had seen by trick three. If West had been able to take the nine of clubs, it would have meant that the diamond suit was bound to produce five tricks. Either the diamonds would break, or they would lie with East and could be picked up by means of a finesse.

Then there are those curious preparatory finesses. On the next hand you have to take one finesse against West and two against East in the same four-card suit.

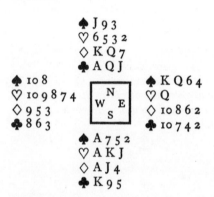

West leads the ten of hearts against your contract of six no trumps. When you cash a second top heart East discards a club.

Prospects are not good, but if East has K Q doubleton in spades you can play the ace and a small spade and eventually catch West in a pretty criss-cross squeeze in the majors.

An alternative chance is that West has 10 8 doubleton in spades, so you begin with the deuce of spades from hand to test the position. If West plays the four or the six, you will try for the criss-cross squeeze. But when West plays the eight, you finesse the nine, and lead the jack of spades from dummy on the second round. Subsequently, you can lead the three of spades from the table and take a further finesse against the six. Isn't this the weakest four-card suit with only one loser?

Note that if West holds 10 8 6 4 in spades he may try to false-card you into the losing option by playing his eight on the first round. After cashing three rounds of clubs and the ace and king of diamonds, however, you should have a good idea of what is going on.

Your finesse may be only a threat, never actually taken. When you lead the two in this diagram, for instance, the threat of the finesse forces West to play an honour card. Of course, you must be firm in your resolve to put in dummy's seven if West plays the six.

```
            A 7
          ┌───────┐
          │   N   │
 K Q J 6  │ W   E │  5 4 3
          │   S   │
          └───────┘
           10 9 8 2
```

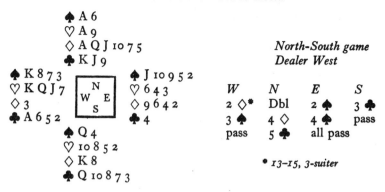

```
            ♠ A 6
            ♡ A 9
            ◇ A Q J 10 7 5
            ♣ K J 9                        North-South game
                                            Dealer West
♠ K 8 7 3       ♠ J 10 9 5 2
♡ K Q J 7       ♡ 6 4 3          W     N     E     S
◇ 3             ◇ 9 6 4 2        2 ◇*  Dbl   2 ♠   3 ♣
♣ A 6 5 2       ♣ 4             3 ♠   4 ◇   4 ♠   pass
            ♠ Q 4                pass  5 ♣   all pass
            ♡ 10 8 5 2
            ◇ K 8                      * 13–15, 3-suiter
            ♣ Q 10 8 7 3
```

West leads his singleton diamond to your king. The bidding has given you a blueprint of the distribution, and it is clear that you cannot afford to play trumps. If you do, West will hold up his ace until the third round and switch to hearts, and you will be unable to avoid the loss of two heart tricks.

Instead, you must play hearts yourself, using the finesse threat in dummy to force an honour card from West, winning with the ace and continuing with the nine of hearts. You win the trump return in hand and lead the ten of hearts for a ruffing finesse, discarding a diamond from dummy if West refuses to cover. After ruffing the fourth heart with the king of clubs, you can play trumps, and the way is clear to eleven tricks.

East deals and opens two hearts, and you eventually play in six spades.

Ruffing the heart lead, you play five rounds of trumps, discarding hearts from dummy, and West comes under pressure. Since you still have two entries, he cannot afford to throw a diamond and therefore parts with two clubs. Now the ace of clubs, a diamond to the queen and ace, the king of clubs, a club ruff, and another

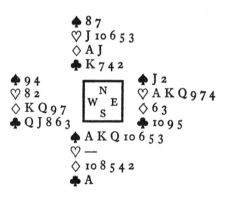

```
            ♠ 8 7
            ♡ J 10 6 5 3
            ◇ A J
            ♣ K 7 4 2
♠ 9 4                   ♠ J 2
♡ 8 2                   ♡ A K Q 9 7 4
◇ K Q 9 7               ◇ 6 3
♣ Q J 8 6 3             ♣ 10 9 5
            ♠ A K Q 10 6 5 3
            ♡ —
            ◇ 10 8 5 4 2
            ♣ A
```

diamond. If West plays low he allows access to the established club; if he plays the king he has to concede two further diamond tricks on his return.

Not much guesswork was needed. You saw ten high-card points and a fine heart suit in the East hand. With a diamond honour as well he would have opened *one* heart, not two.

The next hand has a point about finessing and also one about 'changing your tack'.

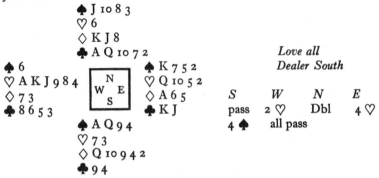

```
                    ♠ J 10 8 3
                    ♡ 6
                    ◇ K J 8
                    ♣ A Q 10 7 2                 Love all
    ♠ 6                        ♠ K 7 5 2          Dealer South
    ♡ A K J 9 8 4    ┌─────┐   ♡ Q 10 5 2
    ◇ 7 3            │  N  │   ◇ A 6 5
    ♣ 8 6 5 3        │W   E│   ♣ K J          S      W      N      E
                     │  S  │                  pass   2 ♡    Dbl    4 ♡
                     └─────┘                  4 ♠    all pass
                    ♠ A Q 9 4
                    ♡ 7 3
                    ◇ Q 10 9 4 2
                    ♣ 9 4
```

West cashes the king of hearts and switches to a club. You go up with the ace and run the jack of spades successfully. Then you try to force out the ace of diamonds, but dummy's king is allowed to hold the trick. The risk of a diamond ruff compels you to revert to trumps, so you lead the three of spades and play . . . what from your hand? The nine or the queen?

On a 3–2 trump break it makes no difference, but the queen is the correct card to cater for a 4–1 break. West shows out on the second spade and the hand becomes difficult. You cannot afford to ruff your heart at this stage, for East would then hold up his ace of diamonds until the third round and return a third heart, giving you a deadly ruff and discard. So you play a diamond to the jack and East, as expected, holds off. If you continue with a third diamond, East will find his alternative tack, returning a low trump to kill your heart ruff. You must therefore try a new tack yourself, switching to the two of clubs and establishing the clubs as trump-substitutes.

Now you see the point of keeping the nine of spades in your hand. If you had kept the queen instead, a trump lead from East would nail you down in your own hand and you would have

```
                    ♠ 10 8
                    ♡ —
                    ◇ 8
                    ♣ Q 10 7 2
    ♠ —                        ♠ K 7
    ♡ A J 9 8        ┌─────┐   ♡ Q 10 2
    ◇ —              │  N  │   ◇ A
    ♣ 8 6 5          │W   E│   ♣ K
                     │  S  │
                     └─────┘
                    ♠ A 9
                    ♡ 7
                    ◇ Q 10 9
                    ♣ 9
```

to lose two more tricks. But against the 'airy' trump position of the diagram East is helpless. No matter what he returns you can make ten tricks.

The setting up of side-suit tricks for use as trump-substitutes can be of value on many hands.

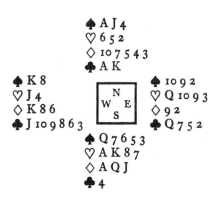

♠ A J 4
♡ 6 5 2
◇ 10 7 5 4 3
♣ A K

♠ K 8   ♠ 10 9 2
♡ J 4   ♡ Q 10 9 3
◇ K 8 6   ◇ 9 2
♣ J 10 9 8 6 3 ♣ Q 7 5 2

♠ Q 7 6 5 3
♡ A K 8 7
◇ A Q J
♣ 4

You play in six spades on the lead of the jack of clubs. The diamond finesse loses to West and another club comes back.

For your slam to have a chance you need to find the diamonds breaking kindly and the doubleton king of spades with West.

Discard a diamond honour on the second club, come to hand in diamonds, and lead the five of spades for a finesse of the jack. Continue with the ace of spades, unblocking the six from hand. Now you make use of the three diamond winners on the table – two for heart discards and one as a trump-substitute to force out East's trump. As soon as East ruffs, you over-ruff and return to dummy by leading the three of spades to the four. Then you can enjoy the rest of your discards.

Plain suit winners may sometimes be used to take a deep finesse in trumps, as in the next hand.

West leads the jack of clubs against your contract of six diamonds.

Clearly you can deal with four trumps on your right provided that you play the king of diamonds on the first round. Then you can pick up the trumps by finessing twice against East. But that is not enough to bring home the slam, for you also need discards on the hearts. If you lead a diamond at trick two, you will go down. First you must lead the heart to set up your trump-substitutes.

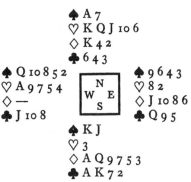

♠ A 7
♡ K Q J 10 6
◇ K 4 2
♣ 6 4 3

♠ Q 10 8 5 2   ♠ 9 6 4 3
♡ A 9 7 5 4   ♡ 8 2
◇ —   ◇ J 10 8 6
♣ J 10 8   ♣ Q 9 5

♠ K J
♡ 3
◇ A Q 9 7 5 3
♣ A K 7 2

Win the club return and lead the five of diamonds to the king, and when the bad break comes to light, you are in a position to use the heart winners to force out East's trumps. East will ruff the third heart high to stop you discarding your last club loser, but you over-ruff, play a spade to the ace, and lead another heart. Again East must ruff, and after over-ruffing and drawing his last trump, you can enter dummy with the four of diamonds to take your discard on the last heart.

'Take your finesses . . .' advised Aunt Clara, but she later added the qualification: '. . . unless you can avoid them.'

Here is a finesse you shouldn't take.

♠ A
♡ Q J 10 8
◇ A K J 10 5
♣ 7 4 3

```
    N
 W     E
    S
```

♠ 10 6 2
♡ A 5 4
◇ Q 4
♣ A K Q 10 2

A spade is led against your contract of six clubs. You play a club from dummy at trick two, and East follows with the five.

At first glance it may seem a good idea to finesse the ten, protecting against the guarded jack of clubs in the East hand.

But this is not the safest of safety plays. Suppose East has all five clubs! That's right. The only correct card is the two of clubs from your hand. You will subsequently be able to ruff a spade, finesse in trumps if necessary, and claim your slam.

You may be offered a 'free' finesse on the opening lead, but you cannot be forced to take it.

West leads the ten of hearts against your contract of three no trumps.

If you cover the ten and the king comes up, you'll have another potential finesse against the nine. Nevertheless, don't do it. You may be sorry if you win the first trick in dummy and then discover that the diamonds don't behave. Play the eight of hearts from dummy and win with the ace, and tackle the diamonds the sure five-trick way – by leading the four from your hand. If West shows out and East keeps his king for the fourth round, enter dummy in clubs and clear the diamonds, discarding a spade from hand. After a club return you can make sure of nine tricks by playing the queen of hearts. Three no trumps is 100% this way.

♠ Q 7
♡ Q J 8
◇ Q J 7 6 3 2
♣ A K

```
    N
 W     E
    S
```

♠ K 10 8
♡ A 7 3
◇ A 9 4
♣ J 10 6 5

You may have to reject the finesse at trick one for a different reason.

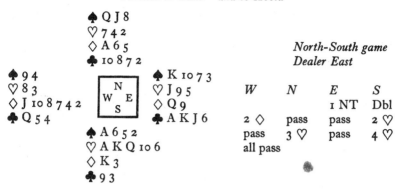

♠ Q J 8
♡ 7 4 2
◇ A 6 5
♣ 10 8 7 2

North-South game
Dealer East

♠ 9 4
♡ 8 3
◇ J 10 8 7 4 2
♣ Q 5 4

♠ K 10 7 3
♡ J 9 5
◇ Q 9
♣ A K J 6

♠ A 6 5 2
♡ A K Q 10 6
◇ K 3
♣ 9 3

W	N	E	S
		1 NT	Dbl
2 ◇	pass	pass	2 ♡
pass	3 ♡	pass	4 ♡
all pass			

West leads the nine of spades, and when dummy goes down you see that three no trumps might have been easier. In four hearts you must try to ruff a spade in dummy after drawing two rounds of trumps.

You may play the queen of spades, intending to hold up your ace when East covers with the king, but East can counter neatly by playing the three of spades instead of the king. You will then be unable to negotiate the spade ruff. If you concede a spade before drawing trumps, West will get a ruff. And if you draw two rounds of trumps before giving up a spade, East will play a third trump to leave you with four losers.

The way to keep control of the situation is to play the eight of spades from dummy, allowing West to win the first trick with his nine.

An early finesse with Q J x opposite A x x will often prove to be a mistake. For one thing it may commit you prematurely to a particular line of play.

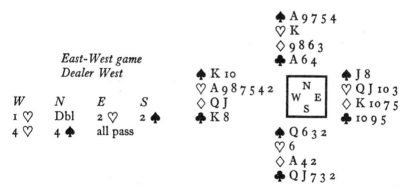

♠ A 9 7 5 4
♡ K
◇ 9 8 6 3
♣ A 6 4

East-West game
Dealer West

♠ K 10
♡ A 9 8 7 5 4 2
◇ Q J
♣ K 8

♠ J 8
♡ Q J 10 3
◇ K 10 7 5
♣ 10 9 5

♠ Q 6 3 2
♡ 6
◇ A 4 2
♣ Q J 7 3 2

W	N	E	S
1 ♡	Dbl	2 ♡	2 ♠
4 ♡	4 ♠	all pass	

West leads the ace of hearts and switches to the queen of diamonds. You let him have this trick but win the next diamond with the ace. Clearly you have to play for West to hold both black kings. But if, at this point, you play the queen of clubs to the king and ace, West is likely to see the danger of a throw-in and it may occur to him to drop his king of spades under dummy's ace. You will then avoid a trump loser but you will have to lose a club and a diamond.

There is no need to strip West of his clubs before throwing him in, so leave the clubs alone; just lead a low spade at trick four. If West plays the king, you can draw trumps and concede a trick to the king of clubs. If West plays the ten, you win with the ace and return a spade to the queen and king. On the forced heart return you pitch a club from dummy and ruff in hand. Now the queen of clubs to the king and ace, a club back to the jack, a club ruffed high, and you return to hand with the six of spades to cash two long clubs and discard dummy's diamonds.

This type of manoeuvre may lead to a squeeze ending.

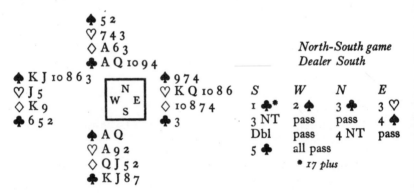

West leads the jack of hearts, East plays the queen, and you drop the nine. The nine of spades comes back, and you go up with the ace. After three rounds of trumps, the distribution is clear. You might play a diamond to the ace and duck on the way back – for one down. Or you could strip West of his diamonds, cash the ace of hearts and exit with the queen of spades – also for one down. The one trick you gain from the ruff and discard isn't enough. But if you could squeeze East into the bargain . . .

That's it. Leave the diamonds alone. Just cash the ace of hearts and exit with the queen of spades. If West refuses the trick, you can then play the ace of diamonds and duck a diamond. But West is likely to win the king of spades and now he has a choice. The diamond return concedes one trick immediately, and a second trick materializes when East is squeezed on dummy's second club. The spade return fares no better. You throw the heart from dummy and ruff in hand. The queen of diamonds is played to the king and ace, and East is squeezed as before on the play of the trumps.

All three diamond honours are needed for entry and re-entry in the end-game, so an early diamond finesse is taboo.

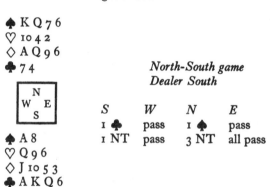

You remember a hand from the distant past on which an early diamond finesse would not have been a good idea.

♠ K Q 7 6
♡ 10 4 2
◇ A Q 9 6
♣ 7 4

North-South game
Dealer South

```
N
W   E
S
```

♠ A 8
♡ Q 9 6
◇ J 10 5 3
♣ A K Q 6

S	W	N	E
1 ♣	pass	1 ♠	pass
1 NT	pass	3 NT	all pass

West led the five of hearts to the jack and queen. Most players would look no further than the diamond finesse, but the declarer was a talented young pianist who was capable of producing virtuoso performances at the card table as well as in the concert hall. He gathered in the first trick and, in the same motion, flicked a second heart on to the table. West started rattling off heart tricks but declarer, apparently unconcerned, occupied himself by talking in low tones to his pet tortoise. This annoyed dummy to the point where he requested South, rather sternly, to pay more attention to the game.

'Take it easy,' declarer replied. 'The poor fellow is just going to squeeze his partner.'

And so it proved. West took four heart tricks, and East succumbed quickly.

George, your pianist friend, earned your everlasting respect by his lightning analysis on this hand. He reasoned that West was unlikely to hold a five-card heart suit headed by the ace and king *and* the king of diamonds, because of his failure to overcall one club. That being the case, it could not be right to take the diamond finesse. The only thing

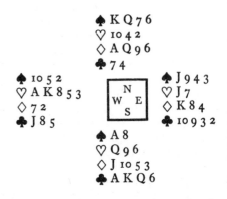

♠ K Q 7 6
♡ 10 4 2
◇ A Q 9 6
♣ 7 4

♠ 10 5 2   ♠ J 9 4 3
♡ A K 8 5 3   ♡ J 7
◇ 7 2   ◇ K 8 4
♣ J 8 5   ♣ 10 9 3 2

♠ A 8
♡ Q 9 6
◇ J 10 5 3
♣ A K Q 6

that might help was an immediate sacrifice of tempo in an effort to break communications. George's gambit of returning a heart forced the defenders to commit themselves: if four heart tricks were taken, a potential squeeze position could be established; if the hearts were abandoned, the diamond finesse could be taken in safety.

On the actual hand West squeezed his partner – what we might term a 'fratricide' or 'cannibal' squeeze. Of course, it was not really necessary for East to have four cards in each of the black suits. If he controls just one of the black suits, he can still be squeezed, provided that South reads the position and plays off his winners in the right order after winning the diamond switch.

The only case in which East cannot be squeezed is where West has 4–5–0–4 distribution, but then West himself will be squeezed when declarer cashes the ace of diamonds. That might appropriately be termed a 'suicide' squeeze.

At the time the concept of cutting communications by returning the enemy suit was new to you. You were enormously impressed by your pianist friend's play, and for weeks, for months, thereafter you went out of your way to lead back the opponents' suits on the slightest pretext. Naturally, this cost you lots of tricks and many humiliations. You can still remember vividly those painful, undignified occasions when you tried to be a hero and drowned instead in a sea of ridicule.

Yet perhaps those sad trials were not altogether in vain. Years later you could hardly have found the winning line in quite the prettiest hand you ever played if you had not been so deeply infatuated with 'George's Gambit'.

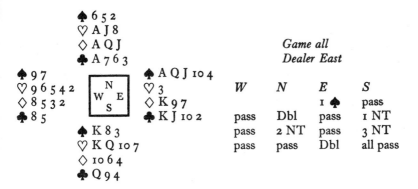

♠ 6 5 2
♡ A J 8
◇ A Q J
♣ A 7 6 3

Game all
Dealer East

W	N	E	S
		1 ♠	pass
pass	Dbl	pass	1 NT
pass	2 NT	pass	3 NT
pass	pass	Dbl	all pass

West led the nine of spades to his partner's ten, and you had to take some time to consider the position. On the bidding it was clear that East had all the high cards. You could count only seven top tricks, but you saw that if you could remove East's hearts and then throw him in with a spade, he would have to give you an extra trick on his minor suit return. Clearly you had to win the first spade, or else East would remove your exit card.

The throw-in would provide an eighth trick, and the ninth would have to come from a Vienna Coup and squeeze. You needed to arrive at a seven-card end-position; three clubs and three diamonds had to be kept in dummy, plus a heart for the re-entry. That meant that only one heart could be cashed, for you would need to discard a heart from dummy on the long spades. Your plan could not succeed, in fact, unless East had a singleton heart.

So be it! You played a heart to the ace and returned a spade, and East took his four spades to leave the position shown in the diagram. After much meditation, East switched to the king of clubs. That destroyed the Vienna Coup, but a criss-cross squeeze came to your aid. Winning the ace of clubs, you played three rounds of hearts, discarding the queen and jack of diamonds from dummy

Three no trumps doubled and made! And you immediately lost a bet.

'That was lucky,' said East, pretending to be unimpressed. 'If my partner had not led the spade . . .'

♠ —
♡ J
◇ A Q J
♣ A 7 6

♠ —
♡ 9 6 5
◇ 8 5
♣ 8 5

♠ —
♡ —
◇ K 9 7
♣ K J 10 2

♠ —
♡ K Q 10
◇ 10 6
♣ Q 9

'But you doubled for the spade lead, didn't you? Anyway, the contract is cold on any lead.'

'Want to bet?'

So you laid a wager and set out the cards to examine the possibilities. On a club lead you play low, and East can later be strip-squeezed. On a diamond lead you go up with the ace and play a small club, and again you have no problems.

But, alas, the lead of the spade *seven* beats you! East plays the ten, you win with the king and cross to the ace of hearts. But on your spade lead from dummy East plays the four, allowing West to win with the nine. Now the contract must go down, no matter what West returns. Even a second heart from West defeats you – in a perverse kind of way, simply by restricting your elbow-room.

Although one might expect these squeeze positions to be comparatively rare, in practice, opportunities arise with surprising frequency. This is because three no trumps is a popular contract, the lead is often from a five-card suit, and the declarer is quite likely to have eight top tricks with only one stopper in the enemy suit. Conditions are thus exactly right for the tempo gambit of returning the opponents' suit. Once the defensive communications have been cut, declarer may be able to establish his ninth trick without risk. And if the defenders cash four tricks in their long suit, they rectify the count against themselves and there is a good chance that someone will be squeezed.

Here is a further example of the 'suicide' variety.

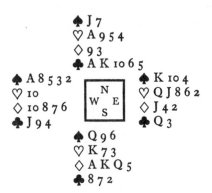

♠ J 7
♡ A 9 5 4
◇ 9 3
♣ A K 10 6 5

♠ A 8 5 3 2
♡ 10
◇ 10 8 7 6
♣ J 9 4

♠ K 10 4
♡ Q J 8 6 2
◇ J 4 2
♣ Q 3

♠ Q 9 6
♡ K 7 3
◇ A K Q 5
♣ 8 7 2

South plays in three no trumps, and West leads the three of spades to the seven, ten and queen. Realizing that he cannot afford to lose a trick outside spades, South returns a spade to East's king. East may try a shift to a diamond at this point, but it avails him nothing. South wins and patiently continues with a third spade. The defence is now helpless, for if West abandons spades South can develop the clubs by ducking a trick to East. West therefore cashes his winners, involuntarily tightening up the position against himself, and he is eventually squeezed in the minor suits.

The contract does not have to be three no trumps, of course.

You open one club with the South hand. After West has bid hearts and East diamonds, you reject the humdrum contract of three no trumps in favour of a more exciting venture in five clubs.

West leads the queen of diamonds and when you cover, dummy's king is allowed to hold the trick. The only counter to this defence is to play back a diamond immediately. If East fails to take his two diamond

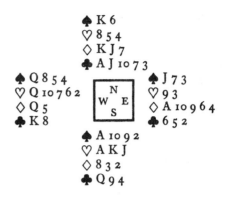

tricks, you can later play on spades, losing a trick to West but getting two discards from dummy. So East will take his two diamond tricks, and West will subsequently come under pressure in the following ending:

On the penultimate club from dummy you discard the jack of hearts, and West is caught in a ruffing squeeze.

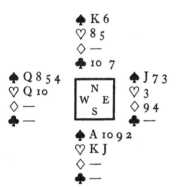

Back to three no trumps for the next hand and a progressive squeeze.

North-South game
Dealer South

S	W	N	E
1 ◇	pass	1 ♡	pass
2 ◇	pass	3 ♣	pass
3 NT	all pass		

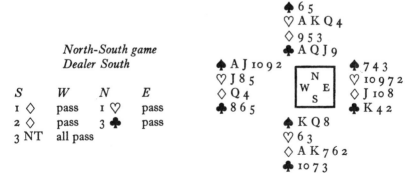

West leads the jack of spades, and when you hold off he continues with the ten of spades to your queen. You have seven top tricks, and the obvious way of trying for your contract is by taking the club finesse.

However, your table presence may tell you that West would have bid one spade if he had held the king of clubs as well as a decent spade suit. In that case your only chance is to return the king of spades at trick three. On the long spades you discard two clubs and a diamond from dummy (not two diamonds, for then East discards a heart and West switches to diamonds). East is squeezed in three suits and has to establish one of your menace cards. And you promptly use the established winner to squeeze him again for the ninth trick.

Note that it does not suffice to win the first spade and return the suit; West will lead a club at trick three.

As in all squeeze situations, each particular hand may have its own small complexities.

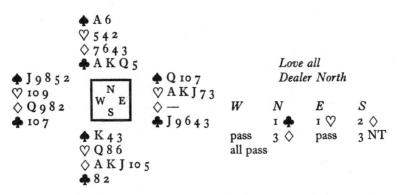

```
              ♠ A 6
              ♡ 5 4 2
              ◇ 7 6 4 3
              ♣ A K Q 5                    Love all
♠ J 9 8 5 2        ♠ Q 10 7               Dealer North
♡ 10 9        N    ♡ A K J 7 3
◇ Q 9 8 2   W   E  ◇ —           W     N     E     S
♣ 10 7         S   ♣ J 9 6 4 3                1 ♣   1 ♡   2 ◇
              ♠ K 4 3              pass     3 ◇   pass  3 NT
              ♡ Q 8 6             all pass
              ◇ A K J 10 5
              ♣ 8 2
```

West leads the ten of hearts which runs to your queen. When you cash the ace of diamonds, East discards a club.

Well, you have eight top tricks and it looks as though you should be able to squeeze both defenders – East in clubs and spades, West in diamonds and spades. A heart return will sever the link between the enemy hands.

However, if you play a heart at trick three, dummy is bound to be squeezed first. Since the spade menace is in your own hand, the minor suit menaces must be kept in dummy – the fourth club and the third diamond. But on the play of the last heart dummy will have to give up one of these cards.

You should therefore begin your double squeeze (which is non-simultaneous, anyway) by cashing your second diamond winner. This squeezes East out of his spade guard. And now, at trick four, the heart. On the last heart dummy can throw the small club which has served its purpose and is not needed any more. A simple squeeze against West in spades and diamonds produces the ninth trick.

Sometimes it looks for all the world as though the defenders have signed a suicide pact.

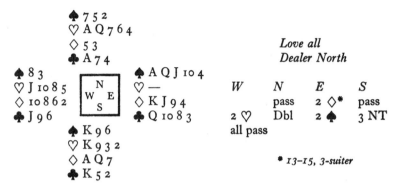

♠ 7 5 2
♡ A Q 7 6 4
◊ 5 3
♣ A 7 4

Love all
Dealer North

♠ 8 3
♡ J 10 8 5
◊ 10 8 6 2
♣ J 9 6

♠ A Q J 10 4
♡ —
◊ K J 9 4
♣ Q 10 8 3

♠ K 9 6
♡ K 9 3 2
◊ A Q 7
♣ K 5 2

W	N	E	S
	pass	2 ◊*	pass
2 ♡	Dbl	2 ♠	3 NT
all pass			

* *13–15, 3-suiter*

A spade is led to the ten and king (if you hold up, a diamond or club shift kills you). You play the king of hearts, and East discards a club. What now? Ace and queen of hearts? East will have to abandon one of the minors: if he chooses to let go diamonds, you will have easy club discards from both hands on the fourth spade and West will eventually be squeezed in the red suits. But East may choose to throw clubs on the hearts, in which case you will have to squeeze West in hearts and clubs. After cashing his spades, however, East will exit with a club and your squeeze will fail because you have been unable to take the diamond finesse.

Should you then take the diamond finesse before giving up the lead in spades? No good! East shifts immediately back to diamonds to establish an extra trick *and* entry in that suit.

So it seems that you must retain at least one heart honour in dummy and aim for a more complicated double-suicide ending. A heart to the queen and a spade to East. On the fourth round of spades you discard a heart, and the continuation depends on West's discard.

If West pitches a club, so does dummy. On the last spade you can throw hearts from both hands while West throws

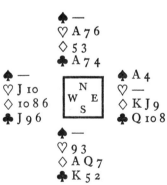

♠ —
♡ A 7 6
◊ 5 3
♣ A 7 4

♠ —
♡ J 10
◊ 10 8 6
♣ J 9 6

♠ A 4
♡ —
◊ K J 9
♣ Q 10 8

♠ —
♡ 9 3
◊ A Q 7
♣ K 5 2

[45]

another club. Now, whatever East leads, you play the king and ace of clubs to force a diamond discard from West, and the play of the ace of hearts squeezes East in the minor suits.

If West discards a diamond on the fourth spade, so does dummy. East must play his last spade, or else you set up a long heart. You discard a club from hand and a heart from dummy to leave this position:

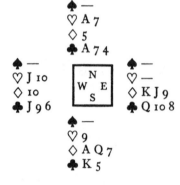

You take a club shift with the king and cross to the ace of hearts, forcing East to give up clubs. Two rounds of diamonds then put the screws on West.

If East chooses to exit with a diamond, it is West who is squeezed first. The second diamond compels him to part with a club, the small heart is thrown from dummy, and the ace of hearts fixes East.

Had this been a simultaneous double-suicide squeeze, we could have called it a lovers' leap. As things are, it seems more like a Romeo-and-Juliet type of confused death-succession.

Here is an example of a tempo sacrifice for strategic purposes. By cutting the link between the defenders' hands, you threaten with an 'invisible' squeeze against the defensive options.

```
              ♠ 8 5 4
              ♡ 10 7 6 4 2
              ◇ 10 4
              ♣ J 6 3
♠ 10 9 7 6   ┌──────┐   ♠ K Q J 2
♡ Q J 8 3    │  N   │   ♡ —
◇ 7 3        │W   E │   ◇ A 9 8 5 2
♣ 8 5 2      │  S   │   ♣ A 10 9 4
             └──────┘
              ♠ A 3
              ♡ A K 9 5
              ◇ K Q J 6
              ♣ K Q 7
```

North-South game
Dealer East

W	N	E	S
		2 ◇*	Dbl
2 ♡	pass	2 ♠	2 NT
all pass			

* *13–15, 3-suiter*

West leads the ten of spades to his partner's jack, and East continues with the queen of spades to knock out your ace.

An immediate attack on one of the minor suits will lead to failure, for by taking his ace at the right moment and returning the suit East will establish a sixth trick for the defence. But the play of the king of hearts applies pressure. If East throws a club or a diamond, you can safely knock out the ace of that suit.

East therefore discards the king of spades. Now you cross to the ten of diamonds (not the jack of clubs, for you are planning to concede a tempo and need to retain a double guard in both minor suits). East cannot afford to release the ace of diamonds, and now you cut the defenders adrift by playing the eight of spades. When West cashes his last spade East has to give up a potential long-card winner in one of the minors.

What has happened is that you have denied the defenders the elbow-room they needed for the manoeuvre of setting up a long card. If you had played anything but the eight of spades at trick five, you would have been defeated. The next deal shows that this elbow-room is a real and essential thing, not just a figure of speech.

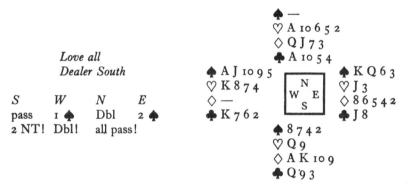

Needing a game swing, you decide to stick it out in this delicate contract of two no trumps. Three or four diamonds? Yes, but that would not be doubled.

West leads the jack of spades, and East overtakes with the queen. If the defenders go on to cash five spade tricks, you just keep three hearts and three clubs in dummy, and the forced lead from West will yield two extra tricks in the suit he opens up. East therefore shifts to a 'backward-tempo' tack by returning a diamond, and you proceed on a similar tack by playing back the eight of spades to the nine and king. West had to discard a club or a heart on the diamond lead, and you are careful to keep four cards in dummy of the suit he discarded. Another diamond from East; you win and play the seven of spades. Fortunately, your spades are just strong enough for this doubled contract of two no trumps. West has to win the trick, and

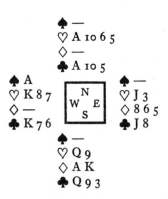

```
              ♠ —
              ♡ A 10 6 5
              ◇ —
              ♣ A 10 5
♠ A                      ♠ —
♡ K 8 7      ┌──────┐    ♡ J 3
◇ —          │  N   │    ◇ 8 6 5
♣ K 7 6      │ W  E │    ♣ J 8
             │  S   │
             └──────┘
              ♠ —
              ♡ Q 9
              ◇ A K
              ♣ Q 9 3
```

if he cashes two more spades you will gain two tricks from the end-play. But West may decide to lead the five of spades to his partner's six, leaving the diagram position.

Well, you win the diamond return, throwing a club from dummy, and play the queen of hearts. It makes no difference whether West covers or not. East is thrown in on the next round of hearts and has to concede your eighth trick whether he returns a diamond or a club.

If the defenders had been able to play a third round of diamonds before the fourth round of spades, you would have been defeated. Although dummy appears to have plenty of 'idle' cards, the third diamond squeezes you out of the vital elbow-room needed for your throw-in, which requires at least a six-card ending. After three rounds of diamonds and five rounds of spades, only a five-card ending is possible – you are forced to give up one of dummy's extended menaces.

Well, that would have happened if you had foolishly led the *four* of spades at any time. Or if you had started with 8 6 4 2 in spades. But then, of course, you would not have bid two no trumps!

So, apparently, there are squeezes against values that are not plainly visible – against planned strategies, defensive options, menaces, elbow-room, ideas, phantoms, abstractions. Perhaps we should try to identify the simplest kind of non-material devices.

3

Entry Squeezes

'Why are squeezes always inexorable?' asked Alec.

A hot and glassy calm had descended on the big lake that afternoon and you were lying on the foredeck, drinking beer and soaking up the sun while you waited for the first breath of the evening breeze that would enable the *Cormorant* to get under way again.

You knew what Alec meant, of course. It is hardly possible to pick up a bridge book or magazine these days without reading something like: '. . . on the play of the last trump East was inexorably squeezed in spades and diamonds.'

'Time for a change,' you agreed. 'For the next few years our squeezes will be ineluctable.'

Alec became thoughtful. 'When I was in prison . . .'

You waited patiently when he lapsed into silence, and after a while he continued with his story. His fellow-prisoners had been a rough and ugly bunch, and from choice Alec had spent most of his time in solitary confinement. But one day when he was out with a working party he had stumbled upon a battered copy of a Norwegian magazine. Later, in the dim light of his cell he had read it from cover to cover – quite a task, since he knew no Norwegian. The only thing that made any sense to him was a bridge problem.

You smiled. 'Do you remember the hand?'

'Of course I do. It was a straightforward squeeze hand – nothing out of the ordinary – but it gave me an idea. I began to wonder if a squeeze could work against seemingly immaterial cards.'

'It certainly can,' you said, sitting up and reaching for pencil and paper. A hand that you had played recently had started you thinking along similar lines.

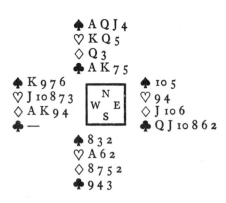

West had opened the bidding with one heart, and you eventually became declarer in a contract of three no trumps.

West began with the king, the ace, and the four of diamonds, and you discarded a club from the table.

The contract looked almost hopeless. The only immediate chance you could see was to find West with the doubleton king of spades and 2–6–3–2 (or 2–7–3–1) distribution. In that case the spade finesse would bring your total up to eight tricks, and whether East cashed the last diamond or not you might be able to squeeze him for the ninth trick.

At trick four East switched to the queen of clubs, however, and West's discard of a small heart put an end to that plan, for if West had no clubs he could hardly be short in spades as well. Hoping for a defensive error, you won the king of clubs and returned the low club. West concluded, quite correctly, that if you held four hearts to the ace he would soon be subjected to a progressive squeeze in three suits. Accordingly, he discarded another heart, which did the defence no harm.

East continued clubs and West had to find another discard in this position. He was not really in any trouble. If he had thrown a spade, for instance, you would have had no chance of making eight tricks let alone nine. Even a discard of the master diamond would have defeated three no trumps.

But West considered his heart holding to be worthless and threw another heart. That proved to be a fatal mistake. While West's third heart was not a guard in any ordinary

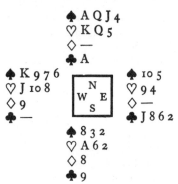

sense, it held great power, for it prevented you from securing two heart entries to the closed hand.

Once West had parted with a third heart your problems were over. You cashed the heart king and then overtook the heart queen with your ace. After a successful spade finesse you were able to lead the five of hearts to your six, making use of the extra entry and giving force to your remaining diamond which now acted as a menace. On this trick West was ineluctably squeezed in spades and diamonds and you took the balance of the tricks.

The hand is flawed in that West could have defeated the squeeze by proper discarding. But there is nothing impossible in the idea of a genuine squeeze against 'immaterial' cards in order to gain an extra entry. You remember a hand from a pairs tournament.

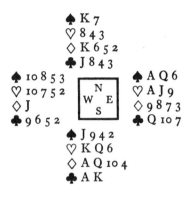

♠ K 7
♡ 8 4 3
◊ K 6 5 2
♣ J 8 4 3

♠ 10 8 5 3   ♠ A Q 6
♡ 10 7 5 2   ♡ A J 9
◊ J   ◊ 9 8 7 3
♣ 9 6 5 2   ♣ Q 10 7

♠ J 9 4 2
♡ K Q 6
◊ A Q 10 4
♣ A K

The South players, many experts among them, became declarer at two or three no trumps, generally after East had opened the bidding.

The West players favoured their stronger major and attacked with the three of spades. East won the first two tricks and continued with a third spade to declarer's jack, a club being discarded from dummy. The ace and queen of diamonds were cashed, West discarding a heart.

At this point the lines of play diverged, but no declarer made more than eight tricks. Yet here was a golden opportunity for the entry squeeze. If South concedes his remaining spade to West, discarding a heart from dummy, East is crushed in three suits. Clearly East cannot give up a club, and if he parts with a heart, one lead from dummy suffices to establish two heart tricks for declarer. So East is forced to discard one of his 'useless' diamonds – and declarer now has two diamond entries to dummy and can lead twice towards his heart honours.

Those silly little diamonds in the East hand have a function after all. Idle, irrelevant or immaterial as they

♠ —
♡ 8 4 3
◊ K 6
♣ J 8 4

♠ 10   ♠ —
♡ 10 7 5   ♡ A J 9
◊ —   ◊ 9 8
♣ 9 6 5 2 ♣ Q 10 7

♠ 9
♡ K Q 6
◊ 10 4
♣ A K

may be called, by their mere existence they also serve. They stand and wait, in the way, blocking traffic, hindering enemy lines of communication. And having this value, however silent and hidden, they are subject to the pressure of a squeeze.

Developing the theme, you realize that declarer may be required to un-block the entry suit in order to achieve a satisfactory entry squeeze position.

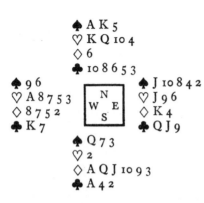

Bidding aggressively, you reach a contract of six diamonds after West has overcalled in hearts and has been raised by East.

The opening lead of the nine of spades gives you your chance. You win in dummy with the ace and . . .

Before we continue, let's look at the four hands and examine your prospects. There are four potential losers – a heart, a diamond and two clubs. The diamond loser will disappear after a finesse, and the heart loser will also vanish since West cannot afford to pop up with the heart ace on the first round of the suit. So you are faced with the problem of reducing two club losers to one.

Accordingly, upon winning the ace of spades, you unblock the seven from your own hand. No doubt in days to come this will be considered a routine play of the garden variety, hardly worth a mention in the daily newspaper column. But today, perhaps there are one or two players who would not think of it.

The rest is not too difficult. You finesse in trumps and draw four rounds, discarding clubs from the table. When you throw a further club on the fifth round of trumps, what is East to do? If he throws a club, you can lead a heart to the king (West is forced to duck) and then give up a club, establishing your twelfth trick in clubs. If East parts with a heart, the play is a heart to the king and then the queen of hearts for a club discard, smothering the jack and establishing the ten of hearts for a second discard.

So it comes to pass that East discards another of his 'useless' spades. You lead a heart to the king, ruff the four of hearts, overtake the queen of spades with the king and play the queen of hearts, pinning the jack as you discard a club from your hand. West wins with the ace but can do nothing to defeat the contract. Your carefully preserved three of spades allows you to cross to dummy with the five, and the ten of hearts is your twelfth trick.

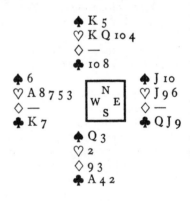

' "Carefully preserved" is as bad as "inexorable",' grumbled Alec.

'Clichés are always with us.' You told him the story of the foreign writer in search of literary variation who wrote: '. . . declarer was able to enter dummy with his thoughtfully pickled two of clubs.' The English language is full of little traps for the unwary.

As further complications are introduced, the plot grows thicker. You recall one of the standard textbook themes in which declarer attempts to gain two entries to dummy from this combination. West holds the king of spades and South leads the deuce, putting in dummy's jack and gaining the required two entries. Then, on the next page West foils the plan by putting up his king on the first round of the suit, blocking out the second entry. But on the *final* page . . .

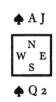

♠ A J

♠ Q 2

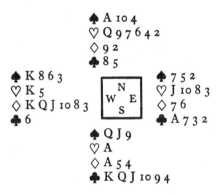

```
              ♠ A 10 4
              ♡ Q 9 7 6 4 2
              ◇ 9 2
              ♣ 8 5
♠ K 8 6 3                    ♠ 7 5 2
♡ K 5              N         ♡ J 10 8 3
◇ K Q J 10 8 3   W   E       ◇ 7 6
♣ 6                S         ♣ A 7 3 2
              ♠ Q J 9
              ♡ A
              ◇ A 5 4
              ♣ K Q J 10 9 4
```

West, who has bid and rebid diamonds, finds the best lead of his trump against your doubled contract of five clubs. On a diamond lead you would have been able either to ruff your third diamond with the eight of clubs or to squeeze West after ducking the first diamond.

East plays the ace and another trump and you draw two more rounds. Now you might play the ace of hearts followed by the nine of spades, intending to put in dummy's ten to gain the needed entry. But rather than give West the opportunity to be a hero by playing his king of spades on the nine, you should plan to squeeze West out of his entry-guard in spades. Simply play off your remaining trumps.

West is forced to keep three diamonds and two hearts, and thus can hold only king and one other spade. You discard a diamond from dummy on the last trump, cash the ace of hearts and lead the queen of spades. When West ducks, you continue with the jack of spades to the king and ace, concede a heart to West, and later enter dummy with the spade ten to cash the queen of hearts and claim your contract.

Sometimes it is not an extra entry you need but a card of re-entry to serve as a final squeeze-card. Here is an example of a re-entry squeeze.

East opens one no trump, you double, West bids two spades, and you eventually play in the ambitious contract of six no trumps.

West leads the nine of hearts to his partner's queen. East returns a diamond (best) to your jack, and you cross to dummy with the ace of hearts in order to run the nine of clubs. A finesse of the queen of clubs comes next, the ace of clubs is cashed, the ten of clubs is over-taken by the jack, and the last club is played for a heart discard.

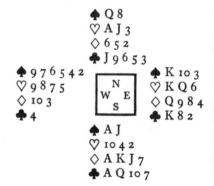

After taking the spade finesse, how can you get back to dummy to squeeze East in hearts and diamonds? The problem is strictly illusory, for if East has kept three diamonds and the king of hearts, he must already have bared the king of spades. This is the position before the play of the last club.

East really has no option but to discard the ten of spades on dummy's last club. Now a spade to your ace and a spade back to the queen forces him to surrender.

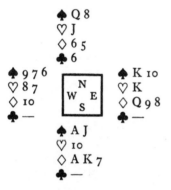

West opens with a bid of one heart, and again you land in six no trumps. The king of hearts is led, and you have to hold off since there is no conceivable throw-in ending. West then switches to his club.

The ace of diamonds is your only apparent entry, and the problem is how to finesse in spades and yet finish in your own hand to effect a red-suit squeeze against West.

Well, this is the sort of situa-

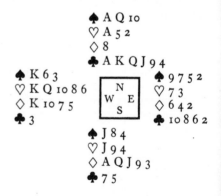

tion in which the re-entry squeeze can come to your rescue. Just run the

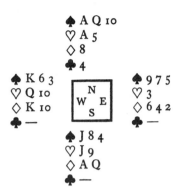

♠ A Q 10
♡ A 5
♢ 8
♣ 4

♠ K 6 3   ♠ 9 7 5
♡ Q 10   ♡ 3
♢ K 10   ♢ 6 4 2
♣ —   ♣ —

♠ J 8 4
♡ J 9
♢ A Q
♣ —

clubs, discarding three diamonds and a heart from hand. West has to keep two hearts and two diamonds and must therefore part with a spade.

Now you play a diamond to your ace, finesse the queen of spades and cash the ace, and the play of the ten of spades to your jack gives West the business.

Now that you are accustomed to playing six no trumps with less than 30 high-card points, let's have a shot at three no trumps with less than 20.

Game all
Dealer East

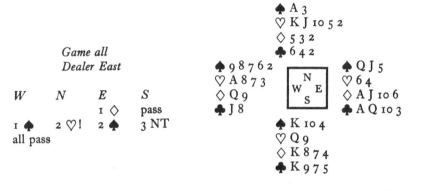

♠ A 3
♡ K J 10 5 2
♢ 5 3 2
♣ 6 4 2

♠ 9 8 7 6 2   ♠ Q J 5
♡ A 8 7 3   ♡ 6 4
♢ Q 9   ♢ A J 10 6
♣ J 8   ♣ A Q 10 3

♠ K 10 4
♡ Q 9
♢ K 8 7 4
♣ K 9 7 5

W	N	E	S
		1 ◇	pass
1 ♠	2 ♡!	2 ♠	3 NT
all pass			

Surprisingly, West decides not to double, and this turns out to be the correct decision in view of his subsequent defence. He leads the nine of spades to the three, jack and king, wins the second round of hearts and continues spades. East fidgets, but in the end doesn't unblock his queen of spades.

Now you manage to execute a most unusual re-entry squeeze by carefully discarding your *sevens* in the minor suits. On the play of dummy's last heart East is helpless. If he throws the queen of spades, you discard in

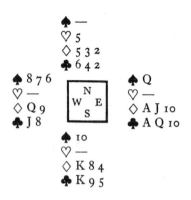

♠ —
♡ 5
◇ 5 3 2
♣ 6 4 2

♠ 8 7 6
♡ —
◇ Q 9
♣ J 8

♠ Q
♡ —
◇ A J 10
♣ A Q 10

♠ 10
♡ —
◇ K 8 4
♣ K 9 5

one minor suit and lead the other. Suppose you throw a diamond and play a club to your king and a club back. East is eventually thrown in and has to concede a trick to your king of diamonds.

East is no better off if he discards a minor suit card (say a diamond). Now you throw a club from hand and play a small diamond, unblocking your eight under the ace. East can now cash the queen of spades and exit in diamonds, but you have the re-entry in dummy for leading towards your king of clubs.

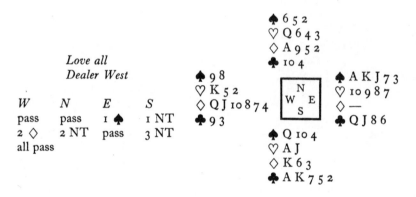

♠ 6 5 2
♡ Q 6 4 3
◇ A 9 5 2
♣ 10 4

Love all
Dealer West

♠ 9 8
♡ K 5 2
◇ Q J 10 8 7 4
♣ 9 3

♠ A K J 7 3
♡ 10 9 8 7
◇ —
♣ Q J 8 6

W	N	E	S
pass	pass	1 ♠	1 NT
2 ◇	2 NT	pass	3 NT
all pass			

♠ Q 10 4
♡ A J
◇ K 6 3
♣ A K 7 5 2

A spade lead would make the contract too difficult, but fortunately West leads the queen of diamonds. East discards a spade and you take your king, returning the suit immediately and allowing West to win with the ten. This time East discards a club, and West switches to the nine of spades, on which East plays the king and you the ten.

East suspects this to be a sly false card from Q 10 8 4, although in fact you have played the ten for quite a different reason. Anyway, East switches to the ten of hearts. This is covered by the jack and king, and West returns a heart to your ace. Now you play a diamond for a finesse of the nine, and when you play the ace of diamonds East is re-entry-squeezed. No doubt he will elect to throw the jack of spades, in which case you play a spade to the ace and *queen*. On winning the return of the queen of clubs in hand, you have a fine re-entry to dummy with the six of spades, which squeezes East in hearts and clubs.

The defenders have missed their way a couple of times, but that does not mean they are palookas. The best of defenders can go wrong in such situations, as indeed can the best of declarers.

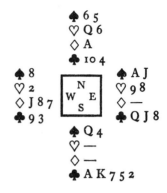

Here is another re-entry squeeze with a point about the defence.

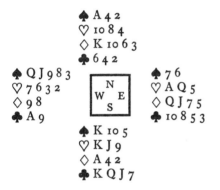

West leads the queen of spades against your contract of three no trumps and you win in hand with the king. Your king of clubs is captured by the ace, and West tries a switch to the nine of diamonds, which you allow to win the trick. You take the second diamond with your ace and play the ten of spades, allowing West to win with his jack, Dummy wins the spade return, and East finds himself re-entry-squeezed in this posi-

tion. A heart discard postpones the agony, but only for a moment. You continue with a small heart from the table, dropping your jack under the ace, and the third round of hearts brings East to his knees.

The point about the defence? Well, this squeeze, like every squeeze, is vulnerable to an attack on the vital entries. Instead of tamely playing a third round of spades when in with the jack, West should have returned his club to take out one of

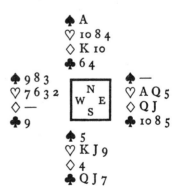

[57]

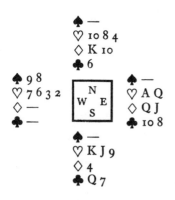

♠ —
♡ 10 8 4
◇ K 10
♣ 6

♠ 9 8   ♠ —
♡ 7 6 3 2   ♡ A Q
◇ —   ◇ Q J
♣ —   ♣ 10 8

♠ —
♡ K J 9
◇ 4
♣ Q 7

the entries in your hand. Now East throws his small heart on the ace of spades, and when a heart is led in the diagram position he plays the *queen*, not the ace.

What is the difference? Just that, after winning with the king, you have to commit yourself as to where you will retain the third-round heart winner. And, according to your choice, East can break up the squeeze by attacking the appropriate entry when he comes in with the ace of hearts. If you play the jack of hearts on the second round and keep the ten in dummy, he will return a club. Otherwise he will return a diamond.

An entry squeeze can sometimes be combined with strip play to produce a throw-in ending.

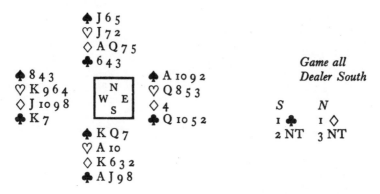

♠ J 6 5
♡ J 7 2
◇ A Q 7 5
♣ 6 4 3

♠ 8 4 3   ♠ A 10 9 2
♡ K 9 6 4   ♡ Q 8 5 3
◇ J 10 9 8   ◇ 4
♣ K 7   ♣ Q 10 5 2

♠ K Q 7
♡ A 10
◇ K 6 3 2
♣ A J 9 8

Game all
Dealer South

S	N
1 ♣	1 ◇
2 NT	3 NT

A spade to the ace and a heart back defeats this contract, but West makes the natural lead of the jack of diamonds. You win with the queen and play a club to the eight and king, and West switches to the eight of spades. You play low from dummy, and your queen is allowed to win (East cannot profit by playing the ace once the king of clubs has gone – you would simply unblock and make nine tricks).

A diamond to the ace is followed by a finesse of the club nine and then the king of diamonds. You lack the entry for a further club finesse, but when you concede the fourth diamond East is caught in an entry strip-squeeze. He has already discarded a heart and a spade on the diamonds, and if he now bares the ace of spades he will allow you to enter dummy with the jack. East therefore discards another heart, and West continues with a spade to the ten and king. Now you can cash the ace of hearts and exit either in spades or in hearts to achieve your throw-in.

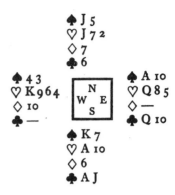

♠ J 5
♡ J 7 2
♢ 7
♣ 6

♠ 4 3
♡ K 9 6 4
♢ 10
♣ —

♠ A 10
♡ Q 8 5
♢ —
♣ Q 10

♠ K 7
♡ A 10
♢ 6
♣ A J

'Here is a curious hand,' you said to Alec. 'Try and find a lead to defeat six no trumps.'

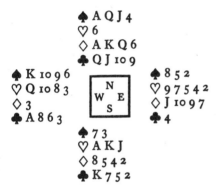

♠ A Q J 4
♡ 6
♢ A K Q 6
♣ Q J 10 9

♠ K 10 9 6
♡ Q 10 8 3
♢ 3
♣ A 8 6 3

♠ 8 5 2
♡ 9 7 5 4 2
♢ J 10 9 7
♣ 4

♠ 7 3
♡ A K J
♢ 8 5 4 2
♣ K 7 5 2

You analysed out loud for Alec's benefit: 'If South is able to finesse twice in spades, he will have eleven tricks, and you will be subjected to a major-suit squeeze for the twelfth trick.

'That rules out a black suit lead, so you consider the obvious lead of the singleton diamond. South wins and plays two more rounds of diamonds, pre-squeezing you out of a spade and a heart. Next comes the queen, jack and ten of clubs, and you

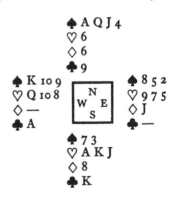

♠ A Q J 4
♡ 6
♢ 6
♣ 9

♠ K 10 9
♡ Q 10 8
♢ —
♣ A

♠ 8 5 2
♡ 9 7 5
♢ J
♣ —

♠ 7 3
♡ A K J
♢ 8
♣ K

have to hold off in order to deny South his extra entry. A fourth round of clubs in the diagram position will now compel you to give something away. A spade return will concede four spade tricks and the contract, but a heart return looks all right. South will make three hearts and two spades, but he will have to lose another trick.

'Are you satisfied with that analysis?' you asked.

'Yes,' he said. 'Well, no . . . wait

a minute. No, I see it now. South won't be so kind as to lead a fourth club. Instead he'll concede the fourth diamond to East, and I'll be decimated by a progressive triple squeeze.'

'So you can't beat six no trumps?'

'I didn't say that,' replied Alec, suspecting the trap. And after a couple of minutes he smiled and continued: 'If I had stopped analysing at the point where I decided that a black suit lead was out, shuffled my five red cards face downwards and picked one at random, I'd have had an 80% chance of beating the contract.'

Yes, an original heart lead defeats six no trumps. It gives declarer his eleventh trick at once, but by cutting the link between the two hands it removes all chance of a squeeze.

It is time to return to the problem that we left you with on page 26. If you remember, partner has rocketed you into a contract of seven no trumps, and West leads the ten of spades.

```
              ♠ J 7 4
              ♡ A K Q J
              ♢ A Q
              ♣ A Q J 6
♠ 10 9 8 6 2   ┌───────┐   ♠ K 3
♡ 10           │   N   │   ♡ 9 7 6 4 2
♢ K J 6        │ W   E │   ♢ 9 8 4 2
♣ K 9 7 3      │   S   │   ♣ 8 5
              └───────┘
              ♠ A Q 5
              ♡ 8 5 3
              ♢ 10 7 5 3
              ♣ 10 4 2
```

Does it seem any easier now? That's right, it's just another entry squeeze, and to give yourself a chance of making the contract you must unblock the seven of spades from dummy at trick one.

Let's assume that East plays the king of spades (not that it makes any difference). You win with the ace, finesse the queen of diamonds, cash the diamond ace and run the hearts. On the fourth heart West is in trouble. A club discard yields thirteen tricks directly, while a further spade discard (blanking the nine) gives you an extra entry to hand. You overtake the jack of spades with the queen, finesse in clubs, then lead the four of spades to your five to squeeze West.

However, what do you do if West throws the diamond king on the last heart, as in the diagram? Spade four to the queen, diamond ten? West throws the spade nine, you discard the spade jack from dummy and cash the established five of spades. At last West is forced to part with a club but – alas – dummy is one-suit-squeezed.

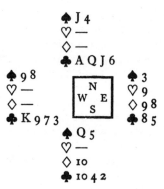

```
              ♠ J 4
              ♡ —
              ♢ —
              ♣ A Q J 6
♠ 9 8          ┌───────┐   ♠ 3
♡ —            │   N   │   ♡ 9
♢ —            │ W   E │   ♢ 9 8
♣ K 9 7 3      │   S   │   ♣ 8 5
              └───────┘
              ♠ Q 5
              ♡ —
              ♢ 10
              ♣ 10 4 2
```

But you don't lead the spade four from dummy in the diagram position, of course. You are now familiar with entry squeezes and it was not for nothing that you unblocked on the opening lead. You lead the jack of spades and overtake in hand, and on the play of the diamond ten West must either part with a club or allow you a re-entry to repeat the club finesse.

The slightest deviation from the correct sequence of plays results in defeat on that hand. You are likely to get the play right only if the characteristics of the entry squeeze are already stored in your memory banks, available for instant recall.

Finally, a double-entry squeeze.

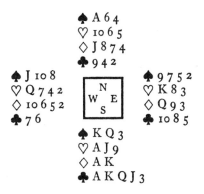

♠ A 6 4
♡ 10 6 5
♢ J 8 7 4
♣ 9 4 2

♠ J 10 8   ♠ 9 7 5 2
♡ Q 7 4 2 ♡ K 8 3
♢ 10 6 5 2 ♢ Q 9 3
♣ 7 6   ♣ 10 8 5

♠ K Q 3
♡ A J 9
♢ A K
♣ A K Q J 3

You play in a sound-looking contract of six no trumps and receive the jack of spades for an opening lead. The fly in the ointment soon becomes apparent – dummy lacks the two entries needed for successive heart finesses.

After winning the king of spades, you play two rounds of clubs, but the ten fails to drop. Now, rather than play East for both heart honours or guess which opponent may hold a doubleton honour, you decide to try for an entry squeeze. You run the rest of the clubs, discarding a diamond from dummy on the fourth round. On the fifth club West is in difficulty. He has to keep three hearts lest you lead a low heart from hand. He also has to hold three diamonds, for if not you can cash your diamond and spade winners and lead a heart from dummy. Whether or not East plays the king, you are now bound to score two heart tricks. Thus West is forced to part with one of his precious spades. (Surely, by this time, no one thinks of West's spades as valueless).

A heart is now discarded from dummy, and the pressure swings around to East. It is necessary for East to guard the diamond queen, and he also has to keep three hearts – otherwise

♠ A 6
♡ 10 6 5
♢ J 8 7
♣ —

♠ 10 8   ♠ 9 7
♡ Q 7 4 ♡ K 8 3
♢ 10 6 5 ♢ Q 9 3
♣ —   ♣ —

♠ Q 3
♡ A J 9
♢ A K
♣ 3

you can establish two heart tricks with just one lead from dummy. So East also is forced to reduce his spade holding to a singleton.

The double-entry squeeze is complete, and the rest is easy. You overtake the queen of spades with the ace and return a heart for a finesse. Winning the diamond return, you re-enter dummy with the six of spades and take a second heart finesse to land the slam.

4

Caught in the Backwash

Choosing presents for your son was always a problem. By the age of ten he had demolished an electric train set, two watches, three radios and a pocket calculator – taking them apart beyond all possibility of repair. When asked why he was so destructive, he would shrug his shoulders and say: 'I wanted to see how it worked.' It was not enough for him to have something happen when he pressed a button – he needed to know why it happened. Eventually you solved the problem by giving him construction kits, so that he could see how things worked by building up instead of tearing down.

Well, it is the nature of man to be curious. A child cannot stop asking 'Why?' any more than he can stop breathing. And the true bridge-player is like the child – once having glimpsed the astonishing beauties of the game, we are driven to find out all there is to know about it. The peculiarly satisfying quality of a bridge hand is that it is a fragment of human experience, a sliver of reality that, unlike most things in life, can be completely understood. We can grasp its meaning, relate it to a larger scheme of things, spot harmony, introduce order. Bridge relieves a small part of our urgent need for clarity. Really, we play and study the game for the same reason Dylan Thomas gave when asked why he wrote poetry: 'For some measure of light.'

If we seek to explain further our fascination with the game, we run up against the limitations of language. For bridge, in a sense, is like the act of love – its delights have to be experienced at first hand. How could a non-player be expected to understand the sweet torment of lying awake in the early hours of the morning while your mind tries to work out new ways of making last night's three no trumps? When an interesting deal arises, it is the inherent mystery that attracts us, not so much whether it ended in triumph or tragedy, in a brilliancy or a blunder. In fact, we sometimes find ourselves playing with great accuracy but without any real understanding of what is happening.

You remember a four-spade hand you played.

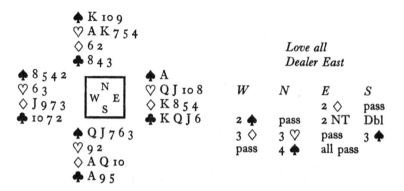

East's opening bid showed a three-suited hand with 12–16 points, and his removal of his partner's non-forcing response specified 1–4–4–4 distribution. The North-South bidding was perhaps a little ragged, but these are relatively uncharted waters.

The opening lead was the three of diamonds, and your ace captured East's king. You played a spade to the nine and ace, ducked the return of the king of clubs, won the club continuation, and embarked on a spectacular dummy reversal and end-play. After taking the club ace, you cashed the top hearts and ruffed a heart high in the closed hand. Entering dummy with a trump, you ruffed another heart high, returned to dummy with your last trump (leaving West with the only remaining trump) and played the established heart. West ruffed, but he was then down to J 9 in diamonds and had to lead into your tenace. Four spades bid and made; well played!

At the time you felt quite satisfied with your line of play, but early next morning you wake up with an uncomfortable feeling that all is not well. Why, you ask yourself, did you duck the first club? It was a routine sort of play; it couldn't do any harm. If your play had been made on a golf-course or a tennis-court, you could relax in the certain knowledge that yours had been the winning shot. But the true bridge-player cannot rejoice in winning if he does not fully understand what took place and why. So you now admit, in the privacy of your own consciousness, that when you ducked the first round of clubs you had not planned the play all the way through. You did not realize at the time that this was a necessary play, nor are you sure of it now. Far from feeling satisfied, you feel almost humiliated. Something happened that you did not understand. Intolerable!

After a while you begin to wonder whether your whole line of play was sensible. You have an uneasy feeling that instead of your leading spades and the opponents' leading clubs it should have been the other way round – you leading clubs and the defenders leading spades. But how could that be right? And why did you think of it?

You thought of it because there was a certain imprint on your memory. Your 6 a.m. reconsideration of the contract has reached the level of abstract analysis. The trouble, your mind now sees, is that East will knock out your club re-entry when he comes on lead with the ace of spades. Thus if you ruff the losing ten of diamonds in dummy, you will be unable to return to the South hand to draw trumps; West's eight of spades will score a decisive trick. Realizing this, your subconscious mind searches its files under 'methods of coping with menacing outstanding trumps' and comes up with a memory imprint, a deal you have once seen – time and place forgotten – fitting the case in hand.

South was declarer at four spades. He ducked the opening lead of the heart king, won the heart continuation, successfully finessed the ten of spades, and led the king of diamonds. West won and shifted to a club: queen, king, ace. Then came a finesse of the spade jack, and when East showed out, South paused to take stock. His problem was similar to the one encountered in the previous deal – no way to return to hand to draw trumps.

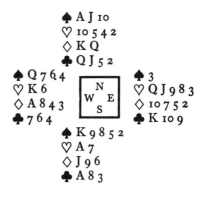

♠ A J 10
♡ 10 5 4 2
◇ K Q
♣ Q J 5 2

♠ Q 7 6 4   ♠ 3
♡ K 6   ♡ Q J 9 8 3
◇ A 8 4 3   ◇ 10 7 5 2
♣ 7 6 4   ♣ K 10 9

♠ K 9 8 5 2
♡ A 7
◇ J 9 6
♣ A 8 3

South countered neatly with a smother play. He cashed the queen of diamonds, then ruffed a heart with the spade king! This seemingly suicidal move was necessary to get the timing right. Declarer continued with the diamond jack (throwing dummy's last heart) and the club jack. Then he exited with the losing club.

Luck held up when West was unable to beat the eight of clubs. East, forced on lead, had to play a red card. South ruffed with the spade nine, and West's queen was blotted out.

Now your conscious mind realizes what your subconscious mind was contemplating when it gave you that uneasy feeling about having tackled the wrong black suit in *your* four spades.

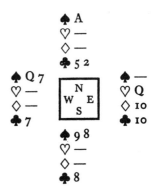

♠ A
♡ —
◇ —
♣ 5 2

♠ Q 7   ♠ —
♡ —   ♡ Q
◇ —   ◇ 10
♣ 7   ♣ 10

♠ 9 8
♡ —
◇ —
♣ 8

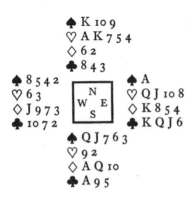

You could have tried to overcome your difficulties with the same type of suicide-ruff smother play. When you won the initial diamond lead, all you had to do was lead a small club yourself. If the defenders return any plain suit, you are home. Cash the remaining minor suit winners, take two top hearts and ruff a heart with a high trump, ruff the ten of diamonds, then ruff another heart with a high trump (a *double* suicide-ruff smother play – whipped cream on the cake!) and you have reached this position (it would have done West no good to under-ruff):

Now you exit with the club loser, and the whole bag of tricks explodes. First, West has to ruff his partner's trick. Next, West is end-played, forced to lead a trump. Finally, the effect of this is that East must take his blank ace and lead a club or a diamond, smothering the life out of his partner's eight of spades. So it's a double suicide-ruff throw-in smother play – and put a cherry on top of that whipped cream.

By now the alarm is ringing and it's time to get up. The ending would have

    ♠ K 10
    ♡ 7
    ♢ —
    ♣ 8

♠ 8 5 4 2   ♠ A
♡ —   N   ♡ —
♢ — W E ♢ 8
♣ —   S   ♣ J 6

    ♠ 7 6 3
    ♡ —
    ♢ —
    ♣ 9

been pretty, and there's nothing double-dummy about playing the hand that way since East was marked with a 1–4–4–4 distribution and the spade ace. Unfortunately, as you have realized for some time, the play does not succeed against best defence. After winning the club, East can simply cash the ace of spades and revert to clubs. Once the ace of spades has gone, the smother play does not work, because when West gains the lead at trick eleven he plays a second trump, establishing a further trick for his eight of spades. Exit the smother play, and you are back again with the situation you faced in real life.

You are up and contemplating your orange juice when you realize that the die is cast. You have just had another recollection, and this one seems to fit. You now think you know how you made your four-spade contract, and it was a very peculiar way indeed. So peculiar that you are not surprised you didn't recognize it. So peculiar that you begin to wonder about similar positions. You know that your mind will not rest until it has explored all the alleys and byways that surround the strange position you reached.

The deal you remembered was this:

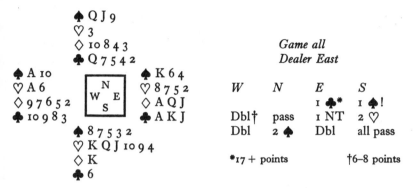

```
        ♠ Q J 9
        ♡ 3
        ◇ 10 8 4 3                Game all
        ♣ Q 7 5 4 2              Dealer East

♠ A 10           ♠ K 6 4
♡ A 6     N      ♡ 8 7 5 2      W    N    E      S
◇ 9 7 6 5 2 W E  ◇ A Q J                  1 ♣*   1 ♠!
♣ 10 9 8 3   S   ♣ A K J        Dbl† pass 1 NT   2 ♡
        ♠ 8 7 5 3 2            Dbl   2 ♠  Dbl    all pass
        ♡ K Q J 10 9 4
        ◇ K                    *17 + points  †6–8 points
        ♣ 6
```

West led the ten of clubs to his partner's jack. Declarer ruffed the second club and tried to slip through the nine of hearts, but West took his ace and switched to ace and another trump. A third trump lead by East would have seen declarer home easily, but the play of the heart suit had alerted East to this danger. He therefore cashed the diamond ace and continued with the queen for South to ruff. Declarer had lost five tricks and seemingly had to lose another – if he drew the last trump, he could not return to the closed hand to run the hearts.

But declarer was not licked. After ruffing the queen of diamonds, he played top hearts and was pleased to see that he could cash three of them without East ruffing in. He was then in a position to deal with East's pesky six of spades.

South ruffed the next heart with dummy's queen of spades – and East was squeezed. If he under-ruffed, the South hand would be high. If he unguarded either minor suit, dummy would be able to lead a *winner*. East would be forced to ruff, but South would over-ruff and cash his winning heart.

The position is simple enough, but it is quite an unusual squeeze. In the first place there is no two-card menace; East is squeezed in three singletons, one of which is a trump. It is unusual also in that East

```
            ♠ Q
            ♡ —
            ◇ 10
            ♣ Q
♠ —                  ♠ 6
♡ —      N           ♡ —
◇ 9 7  W   E         ◇ J
♣ 9      S           ♣ A
            ♠ 8
            ♡ K 4
            ◇ —
            ♣ —
```

is behind the menace cards. Normally you need at least one menace card behind the squeezee; here you don't have one. This suggests the name 'backwash' for our squeeze. The defender is all set to torpedo your contract with his trump, but when he is caught in the powerful backwash of your high ruff his boat capsizes.

The backwash squeeze is a useful way of neutralizing enemy trumps that cannot be drawn. It may help to establish a trump coup, for instance.

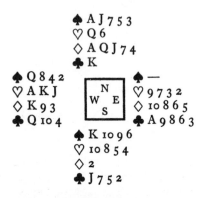

West opened one no trump (13–15), and North tried two diamonds, Astro, showing spades and another suit. South bid two spades, North raised, and South went on to game.

West cashed the two top hearts and shifted to a club. East took his ace and returned the suit for dummy to ruff. Declarer came to hand with the king of spades, inwardly wincing when the bad break revealed itself. He continued with a diamond finesse, cashed the ace of diamonds (discarding a heart from hand) and ruffed a diamond, bringing down the king. Then he led the nine of spades. West naturally covered with the queen, blocking the spade suit in this position:

The problem is familiar by now. Declarer has the rest of the tricks in a sense, but he can't return to the North hand to draw trumps if he cashes the ten of spades. So he doesn't cash it; he uses it to ruff a winning diamond instead! West is backwash-squeezed into a trump coup. An under-ruff allows declarer to re-enter the North hand with a ruff and draw the last trump. Any other discard sets up a winner in the South hand, and on the lead of that winner West has a choice of giving up his potential trump trick at the eleventh or the twelfth trick.

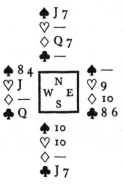

The squeeze was necessary on that hand because the defenders were unkind enough to attack dummy's entries. In some cases there just aren't enough entries in the first place. It often happens that declarer lacks the wherewithal both to draw trumps and to ruff out the side suit. In such hands a backwash squeeze may come to the rescue.

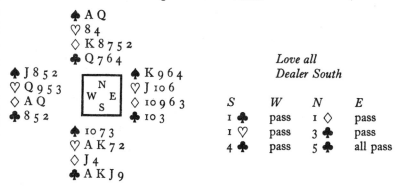

	♠ A Q		
	♡ 8 4		
	◊ K 8 7 5 2		
	♣ Q 7 6 4		

♠ J 8 5 2   ♠ K 9 6 4
♡ Q 9 5 3   ♡ J 10 6
◊ A Q   ◊ 10 9 6 3
♣ 8 5 2   ♣ 10 3

♠ 10 7 3
♡ A K 7 2
◊ J 4
♣ A K J 9

Love all
Dealer South

S	W	N	E
1 ♣	pass	1 ◊	pass
1 ♡	pass	3 ♣	pass
4 ♣	pass	5 ♣	all pass

West led the two of spades, and dummy's queen lost to the king. East returned a trump to declarer's ace. South couldn't hope to ruff three losers in dummy, so he had to plan to set up the diamonds. West played the queen on the first round (denying declarer the use of the king of diamonds as a later entry for a diamond ruff) and won the second diamond with the ace. He returned a trump (naturally retaining his eight) and South was up against it. He could not afford to win in dummy and ruff two diamonds, for that would establish West's eight of clubs. And if he won in the closed hand, he would need three entries to dummy to bring in the diamonds and there were only two.

However, there was still hope if West held the spade jack and the long hearts. South won the second trump in the closed hand, played off the ace and king of hearts, ruffed a heart, ruffed a diamond and played a spade to the ace, leaving:

Declarer led the seven of diamonds and ruffed, establishing the remaining diamond in dummy. On this trick West was backwash-squeezed in a position similar to the one that arose in two spades doubled.

One wonders just how many backwash squeezes have been overlooked in situations that do not quite allow the establishment and cashing of a side suit.

More frequently than with any other area of card-play, you may stumble into backwash country unawares. This is because the play that leads you there is often a routine, every-

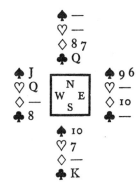

	♠ —	
	♡ —	
	◊ 8 7	
	♣ Q	

♠ J   ♠ 9 6
♡ Q   ♡ —
◊ —   ◊ 10
♣ 8   ♣ —

♠ 10
♡ 7
◊ —
♣ K

day line that involves drawing some but not all of the trumps, ruffing losers, and trying to set up side suits. However, you'd better learn to recognize the landmarks when you get there, otherwise you'll go astray.

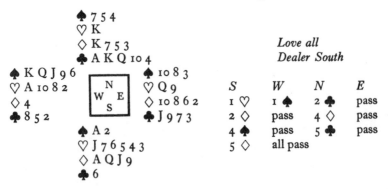

	♠ 7 5 4					
	♡ K					
	◇ K 7 5 3		*Love all*			
	♣ A K Q 10 4		*Dealer South*			

♠ K Q J 9 6   ♠ 10 8 3
♡ A 10 8 2   ♡ Q 9
◇ 4   ◇ 10 8 6 2
♣ 8 5 2   ♣ J 9 7 3

♠ A 2
♡ J 7 6 5 4 3
◇ A Q J 9
♣ 6

S	W	N	E
1 ♡	1 ♠	2 ♣	pass
2 ◇	pass	4 ◇	pass
4 ♠	pass	5 ♣	pass
5 ◇	all pass		

You win the spade lead, play the ace and king of clubs for a spade discard, and concede the king of hearts to the ace. After ruffing the spade return you ruff a heart in dummy, and when the queen appears you are not too happy about stopping in game. It looks like twelve easy tricks. Anyway, you continue with a diamond to your jack and ruff a small heart with the king of diamonds, and now East is slightly reluctant about his discard. This is the position:

East still has a discard to make, and in fact he is backwash-squeezed. If he gives up his exit card in spades, you'll have an easy time. After two rounds of trumps you just switch to hearts, and when East ruffs he has to lead into the club tenace.

East does better to discard a club, for now you will go down if you continue with a trump. To make the contract you have to read the position exactly, playing East for an original holding of four trumps and continuing

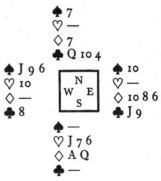

with the queen of clubs for a heart discard. When East ruffs the next club, you over-ruff and play the jack of hearts, throwing the spade from dummy. East can ruff, but he has to yield the last two tricks.

The following is a backwash dummy reversal.

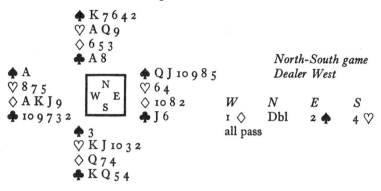

♠ K 7 6 4 2
♡ A Q 9
◇ 6 5 3
♣ A 8

North-South game
Dealer West

♠ A		♠ Q J 10 9 8 5	
♡ 8 7 5		♡ 6 4	
◇ A K J 9	N W E S	◇ 10 8 2	
♣ 10 9 7 3 2		♣ J 6	

♠ 3
♡ K J 10 3 2
◇ Q 7 4
♣ K Q 5 4

W	N	E	S
1 ◇	Dbl	2 ♠	4 ♡
all pass			

West cashes the ace of spades and then the king of diamonds. Seeing his partner's two of diamonds, he switches to a trump and you win in dummy with the nine. You ruff a spade high, West throwing a club, and a trump to dummy reveals the whole distribution. West can hardly have started with six clubs, so he is marked with the remaining trump. In a sense you have ten tricks, but the trouble is that you cannot ruff your losing club in dummy and also enjoy the king of spades.

So you ruff another spade high, and West discards the nine of diamonds. You return to dummy with the ace of clubs and ruff the last small spade in this position:

Caught in the backwash, West has to give up something or other. The jack of diamonds? You play the seven to his ace, win the club return, cash the other club honour, discarding the diamond from the table, and play the queen of diamonds. West has to ruff, and you end up making the king of spades after all.

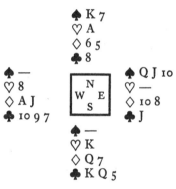

♠ K 7
♡ A
◇ 6 5
♣ 8

♠ —		♠ Q J 10	
♡ 8	N W E S	♡ —	
◇ A J		◇ 10 8	
♣ 10 9 7		♣ J	

♠ —
♡ K
◇ Q 7
♣ K Q 5

The next hand is similar; one needs a little practice to get the hang of these things.

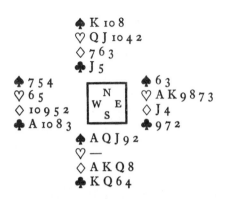

East makes a nuisance of himself with a weak opening bid of two hearts. You bid three hearts, and eventually become declarer in a contract of six spades.

West finds the best lead of a trump, which you win in dummy with the eight. The queen of hearts is covered by the king, and you ruff with the ace of spades. After a club to the jack, you continue with the jack of hearts, ruffing high when East covers with the ace. The king of clubs goes to the ace, and West returns a trump to dummy's ten.

Now your problem is the same as in the last hand. If West has the outstanding trump, you cannot enjoy your heart trick without giving up your minor suit ruff. Nor can you hope to squeeze West by drawing the last trump and cashing your heart, since you have to discard ahead of West.

This is precisely the sort of situation in which the backwash squeeze can help. So, in the diagram position you lead a small heart and ruff in hand, and West's boat is swamped, whether he discards a club, a diamond or his trump.

These situations arise with surprising frequency, but they usually go unrecognized. The declarer who is familiar with such positions has a small but appreciable advantage in practical play.

Anyone who has read a book on advanced play knows that the basic squeezes can often be used to avoid a guess, or at least to increase the amount of information available to declarer. A backwash squeeze may operate in exactly the same manner.

```
              ♠ K
              ♡ 10 4 2
              ◇ 7 6 3
              ♣ —
  ♠ 7                      ♠ —
  ♡ —         N            ♡ 9 8 7 3
  ◇ 10 9 5 2  W   E        ◇ J 4
  ♣ 10 8          S        ♣ 9
              ♠ Q
              ♡ —
              ◇ A K Q 8
              ♣ Q 6
```

Caught in the Backwash

♠ A 10 8 5 4 2
♡ 10 7 3
◇ 9 2   *Game all*
♣ K J   *Dealer South*

	N	
W		E
	S	

♠ 6
♡ K Q J 8
◇ K Q 10 5
♣ A 10 8 3

S	W	N	E
1 ♡	pass	1 ♠	pass
2 ◇	pass	2 ♠	pass
3 ♣	pass	3 ♡	pass
3 NT	pass	pass	Dbl
4 ♡	all pass		

You feared a spade lead after East's lead-directing double of three no trumps, so you removed to four hearts. West begins with a small trump, which looks like a good lead for the defence.

You win the first trick with the eight of hearts and, partly because it's convenient and partly because East seems likely to have more major suit cards than West, you lead a club to the jack, which holds. So far, so good. Now you try a diamond to the king, a club to the king, and another diamond. East plays the diamond ace and leads a trump. West plays the ace and another trump while East discards a spade. You have the lead in the South hand, needing five of the last six tricks from this position:

If either minor-suit honour is unguarded, you can make your contract by dropping it and drawing the last trump. But if, as the bidding suggests, West has a singleton spade, he may have both the diamond jack and the club queen guarded. Is there any way out?

Yes, there is. Don't cash the king of hearts. Instead, lead a spade to the ace and use your king of hearts for ruffing a spade. You lose nothing by this play, except in the wildly unlikely event that West is void in spades and East started with A J x in diamonds. If you were going to guess correctly to drop either the club queen or the diamond jack, you can do it later with

♠ A 10 8 5 4 2
♡ —
◇ —
♣ —

	N	
W		E
	S	

♠ 6
♡ K
◇ Q 10
♣ A 10

equal effect. West will make a trump trick but that's all, because he'll be end-played after taking it. And look what may happen if this is the position:

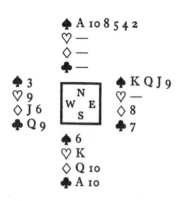

When you ruff the spade with the king of hearts, West is backwash-squeezed. You may, of course, misguess the position – you still have to read West's holding correctly. But you are no worse off than before; you will see another card played before making the decision; you will confirm the exact spade count. And no other play will work in the above ending.

How glad you are that your subconscious mind decided to investigate that four-spade contract! You have come upon a variation on the theme – one that requires declarer to trump a loser with his own high trump, setting up an unnecessary trump trick for an opponent. It might not be easy to find the play at the table, but the nomenclature is clear. This is a Vienna Coup backwash squeeze. South gets his own high trump out of the way in order to set up a winner for West; and then, so to speak, he squeezes him out of it.

Here is a further example of a Vienna Coup backwash.

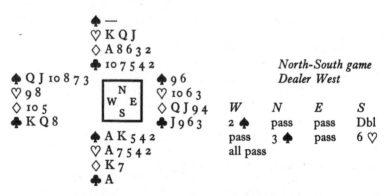

West leads the nine of hearts to dummy's jack, and you take a moment to review your prospects. There are only ten top tricks, and you cannot ruff more than one spade in dummy without setting up a trump trick for the opponents. What about the minors? You lack the entries to set up a club trick, and you don't fancy relying on a 3–3 diamond break. So you decide to ruff two spades after all, trusting that the twelfth trick will appear in the backwash.

[74]

You play a club to your ace and cash the ace and king of spades, impartially discarding a club and a diamond from the table. When you ruff a spade with the queen of hearts East discards a diamond. You return to hand with a club ruff and play a fourth spade in this position:

You apply the Vienna Coup by ruffing with the king of hearts, setting up a trump winner for East but at the same time bringing irresistible pressure to bear upon him.

A discard in either minor permits you to establish your twelfth trick in that suit. Alternatively, East can allow himself to be squeezed out of his trump trick.

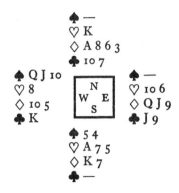

♠ —
♡ K
◇ A 8 6 3
♣ 10 7

♠ Q J 10
♡ 8
◇ 10 5
♣ K

♠ —
♡ 10 6
◇ Q J 9
♣ J 9

♠ 5 4
♡ A 7 5
◇ K 7
♣ —

The next hand is a little more difficult.

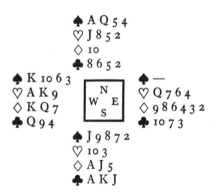

♠ A Q 5 4
♡ J 8 5 2
◇ 10
♣ 8 6 5 2

♠ K 10 6 3
♡ A K 9
◇ K Q 7
♣ Q 9 4

♠ —
♡ Q 7 6 4
◇ 9 8 6 4 3 2
♣ 10 7 3

♠ J 9 8 7 2
♡ 10 3
◇ A J 5
♣ A K J

West opens a strong no trump, East bids two diamonds, you venture two spades and end up playing in four spades doubled.

West cashes the ace and king of hearts, and then switches to the king of diamonds. You win with the ace, play the jack of spades to the king and ace, and return the jack of hearts. When East covers with the queen, you ruff and lead the seven of spades. If West covers, two ruffs in dummy will see you home, but he plays low. Now you try the eight of spades. If West plays low again, he will be strip-squeezed into a club end-play. But, of course, this time West covers with the ten of spades. Why do all the palookas turn into super-experts when playing against you? West has not the faintest idea why he played as he did, yet he has made the ending difficult for you.

This is the position:

One diamond ruff is no use to you, and you are unable to score the established heart in dummy. So, instead, you lead the heart and ruff it with your master trump. This sets up a trump winner for West, but he is backwash-squeezed at the same time. If he under-ruffs or discards a club, you continue with three rounds of clubs. If he parts with a diamond, you ruff out his queen, return to hand in clubs, and play the jack of diamonds.

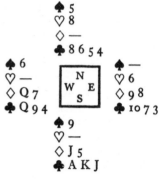

It is possible for a backwash squeeze to gain two tricks in the end-game even when there is no tenace position.

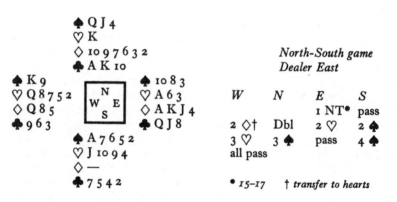

North-South game
Dealer East

W	N	E	S
		1 NT*	pass
2 ◇†	Dbl	2 ♡	2 ♠
3 ♡	3 ♠	pass	4 ♠
all pass			

* *15–17* † *transfer to hearts*

West leads the five of hearts to his partner's ace, and you ruff the return of the king of diamonds. The jack of hearts is covered by the queen and ruffed in dummy. If you knew all four hands at this stage, you could run home on a cross-ruff, but that line would be doomed if the spade king were with East. So you run the queen of spades, hoping to find the finesse right and the clubs evenly divided. West produces the king of spades and makes the awkward return of the diamond queen. On any other lead you could have hoped to draw trumps and play for 3–3 clubs. After ruffing this diamond you can no longer do that.

Since West has already produced two queens and a king, it is not hard to place the rest of the high cards. Is there a play for the contract? You could pitch the ten of clubs on your ten of hearts, cash the top clubs, ruff a

[76]

diamond, ruff a club, etc. . . . but that gives you only six tricks and you need seven. It's a hopeless-looking position – only a miracle can help, a miracle in the form of a Vienna Coup backwash squeeze.

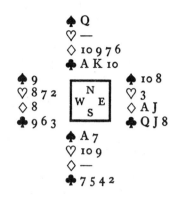

You should cash one high heart to strip East of his last idle card, but you mustn't discard the ten of clubs which is a vital menace card. Throw a diamond from dummy. Now ruff the nine of hearts with the queen of spades. You ruff your heart winner with your trump winner, setting up a trump trick for East but squeezing him out of two tricks simultaneously. If he discards a club or a spade, you play three rounds of clubs. If he parts with a diamond, you ruff a diamond low, cash the ace of spades throwing the ten of clubs, cross to the king of clubs and play diamonds.

Let's move a little closer to home.

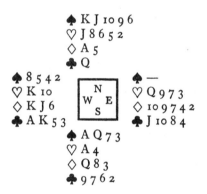

West opened one no trump, North tried an Astro two diamonds (showing spades and another suit), and South jumped to four spades.

West led the club king and, having nothing better to do, forced dummy with a second club. Hearts had to be established, so declarer played ace and another heart. West won and forced dummy again in clubs. Declarer continued with his plan. He ruffed a heart high, then led a low spade to dummy, learning of the unfortunate trump division.

Suddenly a simple hand had become complicated. North was on lead, with declarer needing five of the last six tricks.

Declarer ruffed a heart with the spade ace – and the backwash swirled around West. An under-ruff would let declarer draw trumps; and a diamond pitch (assuming South read the position, which was a near certainty) would allow declarer to keep all-round control by playing a diamond to the ace, then the jack of hearts, throwing a club. West therefore had to part with his club – it wasn't guarding anything but it was his only exit card. Declarer then took two trumps and led

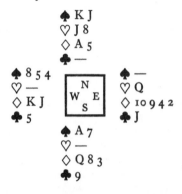

♠ K J
♡ J 8
◇ A 5
♣ —

♠ 8 5 4
♡ —
◇ K J
♣ 5

♠ —
♡ Q
◇ 10 9 4 2
♣ J

♠ A 7
♡ —
◇ Q 8 3
♣ 9

the last heart. West ruffed, but had to concede the last two tricks on his diamond return. Here the backwash acts against a minor tenace and extends to 'idle' exit cards in other suits, much as an ordinary strip-squeeze operates against exit cards, forcing the squeezee into an end-play.

Wait a minute! We've come to the 'secret' of the original deal.

Playing four spades, you won the diamond lead, lost a spade to the ace, ducked the club return, won the club continuation, played ace, king and another heart ruffing high, and led a trump to dummy to reach this position (needing four out of the remaining five tricks):

♠ K 10 9
♡ A K 7 5 4
◇ 6 2
♣ 8 4 3

♠ 8 5 4 2
♡ 6 3
◇ J 9 7 3
♣ 10 7 2

♠ A
♡ Q J 10 8
◇ K 8 5 4
♣ K Q J 6

♠ Q J 7 6 3
♡ 9 2
◇ A Q 10
♣ A 9 5

You ruffed a heart with the spade queen, and West was backwash-squeezed. He couldn't part with a trump – you would draw his last and cash a heart. He couldn't give up a diamond, for you would then drop his jack and continue with the ten of diamonds. When in practice he threw a club, you led a trump to dummy and played the winning heart. West ruffed and had to lead into your diamond tenace.

Now you *know* that you played the hand correctly, and you can see why the club

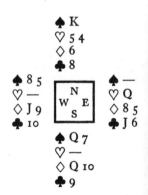

♠ K
♡ 5 4
◇ 6
♣ 8

♠ 8 5
♡ —
◇ J 9
♣ 10

♠ —
♡ Q
◇ 8 5
♣ J 6

♠ Q 7
♡ —
◇ Q 10
♣ 9

duck at trick three was necessary. Suppose you had taken the first club and played the same way. The ending would have been:

You could lead a heart and ruff with the spade queen, but there would be no squeeze. West would throw a club and your contract would go down the drain. In fact, you had to duck the club in order to rectify the count.

Backwash squeezes appear to contain all the familiar elements of ordinary simple squeezes, and to require preparation in the normal way – by rectifying the count, isolating or transferring a menace, Vienna Coup, and so on.

How satisfying to learn all about backwash squeezes as a result of your

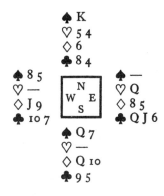

investigation! And what a coincidence that you should have a chance to use your newly-acquired technique in a team match that night – in defence!

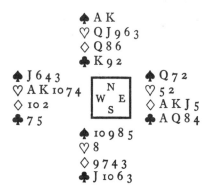

North-South were vulnerable and at both tables North opened one heart. East doubled, South passed, and West gambled a pass because of the vulnerability. At one table North passed, and the defenders took three diamonds, three clubs, and eventually three hearts for a penalty of 800. At your table, North, for reasons best known to himself, made an SOS redouble. South ran to one spade, and you, sitting West, doubled.

Your lead of the ten of diamonds was covered by the queen and king, and East returned a trump to dummy's king. The queen of hearts was led to your king, and you played a second trump to the ace. Declarer ruffed a heart in hand and led a club to the nine and queen, leaving:

Now East could draw South's last trump, cash the ace of clubs and give you a club ruff, but on your next play of the ace of hearts East would be squeezed first and declarer would make a further trick.

Dimly perceiving this, East left the trumps alone, playing ace and another club. You ruffed and found the killing defence – a low heart. This play is as good as any if South has the spade queen and East the ten, and in the actual case when East ruffed with the spade queen South was drowned in the backwash.

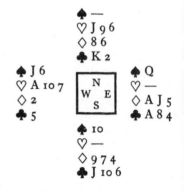

He suffered what must be almost the ultimate indignity of picking up a near-yarborough and being subjected to a squeeze in three suits, including his own trump suit. The defenders took the rest of the tricks; down four, 1100, and a useful gain of 7 i.m.p.

So you have learned something from all this. Not merely a new type of squeeze – another star, albeit a bright one, in a crowded Milky Way – but a useful method of overcoming a bad trump break. The investigation has covered a lot of ground, but you cannot help remembering that there were smother-play possibilities in your original four-spade contract. Surely, then, the backwash squeeze is not the only way of dealing with an annoying enemy trump. You know that you will not rest until you have determined the full range of available countermeasures.

5

Shifting Threats

Your recollections of holidays at your great-aunt Clara's country place are tinged with nostalgia. The summers seemed warmer then than they are now; they seemed better in every way.

You spent hours gathering the bright yellow mushrooms that grew in abundance in the darker corners of the woods, and whole days fishing in the deep pool where the grand-daddy of all trout was reputed to lurk. You never as much as caught sight of him, but somehow that didn't spoil the fun. When you became hot and tired of fishing, you stripped and cooled off in the clear water of the pool.

Why do these memories flash into your mind with such poignancy? You have only to close your eyes and you are again lying on the bank at the foot of the garden, absorbing summer with all your senses, the feel of the mossy turf at your back, the smell of fresh-cut grass, the tang of wild strawberries on your lips, watching a hawk hanging motionless in the cobalt sky, listening to the background murmur of insect noise and the lazy 'chock' of croquet balls from the lawn.

Tea was a picnic meal served under a great chestnut tree, and when the wasps became too troublesome around the jam-pot Aunt Clara and Aunt Alice would launch a two-pronged attack, the one armed with *The Times* and the other with the *Telegraph*. It was rare for a wasp to survive their onslaught.

'One threat isn't quite enough, boy,' remarked Aunt Clara serenely, 'but when you have two, you're in business.'

As usual, she followed up with a bridge analogy, and that is how you came to learn about another method of dealing with troublesome trumps. When an enemy trump stands in the way, preventing by virtue of its rank a complete cross-ruff, declarer's best counter is often the positional trump squeeze.

Here is one of the hands that Aunt Clara showed you.

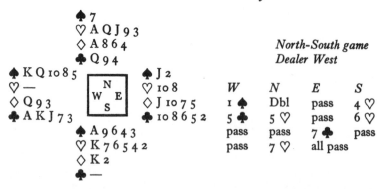

♠ 7
♡ A Q J 9 3
◇ A 8 6 4
♣ Q 9 4

North-South game
Dealer West

♠ K Q 10 8 5   ♠ J 2
♡ —   ♡ 10 8
◇ Q 9 3   ◇ J 10 7 5
♣ A K J 7 3   ♣ 10 8 6 5 2

♠ A 9 6 4 3
♡ K 7 6 5 4 2
◇ K 2
♣ —

W	N	E	S
1 ♠	Dbl	pass	4 ♡
5 ♣	5 ♡	pass	6 ♡
pass	pass	7 ♣	pass
pass	7 ♡	all pass	

Suppose, in the first place, that West leads a top club. If South decides that West's bidding suggests a heart void or that West would have led a trump if he had held one, he may time his play carefully enough to make his contract on a cross-ruff.

Now let's assume that West is made of sterner stuff. He knows South to be void in clubs and North to be short in spades. Since he can't lead a trump himself, his best defence against a cross-ruff is to try to promote a trump trick for his partner. How can he do that? By denying declarer extra entries for minor-suit ruffs in the closed hand. With this in mind, West leads the king of spades.

This leaves declarer an entry short for the cross-ruff, which cannot work if East has two trumps. So declarer might as well draw one round of trumps, hoping to find a 1–1 split.

Does South concede one down when West shows out? Certainly not. A positional trump squeeze will deal with East's outstanding trump and recover the trick that is lost by using two trumps to draw one. On the bidding West is the only defender who can guard spades and clubs, so South organizes the play as follows: spade ace, heart to jack, diamond to king, diamond to ace, diamond ruff, spade ruff with queen of hearts (just in case spades are 6–1), diamond ruff, coming down to this position:

If all dummy's trumps were higher than East's, declarer could cross-ruff and make the rest. However, the rank of East's trump requires that it be dealt with directly. So declarer leads

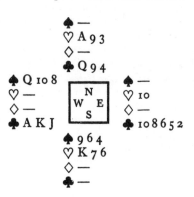

♠ —
♡ A 9 3
◇ —
♣ Q 9 4

♠ Q 10 8   ♠ —
♡ —   ♡ 10
◇ —   ◇ —
♣ A K J   ♣ 10 8 6 5 2

♠ 9 6 4
♡ K 7 6
◇ —
♣ —

[82]

the king of hearts and West, caught between *The Times* and the *Telegraph*, is duly squashed. If West throws a spade, South plays a low heart from dummy and ruffs out the spades. If West parts with a club, South overtakes with the heart ace and establishes his thirteenth trick in clubs.

That was not such a difficult play (although, as a famous chess master used to say, you must *see* it). The essential element is that the removal of the bothersome enemy trump is combined with a squeeze that operates on the trump-drawing trick. The trump suit must have an overtaking position so that the correct hand can be on lead after the squeezee has committed himself. To express this more generally there must be a potential shift of entry on the squeeze trick, hence these squeezes are sometimes referred to as 'entry-shifting squeezes'. In fact, the positional trump squeeze is just one member of a large family of entry-shifting squeezes.

It is perhaps less obvious that the trump matrix must be balanced, that is to say you must have the same number of trumps in each hand when the squeeze card is led.

A x	A x x	A x x x
K x	*K* x x	*K* x x x

Assuming for the sake of simplicity that West is to be squeezed, any of the above matrices will do the trick when the king is led.

But the declarer would have failed on the last deal if he had ended up in something like this position with the lead in the South hand. The difference is that South has ruffed two spades in dummy (one low and one high).

If the lead is on the table, South can recover by ruffing a club and then leading the king of hearts. But if the lead is with South, the squeeze fails, for when the king of hearts is played West can safely discard a club. So a certain degree of care is required in the timing of positional trump squeezes.

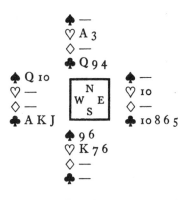

You thought of great-aunt Clara with gratitude when this hand turned up in your student days.

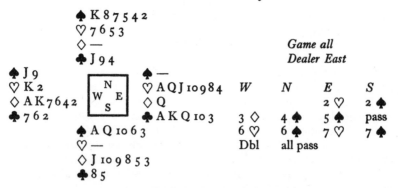

♠ K 8 7 5 4 2
♡ 7 6 5 3
◇ —
♣ J 9 4

Game all
Dealer East

♠ J 9
♡ K 2
◇ A K 7 6 4 2
♣ 7 6 2

♠ —
♡ A Q J 10 9 8 4
◇ Q
♣ A K Q 10 3

♠ A Q 10 6 3
♡ —
◇ J 10 9 8 5 3
♣ 8 5

W	N	E	S
		2 ♡	2 ♠
3 ◇	4 ♠	5 ♠	pass
6 ♡	6 ♠	7 ♡	7 ♠
Dbl	all pass		

West led the king of diamonds, and North banged down his cards
angrily. Yes, he would have doubled seven hearts for a diamond lead and
defeated the contract. Well, you would just have to do the best you could
in your phantom sacrifice. You ruffed the diamond lead, and with the fall
of the queen a ray of hope appeared. After ruffing a heart in hand, you
carefully cashed the queen of spades. When East showed out, you continued with the jack of diamonds, covered and ruffed, a heart ruff, three
winning diamonds, throwing clubs
from dummy, and a diamond ruff on
the table to leave this position:

East had no answer when you led
the king of spades from dummy. In
practice he chose to part with a club,
so you overtook with the ace of spades
and set up the eight of clubs as your
thirteenth trick.

The opportunity was too good to
miss. 'Why didn't you redouble?'
you demanded, fixing partner with a
stern look.

The smallest matrix in which an
entry-shifting squeeze can operate is a four-card ending, such as the one
shown above. The largest? Well, the squeeze can occur at trick two.

♠ K 8
♡ 7 6
◇ —
♣ —

♠ J
♡ —
◇ —
♣ 7 6 2

♠ —
♡ Q J
◇ —
♣ A K

♠ A 10
♡ —
◇ —
♣ 8 5

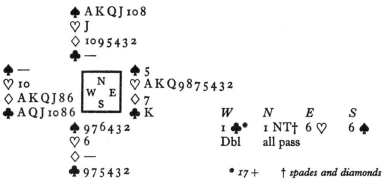

	W	N	E	S
	1 ♣*	1 NT†	6 ♡	6 ♠
	Dbl	all pass		

*17+   † *spades and diamonds*

West leads the heart to his partner's queen, and East has to return his trump to prevent a complete cross-ruff. South plays the nine, and West is squeezed.

This hand shows that the count has to be rectified for the entry-shifting squeeze just as for any other type of squeeze. The ten of hearts is West's only idle card but he has to use it in order to put his partner in for the trump lead, and in doing so he rectifies the count for declarer. Were North the declarer, East's trump lead would force him to use the entry-shifting mechanism too soon, before the count had been rectified. West would discard the idle ten of hearts and there would be no squeeze. Timing is all-important. We shall see shortly that it is sometimes possible to defeat an entry-shifting squeeze by denying declarer the chance to use his mechanism until it is *too late*.

Of course, a squeeze without the count is always possible when there is compensation in the form of extended menaces. Here is an example of an entry-shifting strip-squeeze.

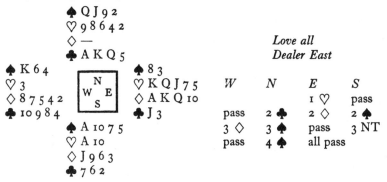

Love all
Dealer East

W	N	E	S
		1 ♡	pass
pass	2 ♣	2 ♢	2 ♠
3 ♢	3 ♠	pass	3 NT
pass	4 ♠	all pass	

West leads the three of hearts to the jack and ace. You return the ten of hearts, and East wins with the queen as West discards the two of diamonds. The trump switch runs to the king, and West plays a second trump to dummy's nine.

Your problem is that you cannot take a ruffing finesse in hearts before drawing the outstanding trump, which will leave you a trick short. And no more than nine tricks are available on a cross-ruff. So you fall back on the entry-shifting squeeze, cashing the three top clubs and leading the queen of spades from dummy in this position:

If East throws a heart, you can establish two heart tricks by ruffing finesse. And if he throws a diamond, you overtake with the ace of spades and lead a small diamond, discarding the club from the table. East must yield the rest of the tricks no matter what he returns.

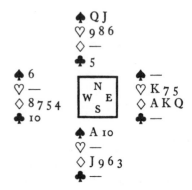

On certain hands it is quickly apparent that the defenders are going to ruin your cross-ruff by leading trumps at every opportunity. Then you must try to arrange the timing so that the final trump lead from one defender squeezes the other in a fratricidal way.

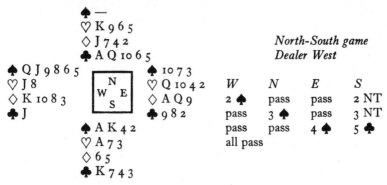

	W	*N*	*E*	*S*
	2 ♠	pass	pass	2 NT
	pass	3 ♠	pass	3 NT
	pass	pass	4 ♠	5 ♣
	all pass			

North-South game
Dealer West

West leads the jack of clubs to dummy's queen. When you play a small diamond at trick two, East plays the ace and returns the nine of clubs. West discards a spade and you win on the table with the ten. Now you have some thinking to do. If East can win the next diamond, he will certainly return his third trump to cut down your ruffs, and you will have to rely on a squeeze for your eleventh trick.

[86]

A red-suit squeeze against East? No good, for West is marked with six spades and one club and therefore six cards in the red suits. Nor is there any chance of a double squeeze, because your spade menace is wrongly placed. The only hope is to find West with four cards in one of the red suits. He is more likely to have four diamonds (out of seven) than four hearts (out of six), and you decide to play for the entry-shifting squeeze in spades and diamonds.

Clearly it would be a mistake to concede a second diamond at this stage. First you must remove West's idle cards and balance your trump position. So you cash the king of hearts, continue with a heart to the ace, play ace and king of spades, discarding hearts from the table, and ruff your third heart in dummy. Now the stage is set.

You play a diamond from dummy, and East finds himself on lead in this position:

East has to return his trump to prevent the threatened cross-ruff. You play the king of clubs, and West is trapped in the now-familiar way. If he lets go a diamond, you overtake with the ace of clubs and ruff a diamond to establish the jack. If West parts with a spade, you retain the lead in your own hand and establish a long spade.

At times you may be short of the entries needed to achieve a balanced trump matrix. Then you will have to enlist the help of the defenders.

```
                    ♠ —
                    ♡ —
                    ◇ J 7
                    ♣ A 6
        ♠ Q J       ┌───────┐      ♠ 10
        ♡ —         │   N   │      ♡ Q
        ◇ K 10      │ W   E │      ◇ Q
        ♣ —         │   S   │      ♣ 8
                    └───────┘
                    ♠ 4 2
                    ♡ —
                    ◇ —
                    ♣ K 7
```

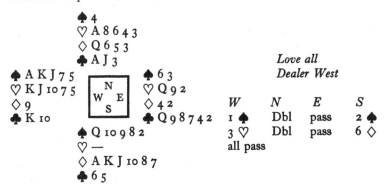

```
              ♠ 4
              ♡ A 8 6 4 3
              ◇ Q 6 5 3
              ♣ A J 3
♠ A K J 7 5   ┌───────┐   ♠ 6 3
♡ K J 10 7 5  │   N   │   ♡ Q 9 2
◇ 9           │ W   E │   ◇ 4 2
♣ K 10        │   S   │   ♣ Q 9 8 7 4 2
              └───────┘
              ♠ Q 10 9 8 2
              ♡ —
              ◇ A K J 10 8 7
              ♣ 6 5
```

Love all
Dealer West

W	N	E	S
1 ♠	Dbl	pass	2 ♠
3 ♡	Dbl	pass	6 ◇
all pass			

West leads the nine of diamonds, and you win in hand with the ten. What now?

Even if you count three ruffs in dummy, you still need a trick from spades to bring the tally up to twelve. Unfortunately, East's last trump is in the way – not because its rank stops a cross-ruff but because its trumping power prevents you from scoring your spade trick. The trump must therefore be drawn and, barring great luck in clubs, the twelfth trick must come from an entry-shifting squeeze against West. In order to achieve the balanced trump position you must ruff three times in the closed hand (since one ruff in dummy is necessary to prepare the establishment of your spade trick). Yet dummy has only two entries that you can use – the ace of clubs and the spade ruff.

Never mind. If West has all three spade honours, as seems likely, he will have to come to your aid whether he likes it or not. Play a club to the ace, discard your second club on the ace of hearts, and ruff a club in hand. Now exit with the ten of spades (or the queen, nine or eight) to put West on lead. A spade return is immediately fatal, so West will have to return a heart for you to ruff, thereby helping to adjust your trump matrix. You continue with the queen of spades, covered and ruffed, ruff the jack of clubs with the ace of trumps, and lead the jack of trumps in this position:

West's hand is destroyed as East's trump is drawn. If West throws a spade, you play the six of diamonds from dummy and ruff out the ace of spades. If West throws a heart, you overtake with the queen of diamonds and establish the hearts.

You realized, of course, that it was

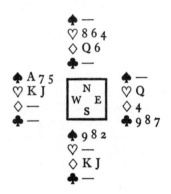

vital to keep the extended menace in hearts. If you had ruffed a heart instead of a club at trick four, West would have defeated you by playing a further heart when in with the spade. The ending would then have been:

When the jack of diamonds is led, West can safely throw a heart, since one extra heart trick is not enough for your slam. After overtaking the trump, ruffing a heart and ruffing a spade, you can cash the established heart, but you have to lose the last trick to the queen of clubs.

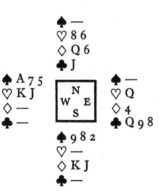

Defending against these positional trump squeezes calls for a great deal of precision. In addition to the normal countersqueeze measures, such as attacking entries, squashing menaces and disrupting the timing, defenders should look out for any chance of destroying the balanced position of declarer's trump suit. And a special form of defence is sometimes available – the double one-suit squeeze. You don't believe there is any such animal? Then take a look at this.

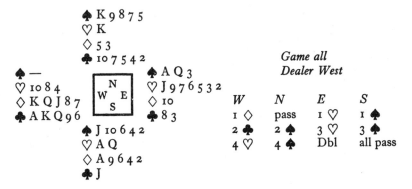

	W	N	E	S
	1 ◇	pass	1 ♡	1 ♠
	2 ♣	2 ♠	3 ♡	3 ♠
	4 ♡	4 ♠	Dbl	all pass

West leads the club king and shifts to the king of diamonds. A quick glance at the four hands shows that declarer needs seven trump tricks from a cross-ruff. Clearly he won't get them, for East will over-ruff a diamond and play two rounds of spades, limiting declarer to six trump tricks. So it's one down, right? Well, we shall see.

On the bidding it's not hard for declarer to place East with all three trumps and West with 0-3-5-5 distribution. South sees the possibility that West may be squeezed while East is drawing trumps. Accordingly, after winning the ace of diamonds at trick two, he makes the far-sighted play of leading to the heart king in order to ruff a club. The reason? To ensure that the North-South trump position will be balanced at the point when East draws trumps.

South continues with the ace of hearts for a diamond discard and a diamond ruff in dummy. Now watch it, East! This is the position with East still to play to the trick of the diamond ruff:

If East over-ruffs and plays trumps to stop the cross-ruff, West can discard his heart on the ace of spades. But when East plays his last trump and South puts on the jack or ten, West is caught in an entry-shifting trump squeeze. So don't be in too much of a hurry to stop the cross-ruff, East, or you will squeeze your partner. Just discard a heart and see what develops. Declarer ruffs a club and ruffs another diamond, reaching this position with East still to play:

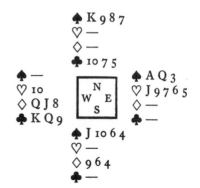

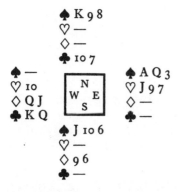

and South hands are both squeezed in spades. By the cards he plays the declarer must reveal which hand will win the twelfth trick, and West discards appropriately to win the last and setting trick.

By waiting until he could play his last trump at a time when declarer had only one trump left in each hand, East destroyed the entry-shifting mechanism. This type of defence requires both vision and patience.

Your adventures in entry-shifting began as a search for a means of

Shall we stop the cross-ruff now? Patience, East! Your time has not yet come. If you over-ruff, West can play the heart ten on your spade ace, but again he will be crushed when you lead your last trump. No, you must discard again. They also serve . . .

So declarer ruffs yet another club and yet another diamond, and with East to play the position is:

Now? Now! East over-ruffs and cashes his ace of spades. West can throw the heart ten, but the North

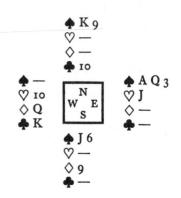

neutralizing a trump that stood in the way of a cross-ruff, and you have discovered the key to the manoeuvre – an equal number of trumps in each hand and an overtaking position in the trump suit. But now a question begins to intrigue you. Is there any reason why this entry-shifting procedure should be confined to plays in the trump suit?

Entry-Shifting at No Trumps

A little study shows that there are three basic situations in which an entry-shifting squeeze can be achieved at no trumps. In each of these diagrams South is on lead needing five of the last six tricks, and East holds immaterial cards.

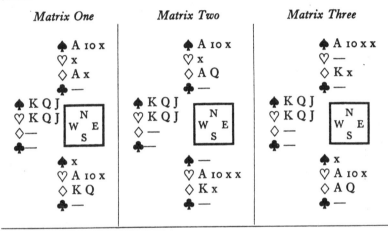

| *Matrix One* | *Matrix Two* | *Matrix Three* |

In each case South is unable to rectify the count for a simple squeeze against West. If he ducks a trick in either major suit, West will return the other major, shattering the linkage between the hands. However, an entry-shifting squeeze comes to the rescue.

In Matrix One West must commit himself when South leads the king of diamonds. When West weakens his holding in one major, South retains the *second* diamond entry in the hand containing that major and establishes the suit by playing the ace and another. Whereas in the positional trump squeeze the entry-shifting mechanism applies to an entry on the squeeze trick, here it is a *later* entry that is shifted.

In Matrix Two the spade void in the South hand makes it essential to win the first diamond in the North hand so as to give power to the spade menace. South leads low from hand, but the card with which he wins the trick in dummy depends on West's choice of discard.

Matrix Three shows the reverse situation – the first trick must be won in the South hand because of North's heart void. South leads the ace of diamonds and can elect to unblock the king or not according to West's defence.

Obviously, the relative ranks of the cards in the entry-shifting suit are crucial. The cards do not have to be the ace, king and queen, but they must be the highest, second-highest and third-highest of the remaining cards in the suit. Where there are entries to both threat suits, as in Matrix One, the entry-shifting suit may take any of the three forms, *K* Q opposite A x, K *x* opposite A Q, or *A* Q opposite K x. But when one hand has an entry-less threat suit, as in Matrices Two and Three, that hand needs the compensation of A Q in the entry-shifting suit.

So much for theory – let's see how it works in practice.

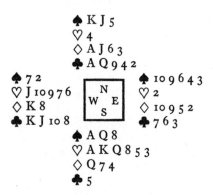

♠ K J 5
♡ 4
♢ A J 6 3
♣ A Q 9 4 2

♠ 7 2
♡ J 10 9 7 6
♢ K 8
♣ K J 10 8

♠ 10 9 6 4 3
♡ 2
♢ 10 9 5 2
♣ 7 6 3

♠ A Q 8
♡ A K Q 8 5 3
♢ Q 7 4
♣ 5

Sitting South, you reach a contract of six hearts, which West greedily doubles.

You remove to six no trumps, whereupon West doubles again and leads the jack of clubs.

Can you teach him a lesson?

You are pleased when the club finesse wins, but not so pleased at having an entry removed prematurely. You come to hand with the ace of spades, finesse the jack of diamonds and cash the diamond ace. Luck is with you when the king falls, and on the third round of diamonds West throws his last spade. Welcome to Matrix Two.

You lead the eight of spades, and it's all over for West.

Having no entry to dummy's threat suit, you had to leave dummy with the equivalent of A Q (in this case K J) in the entry-shifting suit. Indeed, that is why you won the first spade with the ace. Had you won with the queen you would have defeated yourself.

West doesn't care for that

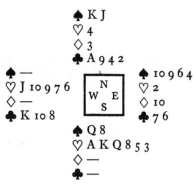

♠ K J
♡ 4
♢ 3
♣ A 9 4 2

♠ —
♡ J 10 9 7 6
♢ —
♣ K 10 8

♠ 10 9 6 4
♡ 2
♢ 10
♣ 7 6

♠ Q 8
♡ A K Q 8 5 3
♢ —
♣ —

result. He grumbles that he would have beaten you if he had led a heart instead of a club. Would you play it again redoubled? Of course you would. West leads the jack of hearts, and you have to win for fear of a club switch (at no trumps, even the entry-shifting squeeze won't save you if you have no entry in *either* threat suit). Now you are in the situation where you lack an entry to the menace suit in the closed hand, so you need Matrix Three, the equivalent of A Q in your own hand and K x in dummy. You take a second round of hearts, finesse the jack of diamonds and cash the ace, and then cash the jack of spades. This puts the spade suit into Matrix Three form,

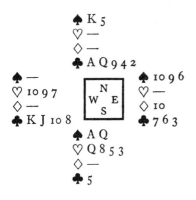

```
            ♠ K 5
            ♡ —
            ◇ —
            ♣ A Q 9 4 2
♠ —                         ♠ 10 9 6
♡ 10 9 7      N             ♡ —
◇ —        W     E          ◇ 10
♣ K J 10 8    S             ♣ 7 6 3
            ♠ A Q
            ♡ Q 8 5 3
            ◇ —
            ♣ 5
```

and you return to the queen of diamonds to reach the proper hand for the entry-shift.

When you lead the ace of spades, West is unable to hold the position.

One further point is worth noting. You could not have reached a winning position in either variation had the spade suit been a mere K x x opposite A Q x instead of K J x opposite A Q x. Remember this the next time someone complains to you about 'wasted values'. One would hesitate to say that entry-shifting potential can be recognized through such overstuffed card combinations, although . . .

You are South and you fear that this may turn out to be another of your eight-trick three no trump contracts. Just look at that duplication in clubs! Rotten luck, partner: if only . . .

West leads the six of spades to the nine and ten. Even with the diamond king onside you have only eight tricks, so you play back a spade, hoping West will cash out and rectify the count for a red-suit squeeze against East. However, West is wise to that game. He takes

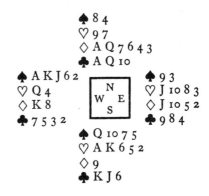

```
            ♠ 8 4
            ♡ 9 7
            ◇ A Q 7 6 4 3
            ♣ A Q 10
♠ A K J 6 2                 ♠ 9 3
♡ Q 4          N            ♡ J 10 8 3
◇ K 8       W     E         ◇ J 10 5 2
♣ 7 5 3 2      S            ♣ 9 8 4
            ♠ Q 10 7 5
            ♡ A K 6 5 2
            ◇ 9
            ♣ K J 6
```

only three spades and then leads the king of diamonds. How annoying! You can't duck to rectify the count, since West will then take the setting trick in spades. Rotten luck, partner: if only . . .

Come now, stop feeling sorry for yourself. If East is 4-4 or longer in the

red suits he can be entry-shift-squeezed. The lead must come through East
and you have no entry to dummy's
suit, so you need Matrix Three with
the North and South roles reversed,
in other words A Q in the North hand
opposite K x.

Can you get the club suit into that
form? Of course. Just cash the ten
first.

You win the diamond king with the
ace, cash the ten of clubs, and continue with the ace of clubs in the
diagram position to squeeze East into
submission.

We saw that a positional trump
squeeze could sometimes be destroyed by a double one-suit squeeze of a
fairly straightforward type. At no trumps the double one-suit squeeze
required to shatter an entry-shifting squeeze is more substantial.

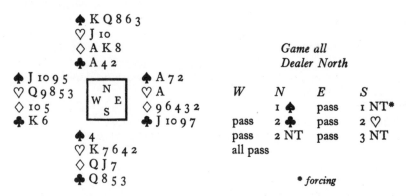

You are East this time, and in the early play you feel that you should
never have shown up for the match. West leads the jack of spades to the
queen and ace. You see that the long-range prospects in spades are unsatis-
factory, so you switch to the jack of clubs, on which South plays the five,
West the six and dummy the two. Thinking declarer may have Q 8 5 in
clubs, you continue with the club ten.

That does not work out too well. Declarer wins the club ace, finesses the
eight on the way back, cashes the club queen, and leads the jack of diamonds
to dummy's king! Next comes a heart to your ace, and you have just one
more chance to break the contract.

A spade lead is no good. Declarer will win and exit with a spade; and even if he guesses wrong, letting you win a trick with the seven, the play of the queen and ace of diamonds will squeeze West.

So you may as well return a diamond. Your diamonds all look the same – worthless – but are they? Suppose you return a low diamond. South plays the seven and achieves Matrix Two, the equivalent of K *x* opposite A Q. If West throws a spade, dummy wins with the eight and sets up the spades; if West throws a heart, dummy wins with the ace and plays on hearts.

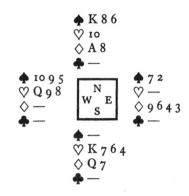

So you don't compound your folly by leading a low diamond. You strike back by leading your nine, injecting some rank into the diamond trick. And this apparently meaningless play – we might call it an elephant in a china shop – wreaks havoc with the delicate mechanism of the entry-shifting squeeze. The North-South hands are double-one-suit-squeezed in diamonds, the appropriate rank matrix cannot be achieved, and the contract fails.

Thus, if the squeeze is timed to occur when a defender leads the entry-shifting suit, an effective defence is sometimes possible.

For example, this position corresponds to Matrix Three but with East on lead.

If East leads the queen of diamonds, South can play the ace and West is squeezed. But if East leads a *low* diamond, the entry-shifting potential is destroyed.

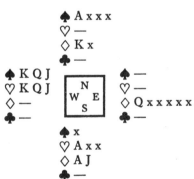

Now interchange the East-West hands, and put West on lead.

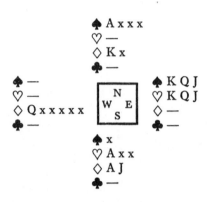

This time declarer needs Matrix Two, with the equivalent of A Q in the South hand. And this time West can destroy the squeeze by leading the *queen* of diamonds.

Does this sort of thing give you an eerie feeling? These positions seem almost supernatural – beyond all familiar aims of card-play, without the frame of reference of the game of bridge. If you haven't got the shivers yet, how will you feel when you discover that the same kind of extra-terrestrial influence can occur earlier than the entry-shifting squeeze trick.

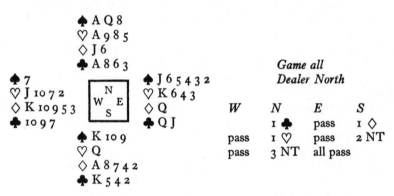

	W	N	E	S
		1 ♣	pass	1 ◇
	pass	1 ♡	pass	2 NT
	pass	3 NT	all pass	

Game all
Dealer North

West led the two of hearts, and you played low from dummy. East won the first trick with the king of hearts and the second trick with the queen of diamonds. He then shifted to the queen of clubs. Reading West for five diamonds and hoping that his hearts included the jack and ten, you planned an entry-shifting squeeze. You won the queen of clubs with the ace and started to unblock by returning the six of clubs. When East played the jack, you let him hold the trick, leaving this position:

A heart return, enabling you to set up your ninth trick in the suit, was too much to hope for. You anticipated the lead of a low spade, and you intended to win with the ten, cash the king of clubs, unblocking dummy's eight, and continue with the five of clubs to extract West's last spare diamond. The play of the spade nine would then catch West in the entry-shifting squeeze.

```
              ♠ A Q 8
              ♡ A 9 8
              ◇ J
              ♣ 8 3
♠ 7                       ♠ J 6 5 4 3 2
♡ J 10 7        N         ♡ 6 4 3
◇ K 10 9 5    W   E       ◇ —
♣ 10            S         ♣ —
              ♠ K 10 9
              ♡ —
              ◇ A 8 7 4
              ♣ K 5
```

But East didn't return a low spade. He unleashed the elephant by leading the jack of spades – straight out of the fourth dimension. Now your hands were double-one-suit-squeezed in spades. No matter how you played, there was no way of arriving at the rank matrix that you needed – the equivalent of K x opposite A Q.

Later, you thought about that jack of spades. Could East have played it by accident, or was it a case of supernatural intervention? Was your contract defeated by unearthly powers?

Non-Euclidean geometries include the Euclidean; complex numbers, with their 'imaginary' qualities, include the real ones; 'surrealism' in art may be a closer approximation of reality than 'realism'. If you find alien and un-explained forces at work in bridge, therefore, you should not write them off as supernatural. That would be an admission of ignorance. Something out of the ordinary is not less but *more* bridge-like than the familiar routine plays, because it includes more of the essential content of the game.

Granted, it was difficult to anticipate East's defence and its devastating effect, but the fact remains that you should have made your contract. Here is the hand again.

The essential nature of your plan was sound – to use an entry-shifting squeeze against West. Had you foreseen the release of the elephant in your china shop, you might have realized that you could counter this defence by transferring the entry-shifting mechanism from spades to clubs. In order to achieve this you must

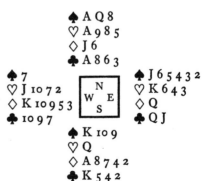

```
              ♠ A Q 8
              ♡ A 9 8 5
              ◇ J 6
              ♣ A 8 6 3
♠ 7                       ♠ J 6 5 4 3 2
♡ J 10 7 2      N         ♡ K 6 4 3
◇ K 10 9 5 3  W   E       ◇ Q
♣ 10 9 7        S         ♣ Q J
              ♠ K 10 9
              ♡ Q
              ◇ A 8 7 4 2
              ♣ K 5 4 2
```

be able to produce Matrix Two, the equivalent of K *x* opposite A Q, out of K 5 4 2 opposite A 8 6 3.

How can this be accomplished? Since you must play either the ace or king of clubs on one of the first two rounds, the matrix has to be 5 2 (or 4 2) opposite A 3. Of course, this matrix will not function while West still holds the club ten, but the problem sorts itself out because the preliminary squeeze forces West to part with the club ten.

When East switches to the queen of clubs at trick three, you should play the four from hand and the six from dummy. Win the next club in hand with the king, unblocking the eight in dummy. Then cash the ace and queen of spades, leaving this position:

When you lead the spade to your king, West is squeezed. If he throws a heart, you can lead the five of clubs to the ace and set up a heart trick; if West throws a diamond, you can establish diamonds and later use the club five as an entry to cash them; finally, if West throws the ten of clubs, as is most likely, you can lead the two of clubs to effect your entry-shifting squeeze.

Thus by changing your entry-shifting suit you are able to erect a barricade to keep that phantom elephant off your premises. Note the delicate manoeuvring that is sometimes required in order to bring the entry-shifting suit into the proper rank-matrix form.

	♠ 8	
	♡ A 9 8	
	◇ J	
	♣ A 3	
♠ —		♠ 5 4 3 2
♡ J 10 7	N	♡ 6 4 3
◇ K 10 9	W E	◇ —
♣ 10	S	♣ —
	♠ K	
	♡ —	
	◇ A 8 7 4	
	♣ 5 2	

Queer Finesses

In the previous deal, when threatened with a defence that could prevent the shaping of the obvious entry-shifting suit (spades) into correct rank-matrix form, you were obliged to prepare an auxiliary entry-shifting suit (clubs). You had to be careful how you played the clubs, but this was only a matter of routine unblocking, taking pains to follow suit with the correct cards.

Sometimes a more complicated manoeuvre has to be performed within the entry-shifting suit itself.

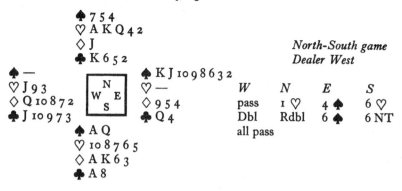

```
        ♠ 7 5 4
        ♡ A K Q 4 2
        ◇ J
        ♣ K 6 5 2                      North-South game
                                       Dealer West
♠ —                 ♠ K J 10 9 8 6 3 2
♡ J 9 3     N       ♡ —                W    N    E    S
◇ Q 10 8 7 2  W  E  ◇ 9 5 4            pass  1 ♡  4 ♠  6 ♡
♣ J 10 9 7 3    S   ♣ Q 4              Dbl  Rdbl 6 ♠  6 NT
        ♠ A Q                          all pass
        ♡ 10 8 7 6 5
        ◇ A K 6 3
        ♣ A 8
```

Not the very best of bidding, perhaps, but this is the sort of thing that happens in a rubber game. You would have taken the money by doubling six spades but for the fact that you were anxious to finish the rubber and get home to bed.

West attacks with the jack of clubs. Are you going to make it to bed? Since East is marked with eight spades, there is obviously a good chance of squeezing West in the minor suits. But if you duck a club to rectify the count, the defenders can lead a diamond to remove your last squeeze entry. You would prefer, if possible, to duck a diamond, making the fourth round of diamonds the threat, but if you do so the defenders will lead another club.

Lacking adequate entries for an ordinary squeeze, you decide to play for an entry-shifting squeeze against West. You have an entry in both threat suits, so any of the three basic matrices will produce a winning end-position, but it is essential that one of the three top heart honours remains in dummy after three rounds of hearts. This is easy enough to achieve if hearts are 2–1. You win the first three rounds of hearts with the ace, king and ten, ending with 8 7 in your hand opposite Q 4, the equivalent of Matrix One.

But if hearts are 3–0, you will need to take a double finesse to achieve the proper rank-matrix. On the bidding the 3–0 division seems highly probable, so you resolve to take what some people may think a 'queer finesse'. (Certainly your partner will think so if East has the jack of hearts!) You win the first trick with the ace of clubs and lead the ten of hearts, running it when West plays low. (It would not help West to cover: you would win in dummy, finesse in spades, and lead the eight of hearts. No matter how West played, you would be able to preserve a heart honour in dummy for the fourth round.) The ten of hearts holds the trick and you breathe a sigh of relief. West gives you an odd look when East shows out, but you don't think West will be amused for long. You continue with a heart to dummy's ace, a spade for a finesse of the queen, a heart to the king and a spade back to the ace, reaching this position:

Now the play of the eight of hearts puts it to West. If he throws a club, you underplay with dummy's four of hearts and continue with the king and another club. If West throws a diamond, you overtake with the heart queen and – careful now – lead *and pass* the jack of diamonds. This is a necessary move in order to deny East an entry in diamonds. (If East were able to cover the jack of diamonds, you would have to overtake and play the suit from the top, hoping that East started with Q 5 4 or that West would fail to unblock.)

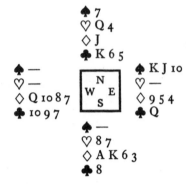

♠ 7
♡ Q 4
◇ J
♣ K 6 5

♠ —
♡ —
◇ Q 10 8 7
♣ 10 9 7

♠ K J 10
♡ —
◇ 9 5 4
♣ Q

♠ —
♡ 8 7
◇ A K 6 3
♣ 8

Be sure that you appreciate the fact that the contract cannot be made without taking a first-round finesse in hearts.

Everything in the world has an opposite. Sometimes you have to reject a normal finesse – take a 'queer non-finesse', as it were – in quest of the proper rank-matrix.

♠ A K 9 6
♡ K 6 2
◇ 5 4
♣ A K 9 5

North-South game
Dealer East

♠ 5 3
♡ 9 8 5
◇ A Q 7 6
♣ J 10 4 3

W	N	E	S
		pass	pass
pass	1 ♣	Dbl	3 ♣
pass	3 ♠	pass	3 NT
all pass			

West leads the queen of hearts, and you play low from dummy. West continues with the jack of hearts, and then the four of hearts to his partner's ace. East switches to the jack of diamonds, and you take a moment to consider the possibilities.

Even with both minor suit finesses right you have only eight tricks, and the ninth will have to come from a squeeze in spades and diamonds. This looks quite a good chance, for on the bidding East may well have something like ♠ Q J x x, ♡ A x x, ◇ K J 10 x, ♣ x x. A simple squeeze will not work, however, since West controls the third round of both suits. If you try to rectify the count by ducking a trick to East in either spades or diamonds, West will simply hang on to his stopper in the other suit and there will be no squeeze.

So what about an entry-shifting squeeze? East is the only one who controls the fourth round of spades and the fourth round of diamonds. If you can force him to commit himself between those two suits and at the same time avoid letting West on lead, you should be able to make this contract.

Suppose you win the queen of diamonds, run the jack of clubs successfully and continue with a small club to the ace. Now the play of the king of clubs will squeeze East as in the diagram:

Unfortunately, the position is complicated by your need to keep West off lead. You will be all right if East throws a diamond on the king of clubs, for you can play the four of clubs from hand and lead the diamond, ducking if East produces an honour and playing ace and another if East plays low. But if East discards a spade on the king of clubs, you will have no way of achieving your avoidance play in spades. You may drop the ten of clubs from hand and play the spades from the top, but East will unblock and West will score the tens of spades and hearts.

You must therefore try for a different entry-shifting ending, one that enables you to return to the closed hand on the squeezing trick if East discards a spade and to stay in dummy if he throws a diamond. Only the equivalent of K Q in dummy opposite A x in your own hand will do, and you can achieve that matrix only if the queen of clubs comes down in two rounds.

Nine tricks cannot be made by taking the club finesse, so you must go against the odds and play for the drop, hoping for the full hand to be something like this.

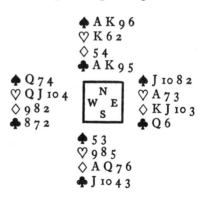

Win the queen of diamonds, lead the jack of clubs to the ace and cash the king of clubs. When the queen drops, you can continue with the nine of clubs, neatly combining your entry-shifting and avoidance threats.

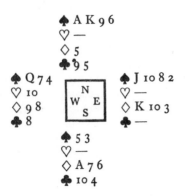

♠ A K 9 6
♡ —
◇ 5
♣ 9 5

♠ Q 7 4
♡ 10
◇ 9 8
♣ 8

♠ J 10 8 2
♡ —
◇ K 10 3
♣ —

♠ 5 3
♡ —
◇ A 7 6
♣ 10 4

If East throws a spade, you over-take with the ten of clubs and lead a spade to dummy's nine. If East pitches a diamond, you retain the lead in dummy and play on diamonds.

Very odd plays are sometimes re-quired in order to establish the appropriate rank-matrix. Suppose, for example, that you need the matrix A Q opposite K x from this spade suit. The only reasonable solution is to finesse the ten on the first round.

♠ A Q 10

♠ K 3 2

And if it occurs to West to put in the jack, you must take care to win with the queen. An alterna-tive play is to lead low to the queen, hoping for a singleton jack in the East hand, but that is well against the odds.

Sometimes you must play with care to avoid blocking your entry-shifting suit internally. Suppose that this is your heart holding and again you need the matrix A Q opposite K x.

♡ A Q 9

It is not good enough to lead low from hand, intending to finesse the nine, because West may be awkward and play the jack. Instead, you must lead the ten and underplay with the nine.

♡ K 10 2

Other considerations may affect your play of the entry-shifting suit. Suppose that you hold these clubs:

♣ A K 7 6 4

♣ J 10 8 5 3

The contract is no trumps and you are planning an entry-shifting squeeze against East requiring the rank-matrix A Q opposite K x. There are many final positions of the clubs that yield the correct matrix. If, for the sake of simplicity, we let 'A' stand for ace or king, 'J' for jack, ten or eight, and '7' for seven or six, we might end with:

♣ A 7   ♣ A 4   ♣ 7 4
        or   or
♣ J 5(3)   ♣ J 3   ♣ 5 3

Now suppose that North has no entry outside the club suit. Since the lead to the squeeze trick must come from the North hand, the third round of clubs must be won there. From this it follows that the first two rounds of clubs must not be won by the ace and king. A careful study of the suit will make this clear. In the first two matrices above the ace or king is needed as the squeeze card. And in the other matrix, 7 4 opposite 5 3, the *third* round of clubs must have been won by the ace or king – it could not have been won by the six, since South's other three cards are all higher than the six. Would you have believed, before experimenting with entry-shifting squeezes, that a 5–5 fit could be blocked?

Since one of the top honours must be saved until at least the third round of the suit, declarer has two choices. He can hope for a singleton queen in either hand and play a top honour (he is doomed if the queen does not fall). Or he can hope to find the club queen onside and finesse the jack on the first round. In most circumstances the immediate finesse will be the better percentage play.

Let's put this club suit into a deal.

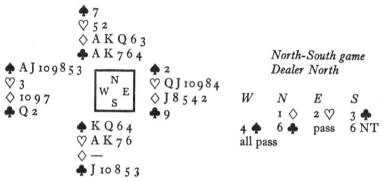

```
            ♠ 7
            ♡ 5 2
            ◇ A K Q 6 3
            ♣ A K 7 6 4                    North-South game
♠ A J 10 9 8 5 3        ♠ 2                 Dealer North
♡ 3          ┌─────┐    ♡ Q J 10 9 8 4
◇ 10 9 7     │  N  │    ◇ J 8 5 4 2
♣ Q 2      W │     │ E  ♣ 9               W      N      E      S
             │  S  │                             1 ◇    2 ♡    3 ♣
            ♠ K Q 6 4   └─────┘           4 ♠    6 ♣    pass   6 NT
            ♡ A K 7 6                      all pass
            ◇ —
            ♣ J 10 8 5 3
```

With so many cards in the major suits, South feared a cross-ruff against six clubs.

West led the three of hearts to his partner's eight. South won with the ace and immediately led the king of spades from hand. West was fairly sure that declarer had a second heart winner, and he saw that to take the ace of spades would rectify the count for a simple red suit squeeze against his partner. He therefore held up his ace, and the declarer had to turn his thoughts towards an entry-shifting squeeze.

Dummy had no outside entry, so the third round of clubs would have to be won on the table. The entry-shifting squeeze required East to have five diamonds, which would leave him with a singleton club. Clearly the percentage play was the first-round club finesse.

South led the jack of clubs, and when West played the two he carefully unblocked the six from dummy. Two more clubs were won by the ace and king, South unblocking with the ten and eight. Then came two rounds of diamonds for spade discards, leaving this position:

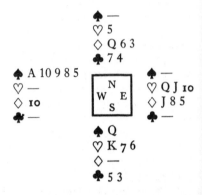

When the seven of clubs was led from dummy, East was faced with the familiar dilemma. A diamond? South would drop the five of clubs and play queen and another diamond. A heart? South would play the three of clubs and continue with the king and another heart.

So here we see another queer finesse that may be the indicated play on any particular hand. An interesting aspect of this club position is that, through what seems an other-worldly transformation, the club queen acquires extra power, assuming the status normally associated with a king. The queen and another club with East would be a 'stopper', just as the king and another is a stopper under more ordinary circumstances.

It is curious to note that Q x of clubs in the East hand defeats both six clubs and six no trumps.

6

Tricks With Trumps

'Stop talking so much. You're making me nervous,' said George to the silent Alec, who smiled good-naturedly and continued to pack tobacco into his ancient pipe.

Your pianist friend had managed to break loose from the concert hall circuit for a couple of days and had travelled down by rail to join you on the *Cormorant*. You were sitting on the terrace of a small hotel overlooking the anchorage, watching the changing patterns of light on the waters of the lake and hoping to see the brief miracle of the green flash as the sun dipped below the horizon. The evening air was soft with the scents of late summer. You stretched contentedly. Good weather, good beer and good companions – what more could a man ask?

The past hour had been spent in an animated discussion of entry-shifting squeezes, with George and you knocking ideas to and fro like ping-pong balls while Alec acted as umpire. The side excursion into no trump territory had been worth while for its own sake, although it had led you away from your original intention of exploring the various ways of dealing with bothersome enemy trumps. Now it was time to return to the main track.

George was scribbling on a paper napkin again. 'Let's see you make four spades,' he said, handing over a diagram. One glance was enough to indicate that the pair of you had been thinking along similar lines.

Entry-shifting trump squeezes are in the nature of redemptive devices – ways of recouping what has been lost through your inability to play a complete cross-ruff. But if you have no more plain suit losers and are threatened only in the trump suit, nothing can save you but a trump-manoeuvre.

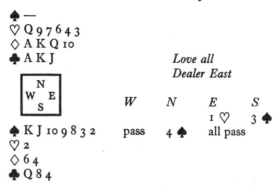

♠ —
♡ Q 9 7 6 4 3
♢ A K Q 10
♣ A K J

Love all
Dealer East

W	N	E	S
		1 ♡	3 ♠

♠ K J 10 9 8 3 2   pass   4 ♠   all pass
♡ 2
♢ 6 4
♣ Q 8 4

West leads the king of hearts to his partner's ace. East continues with a small heart, and you ruff with the jack of spades as West discards a club. What now?

The problem is to avoid the loss of three trump tricks. East is marked with the ace and queen of spades for his opening bid, and it is clear that a direct assault with your high trumps will give you no chance. (Ten of spades to the queen, a heart ruffed with the nine of spades, eight of spades to the ace. Now a further heart promotes a third trump trick for the defence even if the spades are 3–3.) Of course, you could lead a low trump at once, playing East for A Q doubleton in spades. This is an improvement, but surely there is a way to avoid depending on such a specific holding. So you decide to employ what might be called the 'elopement principle'.

Declarer often tries to scramble home in his contract by taking side-suit winners and scoring as many trumps as he can by ruffing. This neutralizes the strength of the enemy trump holding, causing their trumps and side-suit winners to crash together on the last few tricks. You plan to use an extension of this principle, scoring your side winners and *low* trumps at an early stage. In effect, you hope to run the opponents out of tricks on which to get an over-ruff. Your play requires East to hold at least five cards in the minor suits and no singleton – a much better chance than A Q doubleton in spades.

First you play the ace, king and ten of diamonds. If East follows, you ruff with the two of spades, cash the ace and king of clubs, and lead the queen of diamonds. If East follows to this trick, he must have started with 2–5–4–2 distribution, so you ruff high and lead the queen of clubs for East to ruff. Eventually you play your remaining low spade to East's ace, leaving yourself with a solid trump holding. If East discards on the queen of diamonds, you can throw the club queen and lead the club jack from dummy. East must then either allow you to ruff with your remaining small trump or ruff low himself, leaving himself with A Q doubleton and enabling you to over-ruff and lead your small trump with confidence.

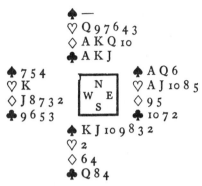

♠ —
♡ Q 9 7 6 4 3
◇ A K Q 10
♣ A K J

♠ 7 5 4   ♠ A Q 6
♡ K   ♡ A J 10 8 5
◇ J 8 7 3 2   ◇ 9 5
♣ 9 6 5 3   ♣ 10 7 2

♠ K J 10 9 8 3 2
♡ 2
◇ 6 4
♣ Q 8 4

In practice, this turns out to be the deal.

East doesn't follow to the ten of diamonds; he discards a club. So you ruff with the two of spades, take the ace and king of clubs, and lead the queen of diamonds. East can't afford to let this go by (you would throw a club and lead a club), so he ruffs with the six of spades. You over-ruff, leaving this position:

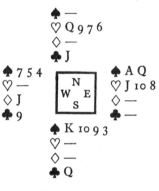

♠ —
♡ Q 9 7 6
◇ —
♣ J

♠ 7 5 4   ♠ A Q
♡ —   ♡ J 10 8
◇ J   ◇ —
♣ 9   ♣ —

♠ K 10 9 3
♡ —
◇ —
♣ Q

Now you play the queen of clubs (not the low trump, for East would win and return a heart and West would discard his last club). East ruffs with the queen of spades and returns a heart, but you ruff high and exit with the three of spades to bring home your contract.

On this hand East has no defence against the elopement play, but it doesn't take much to shift the balance of power. Suppose we interchange the king and queen of spades. The bidding is the same and so is the early play – the heart king overtaken by the ace and a second heart ruffed high.

♠ —
♡ Q 9 7 6 4 3
◇ A K Q 10
♣ A K J

♠ 7 5 4   ♠ A K 6
♡ K   ♡ A J 10 8 5
◇ J 8 7 3 2   ◇ 9 5
♣ 9 6 5 3   ♣ 10 7 2

♠ Q J 10 9 8 3 2
♡ 2
◇ 6 4
♣ Q 8 4

Again your best chance is to try to 'elope' with your small trumps, so you play the ace and king of diamonds and continue as before with the ten. But now East may come up with the winning defence of ruffing high and playing another heart. When you ruff high, West will shed a second club, and you will have no way of preventing the promotion of a third defensive trump trick.

If East goes astray by discarding a club on the ten of diamonds, you can ruff low, play off the ace and king of clubs, and continue with the queen of diamonds. Now East has a second bite at the cherry. Again he can defeat the contract by ruffing high and playing another heart, leaving this position:

After ruffing the heart high you have to lead trumps from your hand. And when East comes in with the ace of spades he plays yet another heart to promote a trick for his partner's seven of spades.

It is worth noting that the best defence against this type of attack is often to ruff high at the earliest opportunity and ram a side suit through declarer.

Playing a winning trump on a plain suit lead, like its less spectacular analogue, the uppercut, has the effect of shifting the relative ranks in the trump suit. Sometimes no further effort is needed once a high trump has been withdrawn from circulation in this way.

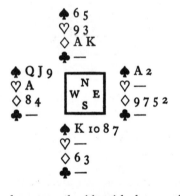

In this diagram spades are trumps, West is on lead, and the defenders need three tricks to defeat the contract.

When West leads the ace of hearts, the defenders make their three tricks if East has the presence of mind to ruff with the ace of spades. That is all it takes to achieve the promotion. West's trump holding automatically becomes worth two tricks once East has stepped aside with the ace of spades.

More often, trump promotion for the defence will be accomplished in two stages – a high ruff, followed by the lead of a plain suit through declarer.

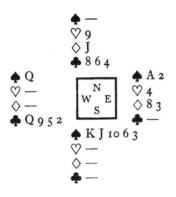

Again spades are trumps, and this time declarer can afford to lose only one trick. The lead is in dummy, and South attempts to enter his hand by means of a club ruff. If he is allowed to do so, he may guess too well at the next trick, leading the king of spades to pin West's queen.

East should not give South the chance, of course. He should ruff dummy's club with the ace of spades and play a heart or a diamond to promote a trick for his partner's queen of spades.

Let us try a further variation on our original four-spade hand.

East opens a heart, you pre-empt with three spades and partner raises to four spades. West leads the king of hearts and continues with a heart for you to ruff.

Again you cannot afford to play trumps and must hope to elope with your trump midgets. This time you need a discard on the diamonds, so you play off the ace, king and queen, discarding a club from your hand. Then you play the ten of diamonds in this position:

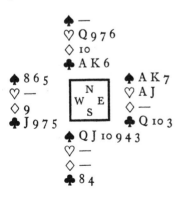

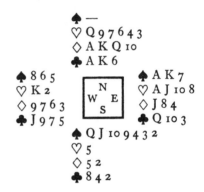

If East discards a club, you ruff with the three of spades and continue with three rounds of clubs, eloping with your four of spades behind East's A K 7.

Yes, but you know that East will ruff the fourth diamond with the king of spades in order to lead a heart. Careful, now. On no account must you throw a second club under the king of spades. If you do, you will eventually have to ruff the second round of clubs and lead trumps from your hand – with disastrous consequences. When East ruffs high with the king of spades you must discard a small spade! Then, after ruffing a heart high, you can ruff the third round of clubs with your other small spade, ending with nothing but trump honours, Q J 10, in your hand.

That's an unusual way of getting rid of a trump loser – by discarding it. In fact, you can have the three of spades all ready to play on dummy's diamond whether East discards a club or ruffs high. Of course, you may dislocate your wrist in snatching it back if East ruffs with the *seven* of spades.

Since we are going to explore elopement plays in some depth, we had better attempt to bring some order to the subject. First, a definition. Elopement play may be defined as a method of scoring tricks (or a threat to score tricks) with trumps that do not have ordinary trick-taking power by virtue of their rank.

The simplest elopements are familiar to all experienced players. The so-called *coup en passant* has a relatively high frequency of occurrence.

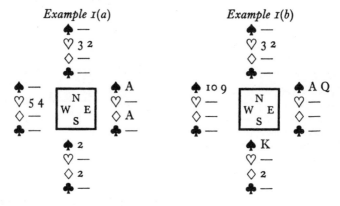

In each case spades are trumps, and when a heart is led from the North hand the declarer elopes with a trump trick. Example 1(a) might be called a 'pure elopement' because the exact rank of South's trump is irrelevant – any trump will do. Example 1(b), however, shows an 'elopement by rank' where the rank of South's trump is vital – nothing lower than the king would allow him to score a trick.

Pure elopements can be subdivided into 'positional' and 'automatic' groups. Example 1(a) shows the positional type, which succeeds by virtue of the fact that East, the defender with the master trump, has to play ahead of South. Interchange the East and West hands and the declarer is unable to score a trick.

Example 1(c) shows the automatic type of pure elopement, which can succeed against either defender. The only requirement is that the defender with the master trump must be obliged to follow to the plain suit lead.

The heart lead from the North hand enables South to elope with the two of spades while West helplessly follows suit.

By its very nature, elopement by rank is always positional.

The next two diagrams show elopement positions which are still basic but not so simple as to be termed *coups en passant*.

Example 1(c)

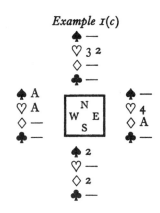

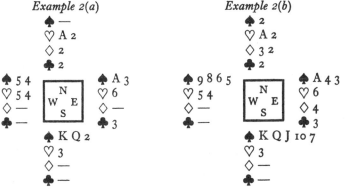

Example 2(a)   *Example 2(b)*

In each case South's trumps (spades again) are superficially strong enough to lead, but East, upon gaining the lead, will play a club to promote a further trump trick for the defence. Instead of leading trumps, South must elope with his low trump by playing the heart to the ace and returning a heart. Example 2(a) is a pure positional elopement; Example 2(b) is an elopement by rank.

We have seen that the basic defence against elopements is to ruff high and threaten declarer's trumps with a side suit. It is up to declarer to keep the door closed against this defence.

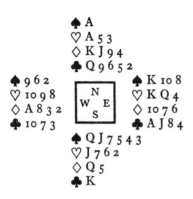

♠ A
♡ A 5 3
◇ K J 9 4
♣ Q 9 6 5 2

♠ 9 6 2
♡ 10 9 8
◇ A 8 3 2
♣ 10 7 3

♠ K 10 8
♡ K Q 4
◇ 10 7 6
♣ A J 8 4

♠ Q J 7 5 4 3
♡ J 7 6 2
◇ Q 5
♣ K

East opens one club; you over-call one spade and, after fighting off game tries from partner, finish precariously in three spades.

West leads the ten of hearts, and you allow East to win with the queen. East cashes the ace of clubs and continues with the four of clubs. You discard a heart from hand, capture the ten with dummy's queen, and play a diamond to the queen and ace. West returns his last club for you to ruff. The threat of an over-ruff on a club lead from East now looms over you and you must play with care.

You cash the king and jack of diamonds, throwing a heart from hand, and you stand at the crossroads. It is tempting to continue with the nine of diamonds, but if you do, East will ruff with the king of spades and lead his last club, giving West the opportunity of discarding a heart when you ruff high. The defenders will then make a second trump trick. But you should not fall into this trap. The nine of diamonds can wait. East is marked with three diamonds and four clubs and there is no hope unless spades are 3–3, so you must play for 3–3 hearts as well.

Play the ace of hearts and ruff a heart. Now a spade to the ace – it would have been fatal to have taken the ace of trumps earlier – and the nine of diamonds for elopement in the diagram position.

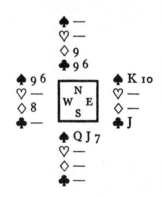

♠ —
♡ —
◇ 9
♣ 9 6

♠ 9 6
♡ —
◇ 8
♣ —

♠ K 10
♡ —
◇ —
♣ J

♠ Q J 7
♡ —
◇ —
♣ —

In practice, of course, misdefence by East may well allow you to make the contract even if you make the mistake of playing the nine of diamonds prematurely.

Sometimes declarer needs only to elope with one small trump.

♠ J 4
♡ 7 6 5 2
◊ 9 7 5 4 3
♣ J 8

♠ 8 5 3
♡ A J 10 8
◊ 10 2
♣ 9 6 5 3

♠ A K 7
♡ Q 3
◊ A J 8 6
♣ 10 7 4 2

♠ Q 10 9 6 2
♡ K 9 4
◊ K Q
♣ A K Q

East opens one diamond, you double, partner responds one heart and you convert to one spade, where the bidding rests.

West leads the ten of diamonds to his partner's ace, and a shift to the queen of hearts nets three heart tricks for the defence. West wisely does not play a fourth heart (which would give you your seventh trick) but exits with the two of diamonds to your king.

Your best chance by far is to ruff the third club low in dummy and lead the seven of hearts for elopement. Try as he may, East can get no more than two trump tricks for his side.

Note that you cannot succeed by playing an early round of trumps. After winning the king of diamonds, for instance, if you play a spade to the jack, East will win with the king and return a diamond. You can ruff high, but West will discard his heart and you will be unable to avoid the loss of three trump tricks.

Automatic elopements are usually simple to play. The main problem is one of recognition, for it is easy to muddle the timing if preparations are not made at an early stage.

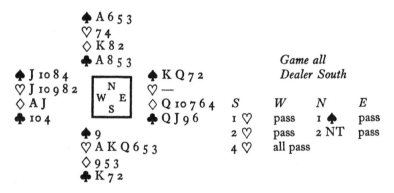

♠ A 6 5 3
♡ 7 4
◊ K 8 2
♣ A 8 5 3

♠ J 10 8 4
♡ J 10 9 8 2
◊ A J
♣ 10 4

♠ K Q 7 2
♡ —
◊ Q 10 7 6 4
♣ Q J 9 6

♠ 9
♡ A K Q 6 5 3
◊ 9 5 3
♣ K 7 2

Game all
Dealer South

S	W	N	E
1 ♡	pass	1 ♠	pass
2 ♡	pass	2 NT	pass
4 ♡	all pass		

West leads the jack of spades to dummy's ace, and your first thought is that three no trumps might have been easier. Partner will not be pleased if it turns out that you have four losers playing in hearts. However, being a careful player and not merely an egotistical one, you ruff a small spade in

[113]

hand before cashing the ace of hearts. Well, well, so three no trumps would
have been at least two down!

In four hearts, even with the diamond ace right, you appear to have a
total of five losers – two trumps, two diamonds and a club. But you soon
prove this to be an illusion. At trick four you play a diamond from hand.
West takes his ace and returns the jack of hearts. You win with the queen,
cross to the king of diamonds, and ruff another spade. The king and ace of
clubs are followed by a ruff of the fourth spade, and then the king of hearts.
The defenders are left in possession of the field, but only two tricks remain –
you have already taken your ten tricks by eloping with all your small
trumps.

Correct timing is vital on such hands. You have to anticipate the possibility of a bad trump break and start at once on the elopement tack. If you
fail to take the precaution of ruffing a spade at trick two, you will perish for
lack of an extra entry to dummy.

It can be only too easy to overlook the chance of an automatic elopement.
How many of your partners would make four spades on the next deal?

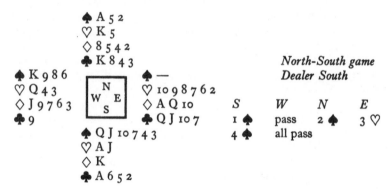

	♠ A 5 2		
	♡ K 5		
	◇ 8 5 4 2		
	♣ K 8 4 3		*North-South game*
♠ K 9 8 6			*Dealer South*
♡ Q 4 3		♠ —	
◇ J 9 7 6 3	N W E S	♡ 10 9 8 7 6 2	
♣ 9		◇ A Q 10	S W N E
	♠ Q J 10 7 4 3	♣ Q J 10 7	1 ♠ pass 2 ♠ 3 ♡
	♡ A J		4 ♠ all pass
	◇ K		
	♣ A 6 5 2		

West leads the three of hearts, and the theme is the same as in the previous
deal. But here the temptation to lead trumps too early is very hard to resist
(try it on your local expert).

The correct play is to win the first trick in hand with the *ace* of hearts and
lead the king of diamonds. Now you will be able to ruff three diamonds
with your small trumps; one when in dummy with the heart king, one when
in with the spade ace, and one when in with the club king (you will play the
ace of clubs first, of course, then a low club towards the king – West cannot
profitably ruff). This line of play cannot lose against any adverse distribution that is consistent with East's overcall.

The big trap to avoid is leading the queen of spades at trick two. It may look harmless enough, but if West covers, as he very well should, you will find yourself short of an entry in dummy to elope with all three of the small trumps in your own hand.

It is not only the automatic type of elopement that requires careful play. The organization of a pure positional elopement may call for a high degree of foresight on the part of declarer.

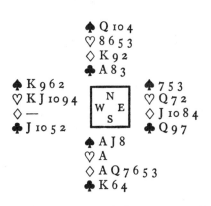

♠ Q 10 4
♡ 8 6 5 3
◇ K 9 2
♣ A 8 3

♠ K 9 6 2
♡ K J 10 9 4
◇ —
♣ J 10 5 2

♠ 7 5 3
♡ Q 7 2
◇ J 10 8 4
♣ Q 9 7

♠ A J 8
♡ A
◇ A Q 7 6 5 3
♣ K 6 4

South opened one diamond and West overcalled one heart. Eventually, a rejected slam try left South in five diamonds.

The opening lead was the two of spades. Declarer won in dummy with the queen and led a diamond to his ace, learning the bad news about the trump division. Hoping to be allowed to bring off a squeeze or a throw-in against West, South cashed the ace of hearts and led a diamond to the nine and ten. East thwarted South's plans by returning a spade, and the contract had to go one down.

Ironically, five diamonds would have been made without difficulty in the absence of the 'helpful' spade lead. On a heart lead for instance, declarer, after seeing the trump break, would have realized the necessity of eloping with three of his small trumps. He would have arranged the play so as to ruff three of dummy's hearts, using the spade queen-ten, the club ace and the diamond king as entries to the table.

In fact declarer should have overcome the awkward spade lead by playing dummy's four to the first trick and winning in hand with the ace. This would have preserved the entries for the elopement in the actual case, and stood to lose at most the chance of an overtrick if the trumps had divided more evenly. (It could hardly have cost the contract, for the bidding would have been different if West had five spades and a diamond void or if East had six spades and a diamond void.)

On certain hands, declarer can manoeuvre to keep his eloping ruff secure against all danger.

Forsaking no trumps for the greater good of elopement demonstration, you open one spade and everyone passes.

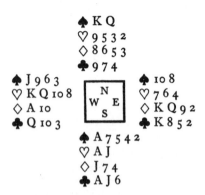

```
              ♠ K Q
              ♡ 9 5 3 2
              ◇ 8 6 5 3
              ♣ 9 7 4
♠ J 9 6 3                    ♠ 10 8
♡ K Q 10 8        N          ♡ 7 6 4
◇ A 10       W       E       ◇ K Q 9 2
♣ Q 10 3          S          ♣ K 8 5 2
              ♠ A 7 5 4 2
              ♡ A J
              ◇ J 7 4
              ♣ A J 6
```

West leads the king of hearts, East plays the four, and you win with the ace. A 3–3 trump break is against the odds and it must be better to try to score your small trumps independently, particularly since East appears to have three hearts. So you return the jack of hearts at trick two. West wins and switches (say) to a trump. You win in dummy, ruff a heart, cross to dummy's second trump, and lead the last heart.

The elopement succeeds easily and automatically as the cards lie, but suppose that instead of switching to a trump West had played the ace and another diamond and East had continued with a third and fourth diamond. To protect your small trumps, you would have to discard a club on the fourth diamond. Then, no matter whether West discarded clubs or hearts on the diamonds and no matter what East returned, your seven tricks would be safe.

If East had held four trumps, of course, you would have had a positional instead of an automatic elopement. And if the trumps had been 3–3 all the time?

Now East would uppercut with the ten of spades on the fourth round of hearts, but you would simply discard a club. And if the defenders continued with four rounds of diamonds, you would throw another club.

You have seen examples of 'loser-on-loser' play to switch a ruff in dummy to a safer suit. Here the same technique is

```
              ♠ K Q
              ♡ 9 5 3 2
              ◇ 8 6 5 3
              ♣ 9 7 4
♠ J 9 6                      ♠ 10 8 3
♡ K Q 10 8        N          ♡ 7 6 4
◇ A 10       W       E       ◇ K Q 9 2
♣ Q 10 3 2        S          ♣ K 8 5
              ♠ A 7 5 4 2
              ♡ A J
              ◇ J 7 4
              ♣ A J 6
```

applied to making elopement ruffs in the long trump hand as safe as possible.

The threat of an automatic elopement may prove a complete answer to a forcing attack by the defenders. It often happens that the defenders seek to prevent the establishment of declarer's side suit by forcing declarer to ruff in hand. This is usually a strong defence, but there are times when the defenders can be faced with a painful dilemma.

Spades are trumps and South, on lead, needs four more tricks. It may seem that he can never establish a heart trick, but let's see what happens when he leads a heart. West wins and returns a club for South to ruff. Another heart is played, and West is in trouble. He can either concede a tempo by switching to trumps, or he can continue clubs and allow South to elope with his last small trump. Either way, South makes his four tricks.

Naturally, it can be more complicated.

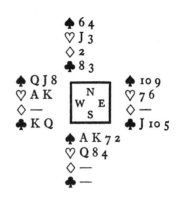

♠ 6 4
♡ J 3
◇ 2
♣ 8 3

♠ Q J 8   ♠ 10 9
♡ A K   ♡ 7 6
◇ —   ◇ —
♣ K Q   ♣ J 10 5

♠ A K 7 2
♡ Q 8 4
◇ —
♣ —

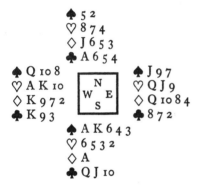

♠ 5 2
♡ 8 7 4
◇ J 6 5 3
♣ A 6 5 4

♠ Q 10 8   ♠ J 9 7
♡ A K 10   ♡ Q J 9
◇ K 9 7 2   ◇ Q 10 8 4
♣ K 9 3   ♣ 8 7 2

♠ A K 6 4 3
♡ 6 5 3 2
◇ A
♣ Q J 10

West opens a strong no trump and, after an auction that is best forgotten, you end up as declarer in three spades doubled.

West leads the two of diamonds to the ten and ace. When you play a heart, West wins with the ten and returns a diamond for you to ruff. You play another heart. If West forces you again, you will eventually elope with a third diamond ruff for nine tricks. If West switches to a spade or a low club, you will play a third heart, and West will again face the 'elopement or tempo' dilemma. So you are bound to make the contract, aren't you?

No, you're not, as you soon discover. West slays you at trick five by switching to the king of clubs! This takes out dummy's only entry and transfers the dilemma to your plate. You are forced to commit yourself between the elopement tack and the trump-drawing-and-heart-establishing tack, and whatever you do is fatal. If you ruff a diamond and concede the third heart, the defenders play trumps. If you duck a trump (or play three rounds of trumps), they force you with a diamond.

Now, for a good, clarifying exercise, try playing the same hand in three hearts. You don't like the trump suit? Still, the contract is unbeatable, even on the best double-dummy lead of the king of clubs.

Suppose the defenders begin with three rounds of hearts. Then you have time to establish and cash your two long spade tricks. If they take only two

rounds of hearts and switch to a spade, a diamond or a low club, you can
elope with three trumps by way of a spade ruff in dummy and two diamond
ruffs in hand. If they switch to the *king* of clubs after two rounds of hearts,
you gain so much tempo that you can make an overtrick! They try just one
round of hearts and then the king of clubs? You ruff the third round of
spades and play hearts, and again you end up with an overtrick.

What about the king of clubs as an opening lead? You win and return a
trump. The defenders must knock out your diamond ace, or else you'll have
an easy time. You ruff out the spades and play another trump, and they have
to return a diamond to force you. Now you cash the clubs and play a
master spade, and whoever ruffs it must return a diamond to let you elope
with your last small trump after all.

Of course, it is the complete mirror-distribution of the defenders' hands
that permits you to succeed. The slightest variation and the defenders
would be able to defeat your three hearts.

Here is another 'tempo or elopement' dilemma.

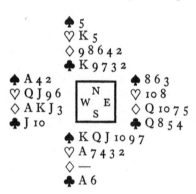

♠ 5
♡ K 5
◇ 9 8 6 4 2
♣ K 9 7 3 2

♠ A 4 2   ♠ 8 6 3
♡ Q J 9 6   ♡ 10 8
◇ A K J 3   ◇ Q 10 7 5
♣ J 10   ♣ Q 8 5 4

♠ K Q J 10 9 7
♡ A 7 4 3 2
◇ —
♣ A 6

Would you like to play in four
spades? It's one down on repeated
diamond leads.

But naturally, your superior bidding lands you in four hearts, where
you can make full use of those lovely
elopable little trumps. While the
spade honours do not like being
forced, the small hearts simply love
it.

You ruff the opening diamond lead
and play a spade to the ace. Already
West is fixed. A trump? You have the
tempo and make ten tricks. Another
diamond? You ruff, cash a high spade, ruff a spade with the five of hearts,
ruff a diamond, play the ace and king of clubs, ruff a fourth diamond, and
finish with a high cross-ruff for ten tricks.

To sum up, when West forces you with a second diamond, you lose
trump control and three of your five spade tricks go to the mice. But you
recover these tricks by three extra trump elopements.

How would you defend a similar 'tempo or elopement' hand?

Playing a *canapé* system at your partner's insistence, you open one diamond in the West seat. East raises to two diamonds, South comes in with two spades, and all pass.

South is likely to have a second suit, so a heart or a club lead could prove disastrous. A diamond? The last thing you want is to force declarer too much. A trump, then? But if he has a second suit to set up, the trump lead may give him a vital tempo.

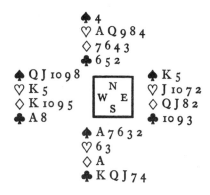

```
              ♠ 4
              ♡ A Q 9 8 4
              ◇ 7 6 4 3
              ♣ 6 5 2
♠ Q J 10 9 8   ┌─────┐   ♠ K 5
♡ K 5          │  N  │   ♡ J 10 7 2
◇ K 10 9 5     │W   E│   ◇ Q J 8 2
♣ A 8          │  S  │   ♣ 10 9 3
              └─────┘
              ♠ A 7 6 3 2
              ♡ 6 3
              ◇ A
              ♣ K Q J 7 4
```

So you lead the ten of diamonds after all; the force may be necessary to prevent the side-suit establishment. South wins and leads the jack of clubs to your ace. Now what?

Your task is to prevent declarer from ruffing three diamonds – and at the same time to force him to ruff one! Not now, obviously, for the two entries in dummy would enable him to complete his three-trick elopement. A trump switch would concede the tempo and also the contract – South would win the second trump and play on clubs. It must be right to attack dummy's entries at this point. So you switch to the king of hearts, and now you are in control. If South ruffs a diamond, you ruff the third club and continue hearts. If he ducks a trump instead, you force him with a diamond return. The elopement is automatic, but the play can be quite complex. Note how the 'tempo or elopement' threat turns the normal defence upside down.

Is it possible to combine pure elopement with squeeze? Why, of course.

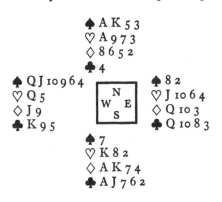

```
              ♠ A K 5 3
              ♡ A 9 7 3
              ◇ 8 6 5 2
              ♣ 4
♠ Q J 10 9 6 4 ┌─────┐   ♠ 8 2
♡ Q 5          │  N  │   ♡ J 10 6 4
◇ J 9          │W   E│   ◇ Q 10 3
♣ K 9 5        │  S  │   ♣ Q 10 8 3
              └─────┘
              ♠ 7
              ♡ K 8 2
              ◇ A K 7 4
              ♣ A J 7 6 2
```

West opens with a weak two-bid in spades, and you eventually become declarer in the ambitious contract of six diamonds.

The queen of spades is led to dummy's king. You continue with the ace of spades, discarding a heart from hand, and then a third spade. East is immediately under pressure. He cannot afford to throw a club, for then you would set up your clubs with two ruffs. If he ruffs with the ten of diamonds, you discard a club, and when you have ruffed two clubs in dummy East will be squeezed in hearts and clubs. So East discards a heart and you ruff. Now you could set up a heart, but that would still be only eleven tricks. You therefore cash the aces of trumps and clubs, ruff a club, and lead dummy's last spade to catch East again in the strange squeeze-cum-elopement. What can East play? A heart? You elope with the seven of diamonds, cash the diamond king and play winning hearts. A club? You elope, ruff a club, return to the diamond king and play winning clubs. A trump? You discard a club, win the red-suit return in hand, ruff a club and return to the other red king. The play of the last trump then squeezes East in clubs and hearts.

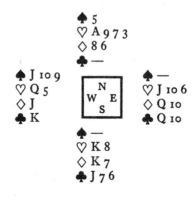

Here is a rather different type of squeeze.

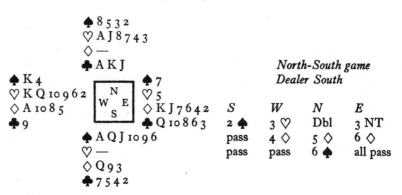

S	W	N	E
2 ♠	3 ♡	Dbl	3 NT
pass	4 ◊	5 ◊	6 ◊
pass	pass	6 ♠	all pass

North-South game
Dealer South

West leads the ace of diamonds which you ruff in dummy. On the bidding, East surely has at least ten cards in the minor suits. When he follows at trick two to your lead of a low heart from dummy, he cannot have all three trumps. Your course is therefore marked. Ruff the heart and cash the ace of spades. When both defenders follow, you are home. A club to the king is followed by the ace of hearts. If East ruffs, he has to concede your twelfth trick in one of the minors on his return. So East will discard whether he has the spade king or not. You throw a club and continue with heart ruff, diamond ruff, heart ruff, diamond ruff and heart ruff (all these ruffs are known to be safe) to reach this intriguing position:

You now lead a club from hand . . . and make your contract no matter how the cards lie. If East has the king of spades, either he has kept clubs (in which case the club ace followed by the heart jack produces a standard *coup en passant*) or he hasn't, in which case the clubs are high.

If West has the king of spades and now holds, for example, the king of spades, the queen of hearts and a diamond, he is squeezed *in one card*. Yes, it's true! He is squeezed in his queen of hearts. If he throws the queen, dummy's heart jack becomes high and you can pitch your losing club on it. If he keeps the queen, you win the club ace and lead the heart jack to elope with the queen of spades.

♠ —
♡ J
♢ —
♣ A J

```
    N
W       E
    S
```

♠ Q
♡ —
♢ —
♣ 7 5

7

Elopement for All

'Not very rare,' mumbled Alec with his mouth half full of steak *au poivre*.

At the small butane stove George wheeled round indignantly. 'What do you mean? Any rarer and it would be raw.'

George always insisted on taking over the galley when he came aboard the *Cormorant*, arguing that this was the least he could do since the need to keep his hands in concert condition prevented him from pulling his weight with the rougher work. The arrangement suited everyone, for George was an excellent cook although highly sensitive to criticism.

Alec waved his fork placatingly. 'Steak's fine. I mean the one-card squeeze.'

Well, there might not be universal agreement on that point, but you knew what Alec meant. All things are relative and there are subtle degrees of rarity. One can argue that one-card squeezes are not rare in the sense that early Picassos are not rare – there must be hundreds of them about. It seems likely that many one-card squeezes have made a brief and hopeful appearance at the bridge table only to sink back sadly into the pack, unrecognized.

The more obscure forms of this squeeze can be really mind-boggling for the defender, even more so than what might whimsically be called the 'ordinary' squeezes against three singletons – those that arise in backwash situations.

```
              ♠ 3
              ♡ K
              ♢ 2
              ♣ —
   ♠ A                 ♠ —
   ♡ A       N         ♡ Q
   ♢ A     W   E       ♢ K
   ♣ —       S         ♣ A
              ♠ 2
              ♡ —
              ♢ 3
              ♣ 2
```

Consider, for example, this annoyance. Spades are trumps and South is on lead. West, with his three aces, is grudgingly prepared to concede declarer a trump trick. But when South leads his losing club, he gets two tricks. West must allow South to make an unexpected heart trick, or a cross-ruff, or an elopement.

So far we have considered only 'pure' elopements. It is natural to wonder what effect it will have on these squeeze positions if 'rank' elopements are permitted. Hold on to your hat.

At first glance it hardly seems possible for South to make three tricks in this position. But South leads a club and West suffers. The discard of a red ace allows a club ruff, a ruff in the other red suit, and a club for a *coup en passant*. Ruffing with the spade ace only delays West's fate. Finally, if West ruffs with the spade queen declarer can, of all things, over-ruff and draw trumps

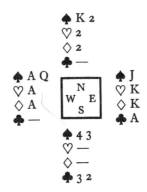

Sometimes the 'pure' and 'rank' aspects of elopement both appear in the same ending.

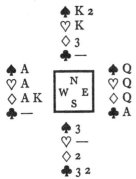

South leads a club and, believe it or not, makes three tricks. If West ruffs, a diamond is thrown from dummy. If West throws a diamond; club ruff, heart ruff, club for *coup en passant*. And if West throws the ace of hearts, dummy ruffs with the two of spades and plays the established heart king for a diamond discard.

There are also elopement endings in which throw-in is an essential element.

If the defenders were on lead against a spade contract, South would not be able to win a single trick. But South has the lead and comes to three tricks when he plays his club. The throw-in occurs if West chooses to discard his diamond. Dummy ruffs the club and South ruffs a diamond. West can over-ruff but must then yield two heart tricks.

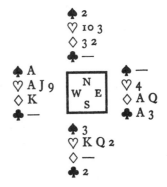

It is not always easy to reach the right position for operating one of these multiple-trick-gainers.

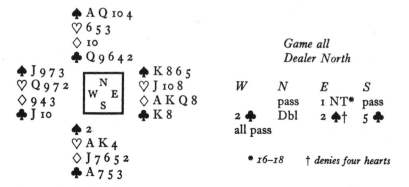

♠ A Q 10 4
♡ 6 5 3
◇ 10
♣ Q 9 6 4 2

Game all
Dealer North

♠ J 9 7 3   ♠ K 8 6 5
♡ Q 9 7 2   ♡ J 10 8
◇ 9 4 3   ◇ A K Q 8
♣ J 10   ♣ K 8

♠ 2
♡ A K 4
◇ J 7 6 5 2
♣ A 7 5 3

W	N	E	S
	pass	1 NT*	pass
2 ♣	Dbl	2 ♠†	5 ♣
all pass			

* *16–18*   † *denies four hearts*

West leads the two of hearts to the ten and king. You play a diamond to East's queen and win the heart return with your ace. How can you avoid the loss of two further tricks?

East is marked with the king of clubs on the bidding, and you must hope that it is accompanied only by the eight. Also, West will need to have the jack of spades to give you a chance for the contract. You cross to the ace of spades and lead the club queen to the king and ace. Then you ruff a diamond, ruff a spade, ruff a diamond, and lead the spade queen from dummy, ruffing away East's king. You are now on lead in this satisfying position:

When you lead another diamond, West cannot extricate himself from your elopement web. If he ruffs, the losing heart is thrown from dummy and the defenders have to allow the elopement of both the six and seven of clubs. If West throws the jack of spades, dummy elopes with the club six immediately, then leads the spade ten for a heart discard, and West cannot prevent the elopement of the club seven. Finally, if West throws a heart, there will be three consecutive elopements on the next three tricks.

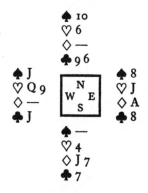

♠ 10
♡ 6
◇ —
♣ 9 6

♠ J   ♠ 8
♡ Q 9   ♡ J
◇ —   ◇ A
♣ J   ♣ 8

♠ —
♡ 4
◇ J 7
♣ 7

Did you notice that East did not put up the strongest possible defence? He could (indeed, should) have defeated the contract by refusing to cover the club queen! This would have given you an 'extra' trump trick but would have denied you the two tricks you gained by the elopement manoeuvre.

Did you also notice that your own play was less than perfect? Try entering dummy by ruffing a diamond rather than leading a spade to the ace. Now, if East covers when you lead the queen of clubs, you can elope as before. And if East ducks, you have the entries to establish a long diamond for your eleventh trick.

The mystery of how the defenders can gain by sacrificing a natural trump trick may be lessened if we examine an ending featuring the same principle.

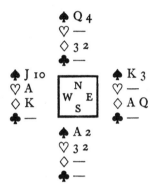

Spades are trumps, dummy has the lead, and South needs three tricks. Neither the spade four nor a diamond will work, but what about the spade queen? If East covers with the king, declarer wins and elopes with both the four and the two of spades. But if East refuses to cover, declarer is helpless. East sacrifices one trick, his side's legitimate trump trick, in order to deny South two elopements – the spade two (which now falls under the queen), and the spade four (which can be over-ruffed by the king).

If you have a handy side winner, you can sometimes pick up the trump suit with this form of elopement threat.

Again spades are trumps. The queen of spades is played from dummy and declarer takes four tricks. If East refuses to cover, South draws trumps and scores his established club. If East covers the queen of spades, South wins with the ace and elopes with both small trumps, playing a heart to the ace, heart ruff, club.

In general, elopement by rank leads to more complicated positions than pure elopement.

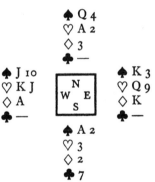

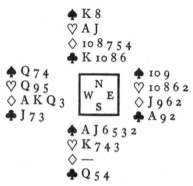

♠ K 8
♡ A J
◇ 10 8 7 5 4
♣ K 10 8 6

♠ Q 7 4   ♠ 10 9
♡ Q 9 5   ♡ 10 8 6 2
◇ A K Q 3   ◇ J 9 6 2
♣ J 7 3   ♣ A 9 2

♠ A J 6 5 3 2
♡ K 7 4 3
◇ —
♣ Q 5 4

West opens with a 13–15 point no trump and, after a series of misunderstandings with your partner, you become declarer at six spades.

West leads the king of diamonds and you ruff the first trick. Clearly you require a miracle or two. You need to find both the heart and the club finesses right with clubs 3–3. And, somehow, you need to score seven trump tricks.

You start by leading a club to the ten, which holds the trick. After ruffing a diamond, you try a second club to the king. This time East takes his ace (it makes no difference if he holds off again) and returns his third club to your queen. You play a heart to the jack, ruff a diamond, cross to the ace of hearts, ruff a fourth diamond, and cash the king of hearts to leave this position:

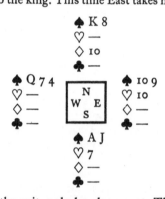

♠ K 8
♡ —
◇ 10
♣ —

♠ Q 7 4   ♠ 10 9
♡ —   ♡ 10
◇ —   ◇ —
♣ —   ♣ —

♠ A J
♡ 7
◇ —
♣ —

When you lead the seven of hearts West has to surrender. What looked like a sure defensive trump trick has melted away.

All textbooks contain examples of this type of situation, where the trumps cannot be picked up by leading the suit, only by elopement. The defensive trump holding is usually given as Q x x opposite J x, and the play is known as the 'Devil's Coup'.

In the last hand East might have tried to break up the position by returning the ten of spades when he was in with the ace of clubs. This would be covered by the jack, queen and king, leaving:

♠ 8
♡ A J
◇ 10 8 7
♣ 8 6

♠ 7 4   ♠ 9
♡ Q 9 5   ♡ 10 8 6 2
◇ A Q   ◇ J 9
♣ J   ♣ 9

♠ A 6 5
♡ K 7 4 3
◇ —
♣ Q

There is not much difference in the ending. As long as you time your sequence of plays correctly, you cannot be prevented from scoring your side suit winners and eloping with the two small trumps in your hand and the eight of trumps in dummy.

A trump return is often the right defence in these situations, however. Suppose that we strengthen the defensive trump holding slightly by giving East the jack in exchange for the ten, and show the position one trick earlier.

If East returns a heart, a diamond or a club, you have the same elopement leading to a Devil's Coup. But the lead of the jack of spades by East produces a trump trick for the defence.

From the viewpoint of our current analysis, the Devil's Coup is a double elopement by rank. This form of ending is possible with a number of different trump holdings, including the following:

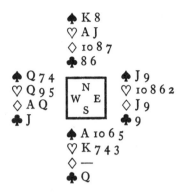

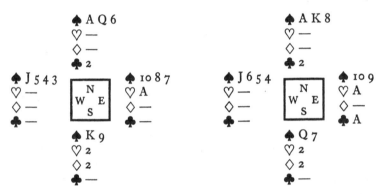

In each case spades are trumps, and South leads his heart to take the rest of the tricks. Like the classical Devil's Coup, these endings can have practical value, although admittedly on rare occasions.

♠ A J 7 3 2
♡ J 8 5 2
◇ A K Q 10
♣ —

With this hand you respond one spade to partner's opening bid of one club. Partner reverses in hearts and later raises spades enthusiastically. You discover that he has two aces, the king and queen of spades, and another king besides.

Naturally you bid the grand slam in spades, and it is only after dummy goes down that you notice that your black jack is in fact the jack of clubs.

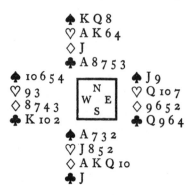

♠ K Q 8
♡ A K 6 4
◇ J
♣ A 8 7 5 3

♠ 10 6 5 4
♡ 9 3
◇ 8 7 4 3
♣ K 10 2

♠ J 9
♡ Q 10 7
◇ 9 6 5 2
♣ Q 9 6 4

♠ A 7 3 2
♡ J 8 5 2
◇ A K Q 10
♣ J

West leads the nine of hearts to dummy's king and East follows with the seven. Now it doesn't look so good. Apparently the heart queen is not going to drop, and the only obvious chance for the contract is to cash the other top heart, discard two hearts on the diamonds, and then try to ruff a heart with dummy's eight of spades. For this line to succeed, you need to find the diamonds no worse than 5-3 and West with precisely 6 5 4 or J 10 9 in spades. In the latter case he may ruff the third heart, but you can still draw trumps successfully.

Is there nothing better than this long shot? What about an elopement? That will require a 4-4 diamond split, but it will succeed in eleven of the twenty possible 3-3 trump divisions – whenever West has none, two or all three of the 'high' spades. You play the ace of clubs and ruff a club, return to the ace of hearts and ruff another club, then hold your breath and play four rounds of diamonds, discarding two hearts and a club from dummy. Now, if trumps are 3-3, you can hope for a position something like this:

When you lead a heart, West has to ruff high to stop a ruff with the spade eight. You over-ruff and lead dummy's club, threatening to elope with the spade seven. When East puts in the spade nine to prevent this, you can over-ruff and finesse dummy's eight of spades to make your grand slam.

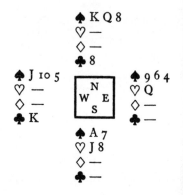

♠ K Q 8
♡ —
◇ —
♣ 8

♠ J 10 5
♡ —
◇ —
♣ K

♠ 9 6 4
♡ Q
◇ —
♣ —

♠ A 7
♡ J 8
◇ —
♣ —

On the actual hand, of course, the end position is rather different, but the elopement still works.

When you lead the heart, West still has to go in with the ten of spades to stop the elopement of dummy's eight. East has to follow suit when the club is led, and West cannot over-ruff the seven of spades.

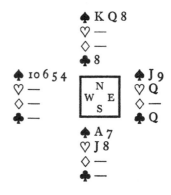

So the elopement also succeeds in three of the fifteen 4–2 breaks (when East has J 10, J 9 or 10 9 doubleton). It is a much better chance than trying to set up a third heart trick – nearly three times as good, in fact.

The practical value of such 'devilish' coups lies not in the ability to bring home apparently impossible grand slams but in the application of the same principles to a wide variety of situations both in attack and defence. The tournament player can improve his bridge vision through closer acquaintance with these positions, quite apart from any pleasure he may derive from contemplating their intrinsic structural beauty.

A knowledge of elopement technique may be helpful in an ordinary cross-ruff hand.

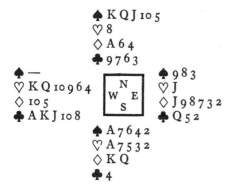

You land in six spades after West has bid strongly in hearts and clubs.

West leads the king of clubs and shifts to the king of hearts. You win with the ace and play a spade to the king, seeing trouble ahead when West shows out. You note regretfully that you could have eloped with twelve easy tricks on an initial heart lead. You note even more regretfully that if your spade ace could be interchanged with one of dummy's spade honours you would be able to overcome the 3–0 trump split with a positional trump squeeze against West. Well, that idea is out, for nothing can overtake the ace of trumps.

Still, it looks like a fairly smooth cross-ruff. At the moment you are on the table, and there are two further entries in dummy (a high trump and the high ruff of a heart), so that you can ruff all three of dummy's losing clubs. And if East trumps a club at any stage, you can over-ruff with the ace and extract his last trump. Never-theless, if you play at all carelessly (for example: club ruff, spade to the ten, club ruff, diamond king and queen, heart ruff with the jack, diamond ace), you will find yourself in a position such as:

North is on lead and East must make a trump trick.

In view of this, you may decide that the best chance is to try for a ruff in hearts with dummy's five of spades, but a much better play is available. Para-doxically, it is safest by far to use a heart ruff with a high trump as the second entry to dummy – in spite of the fact that hearts is the suit in which you are threated with an over-ruff.

So, in the previous line of play, re-place the trump lead to the ten by a heart ruff with the ten, and you will reach this position:

When the club nine is led from dummy, East is helpless. The key factor is the retention of the spade seven: you can either elope with it and thus smother East's trumps without drawing them, or lead your seven to dummy's queen if East prevents the elopement by ruffing a club.

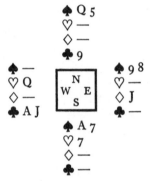

Now take the West seat for a little defensive problem.

You lead the queen of spades against South's contract of four hearts. Declarer wins with the ace, plays the jack of diamonds to dummy's king, and returns the seven of hearts to the nine, jack and queen. What now?

If you appreciate the power of your six of trumps, you will realize that a spade continuation may give declarer problems. Your jack of spades wins, South

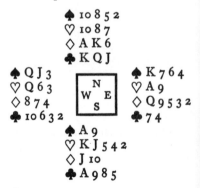

ruffs the next spade, and a trump gives East the lead in this position:

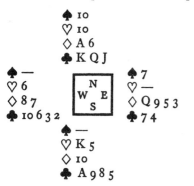

When East leads his last spade, your six of hearts, although not necessarily promoted into a trump trick, is enough to defeat the contract. It either elopes by virtue of its rank, over-ruffing the five, or it causes, through 'elopement menace', a blockage in the North-South hands: if South ruffs high, you discard a diamond.

Declarer could, of course, have made his contract in a number of ways. From the point of view of the present enquiry, it suffices to note that one of these ways is by eloping with the diamond ruff before leading the second round of trumps, thus neutralizing the effect of the club blockage.

This is often a complete answer when declarer is threatened by a defensive elopement. The threat evaporates if declarer can secure his own elopement first.

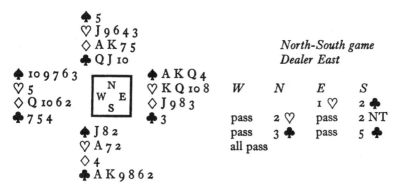

North-South game
Dealer East

W	N	E	S
		1 ♡	2 ♣
pass	2 ♡	pass	2 NT
pass	3 ♣	pass	5 ♣
all pass			

West leads the five of hearts to the eight and ace. Naturally, you play off the top diamonds and discard one of your losing hearts. What next? You need to ruff two spades on the table, but the play of a spade at this point will not be good enough. East will win and play the king of hearts followed by the ten. You will have to ruff high, and West will take the opportunity of discarding his last diamond. The subsequent play will be

an unhappy affair for you. After you have ruffed a spade, ruffed a diamond high, ruffed another spade and cashed the queen of clubs, this will be the position:

With the lead in dummy, you have no way of preventing West from eloping with his seven of clubs.

All this trouble can be avoided by better timing. You need to ruff a diamond with the six of trumps at some stage, and the right time to do so is at trick four, before West has had the chance to make any discards on the

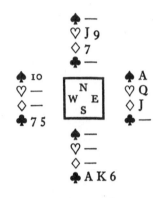

hearts. Once you have eloped with your diamond ruff your worries are over. You exit with a spade and score eleven easy tricks on a high cross-ruff.

♠ 6 4
♡ K 10 4
◇ 8 7 5 3 2
♣ A J 10

♠ 10 7 2   ♠ Q J 8 5
♡ Q 8   ♡ 9 7 6 3
◇ K Q J 9   ◇ 6 4
♣ 8 7 5 2   ♣ 9 6 3

♠ A K 9 3
♡ A J 5 2
◇ A 10
♣ K Q 4

In a rubber bridge tournament match, your opponents have so far been holding all the cards. You need to make a slam on the final deal to win, and eventually you settle in six hearts.

Not surprisingly, West fails to find the killing trump lead. He leads the king of diamonds and you allow him to hold the first trick. Now you are in control of the situation if you play for an elopement. You win whatever West leads at trick two, finesse the ten of

hearts, and cash all the side suit winners ending in dummy. This is the position:

When you lead a diamond from dummy, the heart five acts as an elopement menace, because if East lets you ruff with it you can successfully cross-ruff the rest of the tricks – not quite with high trumps, but with 'eloping' trumps which are high enough. East must therefore ruff with the heart six. You over-ruff with the jack, ruff a spade with the four of hearts, and lead another diamond.

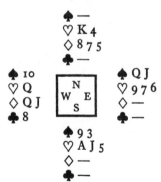

Again East must prevent the threatened ruff with your heart five, so he ruffs with the seven. You over-ruff with the ace and now simply 'draw trumps and claim the rest'. What an easy game, this bridge!

In general, a player who is threatened by a menace has the choice of succumbing to the threat or embracing an alternative disaster. In the last deal the alternative was a fatal weakening of the defensive trump holding, allowing in effect, a dummy reversal. See if you can spot the elopement menace and the alternative on the next hand.

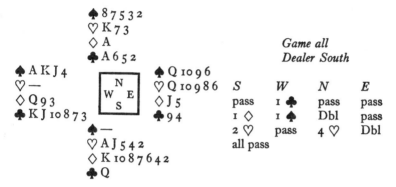

```
            ♠ 8 7 5 3 2
            ♡ K 7 3
            ◇ A                     Game all
            ♣ A 6 5 2               Dealer South
♠ A K J 4            ♠ Q 10 9 6
♡ —          N       ♡ Q 10 9 8 6   S     W     N     E
◇ Q 9 3    W   E     ◇ J 5          pass  1 ♣   pass  pass
♣ K J 10 8 7 3  S    ♣ 9 4          1 ◇   1 ♠   Dbl   pass
            ♠ —                     2 ♡   pass  4 ♡   Dbl
            ♡ A J 5 4 2             all pass
            ◇ K 10 8 7 6 4 2
            ♣ Q
```

West leads the spade king and you ruff the first trick. No doubt East has all five trumps, but if you can ruff a diamond in dummy you should be able to elope easily with ten tricks. So you play a diamond to the ace, return a heart for a finesse of the jack, cash the diamond king (throwing a club from dummy), and play another diamond. If West shows out, you plan to continue: diamond ruff, club ace, spade ruff, diamond ruff with heart king, spade ruff (or club ruff), depending on East's discard, trump ace – for ten tricks.

Prospects look bleak when West turns up with the queen of diamonds, but the rules require you to keep playing. It would be 'self-mate' to ruff with the heart king, so you ruff with the seven. East over-ruffs and forces with a spade. (This is necessary defence. If East returned a heart or a club, you could end spectacularly by overtaking dummy's trump king with the ace and playing diamonds, losing only three trump tricks.) You ruff the spade and lead a diamond, throwing a club from dummy. Again East must ruff and lead a spade. Again you ruff and lead a diamond, throwing dummy's last losing club. The position is:

East has taken three tricks, but he is powerless to take another. If he leads a club or a heart, the South hand is high. And if he plays a fourth round of spades for you to ruff, dummy's long spade becomes established, with the ace of clubs serving as an entry for you to reach the king of hearts and draw the last trump.

Where was the elopement menace? East could have refused to over-ruff when you ruffed a diamond in dummy, but this would have enabled you to elope with the rest of your small trumps.

```
              ♠ 8 7
              ♡ K
              ◇ —
              ♣ A
♠ A                      ♠ Q
♡ —      ┌─────────┐     ♡ Q
◇ —      │ N       │     ◇ —
♣ K J 10 │ W   E   │     ♣ 9 4
         │   S     │
         └─────────┘
              ♠ —
              ♡ A
              ◇ 7 6
              ♣ Q
```

Still, an effective defence was possible. Do you see the difference it makes if East plays the *queen* of hearts when a trump is led from dummy at trick three?

The threat of elopement can be combined with just about any variety of outside threat. Here is an elopement menace allied to a squeeze and two throw-ins.

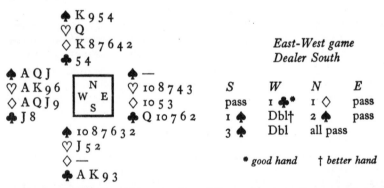

```
              ♠ K 9 5 4
              ♡ Q
              ◇ K 8 7 6 4 2
              ♣ 5 4
♠ A Q J                      ♠ —
♡ A K 9 6    ┌─────────┐     ♡ 10 8 7 4 3
◇ A Q J 9    │ N       │     ◇ 10 5 3
♣ J 8        │ W   E   │     ♣ Q 10 7 6 2
             │   S     │
             └─────────┘
              ♠ 10 8 7 6 3 2
              ♡ J 5 2
              ◇ —
              ♣ A K 9 3
```

East-West game
Dealer South

S	W	N	E
pass	1 ♣*	1 ◇	pass
1 ♠	Dbl†	2 ♠	pass
3 ♠	Dbl	all pass	

* *good hand*   † *better hand*

West leads the king of hearts, then shifts to the ace and queen of spades. You have three top tricks in the black suits and two ruffs in dummy. If you could elope with four diamond ruffs in the closed hand, all would be well. Alas, dummy has only three entries – the spade king and the two ruffs.

Well, you must simply do the best you can: spade king, diamond ruff, ace and king of clubs, club ruff (West throwing a heart), diamond ruff. Now the moment of truth has arrived.

This is the position:

When you lead the nine of clubs West is squeezed. Ruffing is obviously disastrous for him – you would take the rest of the tricks. If West throws a diamond, the bidding marks the winning line: club ruff, diamond ruff, trump to West – and you make the jack of hearts at the end. So West can do no better than throw the nine of hearts on your club. This seems to leave you poorly placed, but you counter by discarding a diamond from dummy.

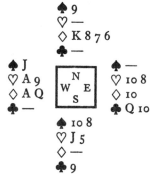

♠ 9
♡ —
♦ K 8 7 6
♣ —

♠ J   ♠ —
♡ A 9   ♡ 10 8
♦ A Q ♦ 10
♣ —   ♣ Q 10

♠ 10 8
♡ J 5
♦ —
♣ 9

Now East, who didn't expect the lead until a week from next Tuesday, is end-played. Let's help him find the strongest defence. A heart is no good – you know that West has the ace, so you play low and the heart jack becomes established as your ninth trick. A diamond also helps you, providing the missing entry needed to complete the elopement: diamond ruff, heart ruff, diamond ruff. So East may as well return a club. You carefully ignore standard ruff-and-discard procedure and trump this in the closed hand, again threatening to complete the elopement. So West is obliged to over-ruff, and now *he* is end-played – forced to concede a trick in the suit he elects to return.

Observe that each opponent in turn was threatened with elopement.

The next example is a double *coup en passant* with a strange twist. Neither defender can interrupt the elopement except at the cost of their only trump trick. And when the elopement is allowed to run its course, the defenders eventually find themselves end-played in trumps. The danger of this deal is that you may be led to believe that nothing is impossible.

♠ A 7 6 2
♡ A 10 6 3 2
♦ A 6 5
♣ 5

♠ Q 10 9 5   ♠ J 8 3
♡ K 8   ♡ J 9
♦ K Q 10 9 2 ♦ J 8 4
♣ Q 7   ♣ J 9 6 4 2

♠ K 4
♡ Q 7 5 4
♦ 7 3
♣ A K 10 8 3

West opened one diamond, North doubled, then . . . But why go through the gruesome details? In the end, West leads the king of diamonds against your contract of six hearts.

There is no lie of the heart suit that will enable you to avoid a trump loser, but it may be possible to set up the clubs for diamond discards in dummy and pick up the trump suit after one of the defenders has used a trump to ruff your long club.

So you win the ace of diamonds, cash the ace and king of clubs (throwing a diamond from dummy), and hopefully lead another club. Your plans receive a set-back when West discards a diamond. (If West trumps, the contract can be made by throwing the losing diamond and later guessing the trump position. If West discards a spade, you can ruff the third round of spades, ruff another club, and play the established spade, discarding a diamond from hand. You can then pick up the trumps, no matter who ruffs the spade or what is returned.)

Now there is no parking place for the losing diamond. But where you can elope there is hope, so you ruff the club, lead a spade to the king and try a fourth club. Again West dares not ruff or part with a spade, so he throws another diamond. After ruffing the club you play the ace of spades and ruff a spade, then lead your last club in this position:

West still can't ruff without giving up the rest of the tricks. If he throws his last spade, dummy's spade will still provide a discard for the losing diamond and the trump suit will be picked up later. So West throws yet another diamond, and you ruff the club in dummy.

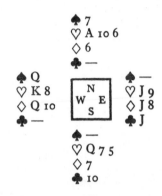

♠ 7
♡ A 10 6
◇ 6
♣ —

♠ Q   ♠ —
♡ K 8   ♡ J 9
◇ Q 10   ◇ J 8
♣ —   ♣ J

♠ —
♡ Q 7 5
◇ 7
♣ 10

When you lead dummy's last spade, the same game is played against East. Whatever kind of coup this is, it's a double one. (Do not overlook the careful timing that is required – the last spade must not be led until all the clubs have been ruffed, lest East discard a club. If you ruff the spade and play a good club, throwing a diamond from dummy, East will ruff and end-play dummy with a diamond return.) If East ruffs the last spade, you discard a diamond and later pick up the trump suit. So East discards a diamond.

You ruff the last spade, and finally you have no more black cards with which to torture the defenders. But you have completed your elopement – you have obtained five ruffs and thus shortened your trumps to the right length for a trump end-play. At this stage all four hands are down to two trumps and a diamond. You lead the diamond that you have so long tried to avoid losing, and the defender who wins the trick is end-played in trumps.

Such deals might be expected to silence the know-alls. Yet you remember many occasions when experts have been all too ready to pontify on this mysterious game we really know so little about.

Once you had reason to approach the world's greatest bridge player (you

Elopement for All

have met him many times over the years—in different places, under different names) with a defensive problem.

```
        ♠ Q 10 5              Love all
        ♡ 7 4                 Dealer East
        ◊ A K J
        ♣ A Q J 6 3       W    N    E     S
♠ A J 6 2                              pass  pass
♡ 10 9 6 3    N          pass  1♣   1♡    1♠
◊ 5 4      W   E         2♡    3♣   pass  4♠
♣ 10 7 2      S          all pass
```

'You lead the heart ten,' you explained. 'East, your partner, takes the king and ace of hearts, dropping declarer's queen, and continues with a third heart. Declarer ruffs in hand with the spade four, discarding the diamond jack from the table, and leads the nine of spades. How would you defend?'

To give him full credit, he didn't snap back a cocksure: 'Ace, then nine of hearts. Wherever declarer ruffs it, he's fixed', but gave serious attention to the problem.

'On the bidding,' he said, 'especially East's original pass, South is marked with the king of clubs. He knows I have the ace of spades, and no doubt he would have considered a first-round finesse against my jack of spades even in the absence of my partner's line of defence. A good declarer will not be fooled into playing my partner for J x x x of spades if I go up with the ace on the first round and return another heart, because he can as easily play me for 4–4–2–3 distribution – ruff the heart in the closed hand, finesse the ten of spades, cash two diamonds and three clubs, and cross-ruff high.

'No sir,' he continued, 'that spade jack of mine is just a red herring. I'll hold off until the third round of trumps, then end declarer's hopes with a fourth round of hearts. By the way, it is not good enough to win the second round of trumps, because when you return the last heart declarer can still end with a high cross-ruff.'

'Thank you,' you said. 'Thank you very much. You know,' you added deferentially, 'I've heard that what you don't know about bridge isn't worth knowing.'

'Who told you that?' he asked eagerly.

'Well . . . um . . . I think *you* did.'

At this he laughed uproariously. The fact is that he is a jolly, good-natured fellow as well as a clever bridge player.

'Well, my friend, I may have said something like that,' he admitted, beaming with self-satisfaction. 'I certainly know enough to avoid the traps in your defensive problems.'

[137]

His smile begins to fade as you point out, respectfully but firmly, that

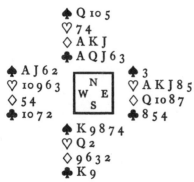

```
                ♠ Q 10 5
                ♡ 7 4
                ◇ A K J
                ♣ A Q J 6 3
♠ A J 6 2                      ♠ 3
♡ 10 9 6 3      ┌─────┐        ♡ A K J 8 5
◇ 5 4           │  N  │        ◇ Q 10 8 7
♣ 10 7 2        │W   E│        ♣ 8 5 4
                │  S  │
                └─────┘
                ♠ K 9 8 7 4
                ♡ Q 2
                ◇ 9 6 3 2
                ♣ K 9
```

there would be no third round of spades for him to take.

After ruffing the third heart in hand, running the nine of spades successfully and continuing with a spade to dummy's ten, declarer has little choice but to abandon trumps.

He cashes two rounds of diamonds and then takes three rounds of clubs, leaving this position with North on lead:

Another club is ruffed with the king of spades, and West faces a three-way losing choice. He can allow the elopement of North's trump queen, the elopement of South's trump nine, or the drawing of trumps.

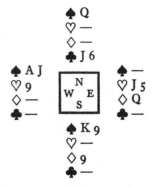

```
        ♠ Q
        ♡ —
        ◇ —
        ♣ J 6
♠ A J              ♠ —
♡ 9     ┌─────┐    ♡ J 5
◇ —     │  N  │    ◇ Q
♣ —     │W   E│    ♣ —
        │  S  │
        └─────┘
        ♠ K 9
        ♡ —
        ◇ 9
        ♣ —
```

'Say, that's cute,' remarked the world's greatest player on seeing this. 'So you can't beat four spades whatever you do.'

Applying the *coup de grace*, you tell him that your wife beat it by two tricks. She didn't want to overkill you (yes, you were the declarer) with a fourth heart lead, so she won the first spade and shifted to diamonds. Needing an extra entry in hand to overcome the apparent 4–1 trump break, you led a club to the nine . . .

Your wife's explanation of why she did not continue hearts was enigmatic rather than instructive. She said: 'You never can tell with these tricky trump things.'

Indeed, it does pay to look into these 'tricky trump things'. A knowledge of elopement technique might have saved a local loudmouth, who fancies himself the best player around your club, from making an ass of himself. He was South on this deal.

Elopement for All

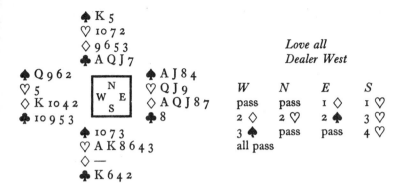

♠ K 5
♡ 10 7 2
◇ 9 6 5 3
♣ A Q J 7

Love all
Dealer West

♠ Q 9 6 2   ♠ A J 8 4
♡ 5   ♡ Q J 9
◇ K 10 4 2   ◇ A Q J 8 7
♣ 10 9 5 3   ♣ 8

♠ 10 7 3
♡ A K 8 6 4 3
◇ —
♣ K 6 4 2

W	N	E	S
pass	pass	1 ◇	1 ♡
2 ◇	2 ♡	2 ♠	3 ♡
3 ♠	pass	pass	4 ♡
all pass			

West led his trump to the ten, jack and king. South played a spade to the king and ace, and East returned the queen of hearts, West discarding a diamond as South won with the ace. Declarer crossed to the queen of clubs in order to lead the second round of spades from dummy, but East hopped up with the jack, cashed his master trump, and played another spade to put the contract one down. You were there when South came forth with this statement:

'There's no way of making it on a trump lead. But they are cold for four spades, anyway.'

A little later the return of his team-mates and comparison of results showed that his second statement was false. Four spades had been bid in the other room, but had been defeated by the simple defence of leading clubs repeatedly. Although East-West appear to have ten easy tricks, there is no way to take them against this defence.

That set you thinking. If the second statement was wrong, perhaps the first was too. Upon examination, it turned out that the declarer had been guilty of a clear misplay. The bidding and early play marked East with 4-3-5-1 distribution. It was a relatively long shot that he would have neither the queen nor the jack of spades, while there was a solid 60% chance that his club singleton would be the ten, nine or eight.

Accordingly, when the 3-1 trump break was revealed, South should have given up the idea of ruffing a spade in dummy in favour of ruffing four diamonds in the closed hand. The king of clubs is led to the ace (not low to the queen, which would enable West later to deny entry status to the club seven), hoping to drop a high spot-card from East. A diamond ruff is followed by another club for a deep finesse of the seven. East has to stand impotently by as South enters dummy four times in clubs and elopes with his four small hearts. If East ruffs a club at any time, South is able to ruff a spade in dummy after all.

8

The Fiercer Trump Squeezes

'Perhaps you should fit an auxiliary motor.'

Alec grunted disdainfully as he peeled off his oilskins and accepted a mug of steaming coffee.

The lake was calm again in the first light of dawn, but you were close to exhaustion after your struggles of the past twelve hours. Needing to put George ashore yesterday, you had run into harbour in the late afternoon just as the storm was building up. You were safely anchored and preparing to batten down for the night when a sister keelboat, crewed by a bunch of rank amateurs, had drifted in. They had dropped anchor too close, fouling your chain, and almost at once the two yachts had started ploughing away, drawing ever closer together in a sickening see-saw motion. You went up and down in the grip of the big swell – one moment two storeys above the other vessel, the next two storeys below. You waited with horror for the moment of crushing impact, but Alec had acted in the nick of time. He howled for canvas, cut loose from your anchor chain, and managed to steer out of the harbour. And all night long as the tempest raged the pair of you fought a grim battle to stay clear of the rocks of the shoreline, using the shortest sail that would keep the *Cormorant* dirigible.

Relief at the narrow escape made you persist. 'Auxiliary power would be useful. It'd be good for . . .'

'Good for palookas, like your super-precise bidding systems.'

Yes, Alec always did like to live dangerously. Rather than rely on auxiliary bidding conventions, he preferred to use brains and ingenuity to deal with emergencies as they arose.

Certainly bridge would be a duller game if we always reached laydown contracts, or contracts that called for no more than a routine display of competence. How can a player improve his card-playing skills if he is never stretched?

If you had bid less boldly and finished in a pedestrian part-score on one particular hand that you remember, you might never have discovered a new and powerful type of trump squeeze.

To set the scene, let us recapitulate. When you first considered positional trump squeezes, you noted that the mechanism failed if the trump position was unbalanced (if you and dummy had different numbers of trumps) at the point of impact.

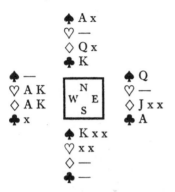

If spades are trumps in this position, for instance, you cannot take the rest of the tricks by leading the spade king.

However, if North has the lead you can adjust the squeeze mechanism by ruffing the king of clubs – not for neatness but because only the symmetrical trump position puts the required pressure on West.

At times you will be denied the entries needed to achieve a balanced trump position, yet you may still be able to squeeze a defender to compensate for your frustrated cross-ruff.

Here we have given West the ace of clubs instead of a small one, and the additional burden is too much for him to carry. However, in this instance, the entry-shifting aspect of the squeeze is unnecessary. With two trump entries remaining in the South hand, it suffices to play a small trump to the ace. It might seem, therefore, that there is no such thing as an unbalanced entry-shifting trump squeeze.

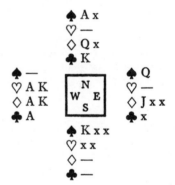

But there is no 'never' in bridge. Here is the hand that you remembered.

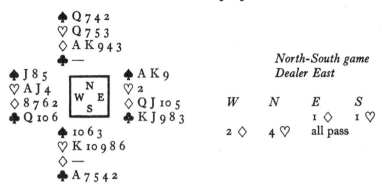

```
        ♠ Q 7 4 2
        ♡ Q 7 5 3
        ◇ A K 9 4 3
        ♣ —
♠ J 8 5              ♠ A K 9        North-South game
♡ A J 4      N      ♡ 2             Dealer East
◇ 8 7 6 2  W   E   ◇ Q J 10 5
♣ Q 10 6     S      ♣ K J 9 8 3      W    N    E    S
        ♠ 10 6 3                              1◇   1♡
        ♡ K 10 9 8 6                   2◇   4♡   all pass
        ◇ —
        ♣ A 7 5 4 2
```

The textbook that recommends a vulnerable overcall of one heart on the South hand has yet to be written. If you had passed, you might have had a later opportunity to buy the contract in two or three hearts, making nine tricks on a simple cross-ruff. But then you would have missed a lot of fun.

West led the eight of diamonds and you discarded two spades on the ace and king. You saw that an immediate cross-ruff of two diamonds and two clubs would land you in dummy – and in trouble. If you conceded a spade at that stage, the defenders would hold you to nine tricks by playing two rounds of trumps.

So you led a spade from dummy at trick three and East won with the king. Recognizing the need to cut down your ruffs, East returned the two of hearts, on which you played the ten and West the ace. West continued with the four of hearts, and you carefully put in the seven from dummy. If East had been able to cover this, his shape would be marked as 2-2-4-5 or 3-2-4-4 and you would be able to establish either the spade queen or a long club as your tenth trick.

But East showed out, discarding a club, and you underplayed dummy's seven with your six. To have any sort of chance, you then had to assume that East started with a 3-1-4-5 distribution and that the position was:

It was clear that you could score the ace of clubs plus five tricks on a cross-ruff – but you needed seven tricks, not six. You could, of course, set up a spade or a diamond in dummy, but that annoying trump in West's hand would prevent you from cashing it.

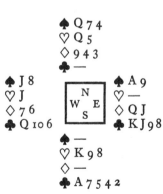

```
        ♠ Q 7 4
        ♡ Q 5
        ◇ 9 4 3
        ♣ —
♠ J 8              ♠ A 9
♡ J        N     ♡ —
◇ 7 6   W   E   ◇ Q J
♣ Q 10 6   S     ♣ K J 9 8
        ♠ —
        ♡ K 9 8
        ◇ —
        ♣ A 7 5 4 2
```

You were therefore forced to consider drawing the last trump. This would cost you a ruffing trick, but East, who guarded three suits, would surely be squeezed out of something. Although you lacked a balanced trump position the squeeze seemed the only chance, so you led the queen of hearts from the table.

In all the positional trump squeezes we studied earlier, the squeeze was 'redemptive'. That is to say, it was a means of recouping what seemed to be rightfully the property of the declarer, a means of overcoming an obstruction to the taking of tricks (such as an enemy trump preventing a cross-ruff). This time, however, when the queen of hearts is led from dummy we see an unbalanced positional trump squeeze gaining in its own right. And the gain, remarkably, is *two tricks*. This is not a progressive squeeze. East does not give up a trick and then suffer a further squeeze on the play of the established winner. He has to give up two tricks on the spot. And the overtaking option on the squeeze trick is necessary to give force to all the menaces. The contract would have failed if you had won the second trump in the closed hand.

So there *is* such a thing as an unbalanced entry-shifting trump squeeze. How does the darned thing work? Well, the form is fairly rigid, for a basic requirement is that just one of the defenders must have double stoppers in three suits. Declarer needs, in the short trump hand, two suits that threaten to develop two tricks. The long trump hand contains the long side-suit, the ace of which must not be cashed lest the opposite hand be squeezed. Here is the basic matrix.

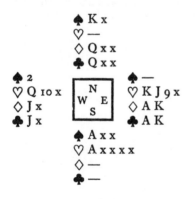

Needing seven tricks with spades as trumps, North leads the king of spades and East cannot hold the position.

Note that these squeezes operate 'without the count'. There are, in fact, three losers at the moment of impact. In this matrix declarer has six winners and two losers, but he deliberately increases his loser count to three by using two trumps to draw one. The squeeze gains two tricks and a trick is given up after the squeeze has taken place, either in the process of establishing the long suit, or, inconsequentially, at the end.

It is important to recognize the chilling implications for the defence in this sort of ending. If West were on lead in the above diagram, it might seem natural for him to lead his trump in an attempt to cut down declarer's ruffs. But the trump is the only lead that allows declarer to make seven tricks. Anything else ensures two tricks for the defenders.

The entry-shifting lead may come from the long trump hand, and the arrangement of menaces may be different, as is shown in this inverse matrix.

North leads the king of spades and again East's defences crumble.

This time, if West were on lead, both spades and diamonds would be taboo.

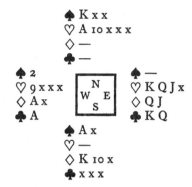

♠ K x x
♡ A 10 x x x
♢ —
♣ —

♠ 2   ♠ —
♡ 9 x x x ♡ K Q J x
♢ A x   ♢ Q J
♣ A   ♣ K Q

♠ A x
♡ —
♢ K 10 x
♣ x x x

In practical play a defender may have only one safe lead at the critical point.

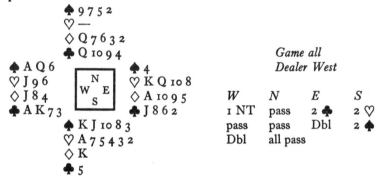

♠ 9 7 5 2
♡ —
♢ Q 7 6 3 2
♣ Q 10 9 4

♠ A Q 6   ♠ 4
♡ J 9 6   ♡ K Q 10 8
♢ J 8 4   ♢ A 10 9 5
♣ A K 7 3 ♣ J 8 6 2

♠ K J 10 8 3
♡ A 7 5 4 3 2
♢ K
♣ 5

Game all
Dealer West

W	N	E	S
1 NT	pass	2 ♣	2 ♡
pass	pass	Dbl	2 ♠
Dbl	all pass		

Sitting West, you decide to go for the penalty, judging game to be unlikely against wild distribution.

You lead the ace of clubs and switch to the four of diamonds. Partner takes the ace and returns his trump, and you capture the jack with your queen. When you continue with the ace of spades partner throws a club, leaving this position:

Declarer's potential cross-ruff tricks have already been sufficiently reduced to five. A third round of trumps would be a mistake, for declarer would play the nine from dummy and East would come under fatal pressure in three suits.

A club return would give South his eighth trick immediately. And on a diamond return South would win with the queen and lead the nine of spades himself to squeeze East.

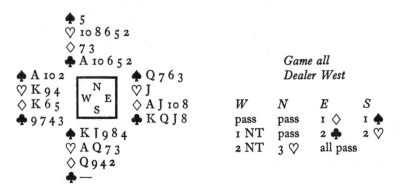

♠ 9 7
♡ —
♢ Q 7 6 3
♣ Q 10 9

♠ 6
♡ J 9 6
♢ J 8
♣ K 7 3

♠ —
♡ K Q 10 8
♢ 10 9 5
♣ J 8

♠ K 10 8
♡ A 7 5 4 3 2
♢ —
♣ —

Only a heart switch defeats the contract. If declarer ruffs in dummy he destroys the entry-shifting mechanism. And if declarer wins with the ace he is doubly ruined. In the first place, dummy is squeezed, forced to give up the two-trick threat in one of the minors. Secondly, quite apart from the squeeze, South is placed in the wrong hand for operating the entry-shift. It is as though you forced declarer to swallow a draught of poison, and then shot him through the heart just to make sure of things.

This sort of overkill is not available when the entry-shifting lead comes from the long trump hand, but the poison can act on its own.

♠ 5
♡ 10 8 6 5 2
♢ 7 3
♣ A 10 6 5 2

♠ A 10 2
♡ K 9 4
♢ K 6 5
♣ 9 7 4 3

♠ Q 7 6 3
♡ J
♢ A J 10 8
♣ K Q J 8

♠ K J 9 8 4
♡ A Q 7 3
♢ Q 9 4 2
♣ —

Game all
Dealer West

W	N	E	S
pass	pass	1 ♢	1 ♠
1 NT	pass	2 ♣	2 ♡
2 NT	3 ♡	all pass	

Partner wins your diamond lead with the ace and returns the jack of hearts to the queen and king. You continue with the four of hearts, and when partner throws the eight of diamonds you realize that he is already in trouble. Dummy's five of hearts wins the trick, and declarer leads the singleton spade to his jack. You win with the ace, and the position is:

[146]

If you continue with the nine of hearts it will be covered by the ten, inflicting the familiar agony on East. And if you cash the king of diamonds, that will be the last trick for the defence. A return of the ten of spades will fare no better. South will win with the king, discarding a diamond from dummy, draw your trump and concede a spade to East.

But the club switch is a killer. If South ruffs in hand, that puts an end to all entry-shifting. And if he wins with the ace, the closed hand is

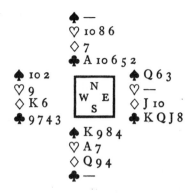

squeezed into weakening one of its own menaces. After winning the club ace, declarer can still continue with the ten of hearts to catch East in an entry-shifting squeeze, but now the squeeze yields only one trick. By following the declarer's discard of the previous round, East can make sure of two tricks for the defence.

On other hands you may have to rely on the shot through the heart.

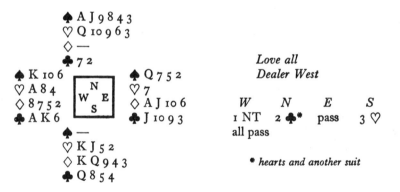

Love all
Dealer West

W	N	E	S
1 NT	2 ♣*	pass	3 ♡
all pass			

* *hearts and another suit*

They say you ought to lead trumps against this sort of bidding, so you start with the four of hearts. South wins with the jack and leads the king of diamonds, discarding a club from dummy. East produces the ace and returns the jack of clubs, and when South plays low you overtake with the king (you must in order to cut down ruffs). When you cash the ace of hearts East discards the club three. What do you know about the hand?

For a start, South is marked with four hearts. And if he had held a spade in his hand he would surely have set about establishing the spades instead of messing about with diamonds. Also, from East's discard it appears that both he and declarer have four clubs. So you can be confident that the position now is something like:

What do you return? A trump is fratricidal, a club suicidal, and a spade allows South to make an overtrick!

Only a diamond defeats the contract – not by squeezing dummy, for dummy can spare a spade. The diamond return wins simply by putting declarer in the wrong hand for his entry-shifting lead. If the diamond is ruffed in dummy, of course the necessary imbalance of the trump position is destroyed, and East can afford to discard a spade when a trump is led from the table.

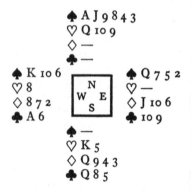

Declarer does not need to have precisely three trumps opposite two to operate an unbalanced entry-shifting trump squeeze. He may have four opposite three, or even two opposite one. Take the South seat for the next hand.

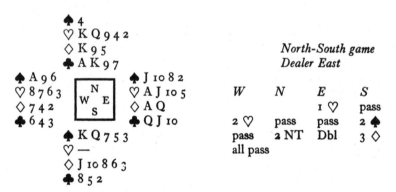

North-South game
Dealer East

W	N	E	S
		1 ♡	pass
2 ♡	pass	pass	2 ♠
pass	2 NT	Dbl	3 ◇
all pass			

West leads the eight of hearts which is covered by the queen and ace. You ruff and play the queen of spades to the ace, and West switches to a trump. When you play low from dummy East takes his queen and continues with the ace. Careful, now! You unblock the jack from hand and the king from dummy. East shifts to the queen of clubs, but the defenders are already helpless when you win in dummy. This is the position:

You can, of course, make your three trumps separately, but that will not give you enough tricks for the contract. And West's trump prevents you from enjoying any extra trick that you set up in the side suits. However, the entry-shifting lead of the diamond nine from dummy squeezes East out of two tricks in whichever suit he elects to give up.

This is a rather different type of entry-shifting squeeze. Move over to the West seat and try your hand at defence.

♠ —
♡ K 9 4 2
◇ 9
♣ A 9 7

♠ 9 6
♡ 7 6 3
◇ 7
♣ 6 4

N
W E
S

♠ J 10 8
♡ J 10 5
◇ —
♣ J 10

♠ K 7 5 3
♡ —
◇ 10 8
♣ 8 5

You lead a trump, of course, thus gaining a vital tempo. East wins two trumps and switches to the queen of clubs. Declarer wins in dummy with the king, plays the queen of hearts and ruffs out East's ace, and then leads the queen of spades to your ace. As a result of this transposition, you are now on lead in the eight card ending of the above diagram.

A trump lead, you know, will wring two tricks from East. A heart will fare no better, for declarer can win with the king, pitching a club from his hand, then lead his squeezing nine of diamonds. The squeeze is still effective since the entry position is unchanged. A spade lead will not work either. Declarer will ruff in dummy, ruff a small heart in hand and lead his last trump to squeeze East 'without the count' in three suits.

A club is the killing return, for it causes the North and South hands to become completely disconnected in the plain suits.

Too many part-scores? Here is a slam.

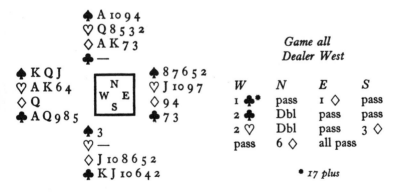

♠ A 10 9 4
♡ Q 8 5 3 2
◇ A K 7 3
♣ —

♠ K Q J
♡ A K 6 4
◇ Q
♣ A Q 9 8 5

N
W E
S

♠ 8 7 6 5 2
♡ J 10 9 7
◇ 9 4
♣ 7 3

♠ 3
♡ —
◇ J 10 8 6 5 2
♣ K J 10 6 4 2

Game all
Dealer West

W	N	E	S
1 ♣*	pass	1 ◇	pass
2 ♣	Dbl	pass	pass
2 ♡	Dbl	pass	3 ◇
pass	6 ◇	all pass	

* *17 plus*

[149]

Nobody doubles and West leads the king of spades. When dummy goes down you see that partner is not quite the fool that he appears to be. You win the ace of spades and cash the king of diamonds. The closed hand is short of an entry for establishing the clubs, but the unbalanced entry-shifting squeeze will come to your rescue. Just ruff a heart and lead the jack of diamonds in this position:

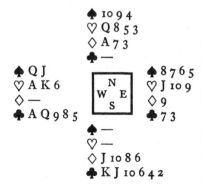

This time you have four trumps opposite three, but the squeeze grips no less firmly. West cannot deny you two extra tricks in one of the side suits.

What would be the result if you led the jack of clubs, instead of the jack of diamonds, in the diagram position? Suicide by poison! West would play low and dummy would be squeezed. On your next lead of the jack of diamonds, West would abandon the suit in which dummy discarded, and the squeeze would gain only one trick.

This prompts you to wonder whether you can succeed against the double-dummy defence of a low club lead. If you run this to your ten, you have to give up one of dummy's double threats; and although you now

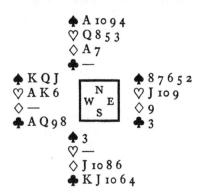

have the entries to establish the clubs, East's nine of diamonds prevents you from enjoying them. However, if you refuse the Greek gift and ruff in dummy at trick one, you can succeed. You cash the king of diamonds and ruff a heart, and a trump from hand squeezes West out of two tricks as before.

The only difference is that the entry-shift is not needed in this position. A diamond to the ace is good enough.

We saw at the foot of page 142 another matrix where no entry-shift was required. But when you run

across one of these positions
there may be a slight variation.
If we extend the side suit in the
long trump hand, for instance,
the entry-shifting aspect may be
essential after all.

Spades are trumps and South
is on lead needing five tricks. It
takes the lead of the king of
spades to apply sufficient pressure
to West.

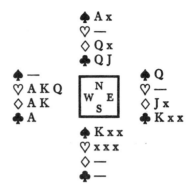

Here is a complete deal to illustrate this ending.

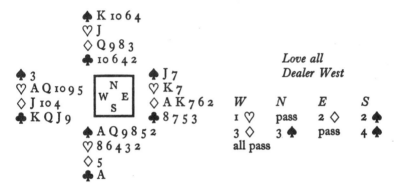

W	N	E	S
1 ♡	pass	2 ◇	2 ♠
3 ◇	3 ♠	pass	4 ♠
all pass			

Love all
Dealer West

West leads the king of clubs to your ace. You lead the singleton diamond,
playing the three from dummy when West puts in the ten. What should
West play at trick three?

Obviously a diamond continuation will give you a trick, but a club may
look safe enough. It isn't. You ruff the club and exit with a heart. A further
club lead from either side of the table yields the tenth trick, so West wins
with the queen of hearts and switches to a trump. You win in hand, ruff a
heart in dummy, play the queen of diamonds and ruff away East's king.

Now you have reached the matrix position, and the entry-shifting lead of the queen of spades leaves West helpless.

So perhaps West was wrong to play a second club at trick three. Should he switch to his trump instead? No, that merely simplifies your task. You win in hand and play a second trump to dummy's king, achieving an instant three-suit squeeze against West without the need for any entry-shift.

The only successful defence – a hard one to find at the table – is to play two rounds of hearts at tricks three and four. By removing an entry from dummy this blunts the effectiveness of your minor suit menaces, and you are unable to avoid the loss of four tricks.

Defenders have a tough time in these situations, for in seeking to avoid one trap they may stumble unexpectedly into another. One of the standard defences against the unbalanced entry-shifting trump squeeze is that of placing the declarer in the wrong hand – the shot through the heart. This is usually deadly, but there is always the possibility that declarer will be wearing a bullet-proof vest.

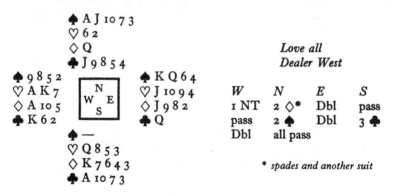

West leads the king of hearts and shifts to the two of clubs. You capture the queen with your ace and play a diamond. West takes his ace and cashes the king of clubs, leaving this position:

East has discarded a heart on the king of clubs, and West has a good idea of the position. He knows better than to lead his third trump or a heart. He considers the lead of a poisoned spade to squeeze the closed hand, but he sees that this would give you a second spade trick. If he led a low spade, the seven would draw East's queen; if he led the nine of spades, you would ruff out East's king and queen and eventually throw West in to lead from his 8 5 of spades into dummy's A 7.

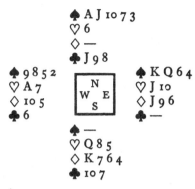

So West decides to shoot for the heart by returning the ten of diamonds. That's annoying. You discard the heart from dummy and win with the king. Now you have the right matrix for the entry-shifting squeeze against East but you are in the wrong hand to operate it. Still, you are not dead yet, and it may be possible to bring pressure to bear on *West*. You ruff a diamond in dummy and return the jack of spades. East covers with the queen and you ruff with the seven of clubs. Now the lead of a fourth diamond places West in an impossible position.

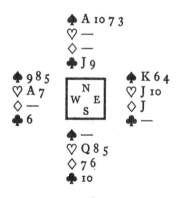

The obvious discard is a heart, but if West parts with his small heart you can discard a spade from dummy, allowing East to have the trick. The rest of the tricks are yours no matter what East returns.

Clearly West cannot gain by discarding his trump, for that lets you score your long diamond as well as three trumps and the ace of spades. And if West throws a spade? You can discard a spade as before; or else ruff the diamond, cash the ace of spades, discarding a heart, and continue with the spade ten, ruffing out East's king. Now the threat of the established spades hangs over West's head and he has to allow you to score the long diamond after all.

This is the first appearance of a squeeze against an 'idle' trump card, and of what we might call a 'non-material' suit establishment (non-material in that the established spades are not used directly, only as a threat). We shall examine these themes more closely later.

Balanced Positions

You started by believing that it took a balanced trump position to operate an entry-shifting squeeze. Then you discovered than an unbalanced trump holding was required when a defender held guards in three suits. But this is not always the case. Even when three suits are involved, it is sometimes the balanced trump position that is needed.

Clubs are trumps and South, on lead, requires five of the last six tricks. A cross-ruff produces only four tricks, and East's trump prevents South from cashing the established heart.

However, when South leads the king of clubs West feels the pinch in three suits and has to yield two extra tricks in one way or another. If he throws a heart or a spade, declarer wins the trump trick in the appropriate hand and sets up the major of West's discard. If West parts with his low diamond, the play of the

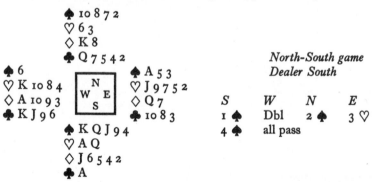

king of diamonds compels him to set up a major for declarer. West may try to avoid this by pitching the *ace* of diamonds, but South can cash the king of diamonds and then let West win a heart trick.

Let us see a complete deal illustrating this type of ending.

North-South game
Dealer South

S	W	N	E
1 ♠	Dbl	2 ♠	3 ♡
4 ♠	all pass		

West leads the six of trumps to his partner's ace. East considers a heart switch, but wisely decides to continue with a second round of trumps. You win with the jack and West discards a heart. If East cannot gain the lead in diamonds you may be able to ruff two diamonds in dummy, but it must be better to play for alternative chances. You cash the ace of clubs, lead a diamond to the king, ruff a club with the queen of spades, and exit with a diamond. East wins, and you receive his trump return in the balanced position, just as you did in some of the two-suit-threat trump squeezes. Only this time West is squeezed in three suits.

You play the nine of spades from hand, and if West parts with a minor-suit card you overtake or underplay accordingly. If West throws a heart, you continue with the ace and queen of hearts, and West has to yield the rest of the tricks whether he returns a club or

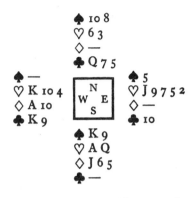

a diamond. The effect is the same if West jettisons his king of hearts under the ace (or on the trump). After two rounds of hearts you concede a diamond.

Sensing that the trump return will squeeze his partner, East may try a heart lead in the diagram position, but it makes no difference. You go up with the ace and lead the nine of spades yourself.

On that hand the contract was unbeatable, but sometimes an effective defence will be possible.

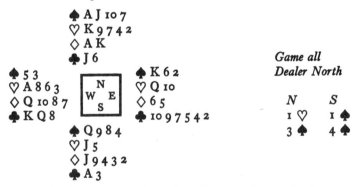

West leads a trump to the jack and king, and you win the trump return in hand with the eight. After a heart to the king, you cash the ace and king of diamonds before conceding a heart to East. Now the defenders may as well resign. Whether East returns his trump or a club, West is going to be squeezed in three suits when you play the queen of spades.

Where did the defence go wrong? An initial club lead is no good, for it is then a simple matter for you to establish dummy's hearts. No, the trump lead was essential for the defence; it was the *second* round of trumps that was the mistake. At trick two East should switch to clubs, attacking the throw-in menace. You

```
                    ♠ A 10
                    ♡ 9 7 4
                    ◇ —
                    ♣ J 6
        ♠ —            ┌──────┐      ♠ 6
        ♡ A 8          │  N   │      ♡ —
        ◇ Q 10      W  │      │  E   ◇ —
        ♣ K Q 8        │  S   │      ♣ 10 9 7 5 4 2
                       └──────┘
                    ♠ Q 9
                    ♡ —
                    ◇ J 9 4
                    ♣ A 3
```

may win and go immediately for the hearts, conceding the second round to East, but the defenders will take their club trick and play another trump, leaving this position:

When you lead a third heart from dummy East will discard a diamond, and you have no way of preventing the loss of a fourth trick.

The best you can do, after winning the ace of clubs, is to play a heart to the king, cash the top diamonds, and take one more trump before exiting in hearts. East wins and plays a club, putting West on lead.

```
                    ♠ A 7
                    ♡ 9 7 4
                    ◇ A K
                    ♣ —
        ♠ —            ┌──────┐      ♠ 6
        ♡ A 8          │  N   │      ♡ —
        ◇ Q 10 8 7  W  │      │  E   ◇ 6 5
        ♣ K            │  S   │      ♣ 9 7 4 2
                       └──────┘
                    ♠ Q 9
                    ♡ —
                    ◇ J 9 4 3 2
                    ♣ —
```

West has two good cards to return. The king of clubs concedes a ruff and discard but limits you to your four trump tricks.

The ten of diamonds has the same effect, since you have to ruff in dummy in order to prevent a ruff by East.

The throw-in element is common to all these balanced three-suit trump squeezes. Here is a different basic matrix.

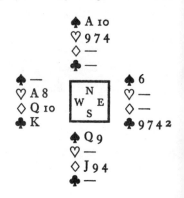

```
                    ♠ A 10
                    ♡ 9 7 4
                    ◇ —
                    ♣ —
        ♠ —            ┌──────┐      ♠ 6
        ♡ A 8          │  N   │      ♡ —
        ◇ Q 10      W  │      │  E   ◇ —
        ♣ K            │  S   │      ♣ 9 7 4 2
                       └──────┘
                    ♠ Q 9
                    ♡ —
                    ◇ J 9 4
                    ♣ —
```

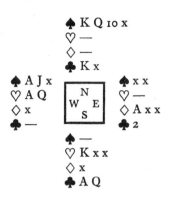

♠ K Q 10 x
♡ —
◇ —
♣ K x

♠ A J x
♡ A Q
◇ x
♣ —

♠ x x
♡ —
◇ A x x
♣ 2

♠ —
♡ K x x
◇ x
♣ A Q

Clubs are trumps and South can come to five tricks by leading the club queen. If West throws a spade, dummy wins and attacks spades. If West discards a heart, the club queen holds and the ace of hearts is ruffed out. And if West releases the diamond, his 'safe' exit card, the throw-in operates. Dummy wins and leads the king of spades, South discarding his diamond. West may hold off, but he has to take the next spade. Note that South cannot succeed by starting with a diamond ruff and returning the king of spades for a heart discard. West will win and play the queen of hearts, and if this is ruffed by the king of clubs East will discard his last spade.

An illustrative deal:

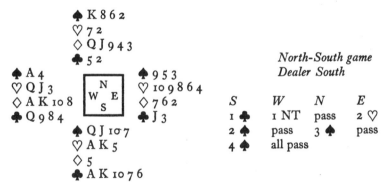

♠ K 8 6 2
♡ 7 2
◇ Q J 9 4 3
♣ 5 2

♠ A 4
♡ Q J 3
◇ A K 10 8
♣ Q 9 8 4

♠ 9 5 3
♡ 10 9 8 6 4
◇ 7 6 2
♣ J 3

♠ Q J 10 7
♡ A K 5
◇ 5
♣ A K 10 7 6

North-South game
Dealer South

S	W	N	E
1 ♣	1 NT	pass	2 ♡
2 ♠	pass	3 ♠	pass
4 ♠	all pass		

West begins with the ace and another spade, East playing low on the second round. Winning with the ten, you lead your singleton diamond. West takes his king and returns the queen of hearts to your ace. It seems likely that West is 4–4 in the minors, and there is no obvious way for you to come to ten tricks. However, if you have seen this sort of situation before, you may realize that there is a chance if East has one of the club honours. Just cash your tops in clubs and hearts, then lead the queen of spades in this position:

Note that it is essential to cash all the side-suit winners before leading the third trump. Otherwise West can escape by throwing a heart.

The entry-shifting squeeze was needed on this hand only because the nine of spades threatened to over-ruff dummy. If East's third trump had been a midget, you could have made your contract more simply and more safely by establishing the club suit.

In the case of the two-suit positional trump squeeze, we observed that when the menaces were unequal it

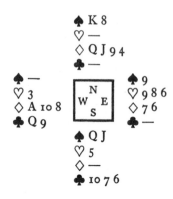

was sometimes necessary to forego ruffing-finesse winners in one suit in order to preserve the balanced trump position. Full compensation for the ignored tricks was provided by additional potential winners in the other threat suit. To remind you of this, here is the ultimate extension of the idea.

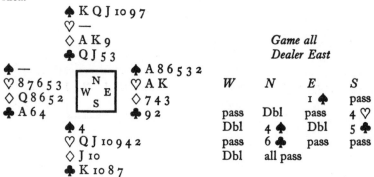

West leads the ace of clubs and continues with a second club to your ten. You finesse in diamonds and cash three rounds, discarding your four of spades. Then the lead of the queen of clubs squeezes East in the majors. A spade discard by East yields only one trick, but that is all you need. If East refuses to give up this one extra trick, you overtake with the king of clubs, happily abandoning four potential spade tricks in dummy because your heart threat will now produce five tricks.

It takes an initial lead of a *low* club to defeat the contract.

The point of this reminder is that unequal threats can also occur in the three-suit positional trump squeezes. Consider this diagram:

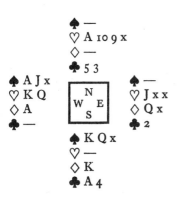

Clubs are trumps, and South leads the four of clubs to win all the tricks. If West throws a spade, South remains in hand to set up the spades by ruffing out the ace, the king of diamonds being discarded on the ace of hearts.

If West throws the diamond ace, a ruffing finesse in spades is enough, for the losing spade is discarded on the ace of hearts.

The extended menace in hearts is used if West discards a heart. South overtakes with the five of clubs, cashes the heart ace, and takes a ruffing finesse against the heart jack to make dummy high.

Many positions are imperfect in that they can be defeated by best defence, but in situations that stem from such tricky matrices the correct defence is by no means easy to find.

Suppose you take the West seat in this diagram. Clubs are trumps and South, who needs the rest of the tricks, leads the club king. Clearly you have to give up something, but if you part with a heart you will regret it. The club king will be followed by a heart ruff and a spade ruff – and the queen of hearts will squeeze you again.

	♠ Q x	
	♡ —	
	◇ A J	
	♣ A x	
♠ A K		♠ x x
♡ A K	N	♡ —
◇ K Q	W E	◇ x x x
♣ —	S	♣ Q
	♠ —	
	♡ Q x	
	◇ x x	
	♣ K x	

Give up a spade or a diamond and the story will have a one-trick-happier ending for you.

Sometimes the defensive options will be less obvious. It is worth remembering that a simple squeeze can be executed at a late stage in the play, and so can the tail end of a repeater. But an entry-shifting squeeze, having a much more delicate mechanism, has to be operated under special conditions which cannot be repeated in the later phases of a compound squeeze. Here is a hand on which a knowledge of this principle is invaluable.

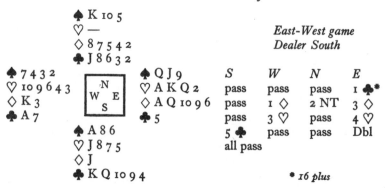

```
            ♠ K 10 5
            ♡ —
            ◇ 8 7 5 4 2         East-West game
            ♣ J 8 6 3 2         Dealer South

♠ 7 4 3 2        ┌─────┐        ♠ Q J 9
♡ 10 9 6 4 3     │  N  │        ♡ A K Q 2        S        W        N        E
◇ K 3            │W   E│        ◇ A Q 10 9 6   pass     pass     pass     1 ♣*
♣ A 7            │  S  │        ♣ 5            pass     1 ◇      2 NT     3 ◇
                 └─────┘                       pass     3 ♡      pass     4 ♡
            ♠ A 8 6                             pass     3 ♡                Dbl
            ♡ J 8 7 5                           5 ♣      pass     pass     Dbl
            ◇ J                                 all pass
            ♣ K Q 10 9 4                                 * 16 plus
```

Partner leads the diamond king and you overtake with the ace in order to return your singleton trump. West duly plays the ace and another trump. The jack is played from dummy on the second round, and you discard . . . well, what *do* you discard?

You find yourself suddenly on a new tack. Had you let South play a complete cross-ruff in the red suits he would have made no more than ten tricks. Now, with one ruff taken away from him, he has only nine tricks, but he is threatening to make his contract by means of what looks like a progressive entry-shifting squeeze.

You are menaced in three suits and something has to go. The spade portion of the squeeze (assuming declarer has the spade eight) can operate later. But a co-ordinated red-suit attack can function only with an entry-shifting mechanism in trumps, and that can occur only right now. If you throw a red card, declarer can set up a trick in the suit of your discard and subsequently use that winner to squeeze you between spades and the other red suit.

But if you throw a spade, the best declarer can do is cash three spades. You will be able to see which hand will win the third spade trick and you will discard accordingly. So the spade discard, immediately sacrificing a trick, is the winning defence.

Bridge, like life, is rich in paradox. You have discovered that a balanced trump position may work in a three-suit squeeze, and it will probably come as no surprise when you learn that it sometimes takes an *unbalanced* trump position to deliver the goods in a two-suit squeeze.

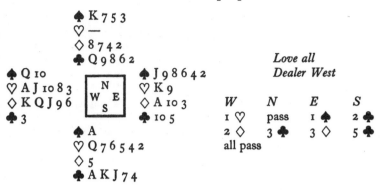

♠ K 7 5 3
♡ —
♢ 8 7 4 2
♣ Q 9 8 6 2

♠ Q 10   ♠ J 9 8 6 4 2
♡ A J 10 8 3   ♡ K 9
♢ K Q J 9 6   ♢ A 10 3
♣ 3   ♣ 10 5

♠ A
♡ Q 7 6 5 4 2
♢ 5
♣ A K J 7 4

Love all
Dealer West

W	N	E	S
1 ♡	pass	1 ♠	2 ♣
2 ♢	3 ♣	3 ♢	5 ♣
all pass			

West leads the king of diamonds and switches to his trump – three, nine, five, king. You ruff a heart, return to the spade ace, ruff another heart, cash the spade king for a heart discard, and ruff a spade with the ace of clubs.

Now, when you lead the jack of clubs in the diagram position, West has no good discard.

A heart? You play low in dummy, ruff a heart, ruff a diamond and concede a heart.

A diamond? You overtake with the club queen, ruff a diamond, and throw West in with a heart, discarding the spade from dummy.

Note that the unbalanced trump position is essential. You could easily have reached a balanced position by

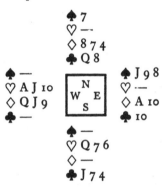

♠ 7
♡ —
♢ 8 7 4
♣ Q 8

♠ —   ♠ J 9 8
♡ A J 10   ♡ —
♢ Q J 9   ♢ A 10
♣ —   ♣ 10

♠ —
♡ Q 7 6
♢ —
♣ J 7 4

ruffing a diamond in your hand at an earlier stage, but then the squeeze would not work.

On the lead of the jack of clubs West discards a heart and you have nowhere to go.

How on earth can you tell whether it is a balanced or an unbalanced trump position that is required?

Well, the difference between this last hand and the two-suit trump squeezes that we studied previously lies in the loser count. Here the count

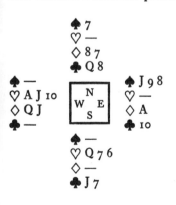

♠ 7
♡ —
♢ 8 7
♣ Q 8

♠ —   ♠ J 9 8
♡ A J 10   ♡ —
♢ Q J   ♢ A
♣ —   ♣ 10

♠ —
♡ Q 7 6
♢ —
♣ J 7

had not been rectified. You had to give up a trick after the squeeze had taken effect, and an element of throw-in was involved.

In general, each of the two types of trump matrix operates in its own area, the balanced one handling two-suit squeezes and the unbalanced one three-suit squeezes. However, to execute a two-suit squeeze without the count it is an unbalanced trump position that is required. And if a three-suit squeeze involves a throw-in menace it is a balanced trump position that you need.

Here is a more complex example of an unbalanced two-suit trump squeeze.

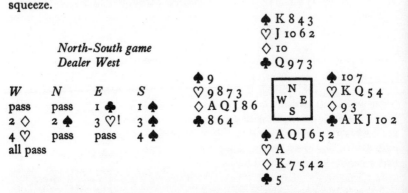

Knowing your opponents to be bold bidders, you pretend to be pushed into game. On the lead of the nine of hearts you play low from dummy and win with the ace. It seems unlikely that you will be able to ruff three diamonds with impunity, so you have to plan some sort of squeeze or throw-in against West. As a first step you lead a club to dummy's nine. You ruff the club return and play a diamond to West's jack. If West plays the eight of

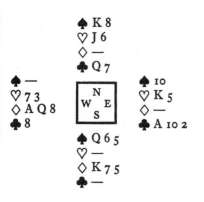

♠ K 8
♥ J 6
♦ —
♣ Q 7

hearts at this point he will soon find himself in trouble. You will cover with the ten, ruff East's queen, ruff a diamond, and play a spade to your ace, leaving this position:

Now the lead of the queen of spades strip-squeezes West into submission. He is forced to part with his exit card in clubs. You play the eight of spades from dummy and concede a low diamond to West, discarding a club from the table, and West has to yield the tenth trick in one of the red suits.

When in with the jack of diamonds West may decide that his best return is a club, but that will not save him.

You ruff the club, ruff a diamond, play a spade to your ace and continue with the queen of spades to squeeze West as before.

If he throws a diamond, you stay in hand, ruff a diamond, ruff yourself back to hand and concede a diamond. If he parts with a heart, you overtake, play the jack of hearts to ruff out the queen, and give up a low diamond to end-play West.

East's club return at trick three gave you the chance to achieve a balanced trump position, but if you had accepted this invitation you would have failed to make the contract.

♠ K 8
♥ J 10 6
♦ —
♣ Q

♠ —
♥ 8 7 3
♦ A Q 8
♣ —

N W E S

♠ 10
♥ K Q 5
♦ —
♣ A 2

♠ Q 6 5
♥ —
♦ K 7 5
♣ —

9

Entry-Shifting Without Trumps

It was the violence of the overnight storm that had put you in mind of the turbulent entry-shifting trump squeezes, and these provided a topic for discussion the next day as you patched up the damage on the *Cormorant* and made your way slowly back to the harbour where Alec hoped to retrieve his lost anchor.

'The build-up of pressure is tremendous,' you concluded, 'especially in the unbalanced three-suit squeezes that gain two tricks instantly.'

'Right,' agreed Alec. 'That takes care of the trump squeezes, but they say that one hand out of three is played at no trumps.'

Well, when we studied the principles of entry-shifting at no trumps earlier we certainly did not exhaust the subject. And the conclusions we reached, while true in general, did not represent the whole truth. We observed, for instance, that at no trumps even the entry-shifting mechanism could not help if there was no entry in either threat suit. Yet we can contradict this statement on the rare occasions when we are allowed to do business with the partner of the squeezee.

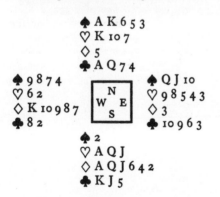

♠ A K 6 5 3
♡ K 10 7
◇ 5
♣ A Q 7 4

♠ 9 8 7 4
♡ 6 2
◇ K 10 9 8 7
♣ 8 2

♠ Q J 10
♡ 9 8 5 4 3
◇ 3
♣ 10 9 6 3

♠ 2
♡ A Q J
◇ A Q J 6 4 2
♣ K J 5

South plays in six no trumps after West has foolishly doubled a temporary effort of six diamonds.

West leads the nine of spades to dummy's king, and declarer burns his bridges by running the clubs. The seven of hearts is led to the jack, and now South cashes the ace of diamonds, leaving himself without an entry in either threat suit! The contract cannot be made without this apparently suicidal move, for it is necessary to extract East's exit card in diamonds.

When the queen of hearts is led in the diagram position, West comes under pressure. If he reduces to two diamonds, the standard procedure operates; the heart ten is played under the queen, the diamond queen forces out the king, and the South hand is high with the ace of hearts as an entry.

If West comes down to two spades, jettison is added to the entry-shifting squeeze repertoire. The heart queen is overtaken by the king, and the play of the ace and

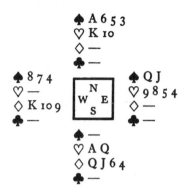

another spade gives the lead to East while South sheds the ace of hearts. East has nothing but hearts to return, and dummy makes the rest.

Even if East had been able to throw one spade (on the fourth club, perhaps) it would not have helped him, since he could then be thrown in on the *second* round of spades while South jettisoned his high heart. A basic form of that situation would be:

South leads the diamond queen at no trumps to win four out of the five tricks.

In all these jettison situations, it is, of course, necessary that the entry-shifting suit be strong enough to withstand both overtaking and jettison. If, in this diagram, East had the jack of diamonds, the defence would prevail.

Compensation for lack of entries may also be found in the form of a third threat. Here are some basic three-suit positions.

South needs five of the last six tricks at no trumps, but there is no link in any of the threat suits. Still, when the low club is led something has to give. West must either relinquish a trick in one of the red suits (in which case dummy plays the club ace), or allow declarer to set up a spade trick while retaining access, through West's forced return, to his red aces (dummy plays the club queen).

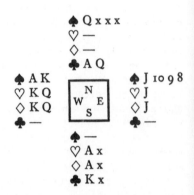

```
            ♠ Q x x x
            ♡ —
            ◊ —
            ♣ A Q
♠ A K                    ♠ J 10 9 8
♡ K Q       N           ♡ J
◊ K Q     W   E         ◊ J
♣ —         S           ♣ —
            ♠ —
            ♡ A x
            ◊ A x
            ♣ K x
```

Here, in another disconnected position, South needs six tricks out of seven. Again the lead of the low club squashes resistance. A spade or heart discard by West leads to a situation similar to that of the previous diagram. If West throws a diamond, the club ace is played, the ace of spades is cashed for a discard of the heart jack, and the club queen is returned to the king. The play of the ace and another diamond then forces East to yield a second trick in diamonds.

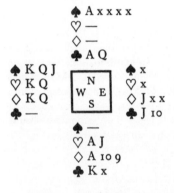

```
            ♠ A x x x x
            ♡ —
            ◊ —
            ♣ A Q
♠ K Q J                 ♠ x
♡ K Q       N           ♡ x
◊ K Q     W   E         ◊ J x x
♣ —         S           ♣ J 10
            ♠ —
            ♡ A J
            ◊ A 10 9
            ♣ K x
```

In this case South needs only five tricks out of the seven. He leads the club queen (not the ace, since West could successfully throw a spade) and West is stuck.

Does West throw a spade? Club king, spade ace for diamond discard, club to ace, and West is strip-squeezed into conceding a heart trick. Does West throw a heart? Any club, low heart to the ace, diamond king ducked. Does West throw a diamond? Small club, ace and another diamond.

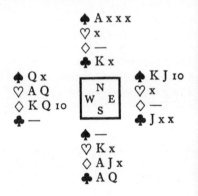

```
            ♠ A x x x
            ♡ x
            ◊ —
            ♣ K x
♠ Q x                   ♠ K J 10
♡ A Q       N           ♡ x
◊ K Q 10  W   E         ◊ —
♣ —         S           ♣ J x x
            ♠ —
            ♡ K x
            ◊ A J x
            ♣ A Q
```

The position is quaint. Declarer can decide to 'cross or stay' on the squeeze trick, but he has a fixed South re-entry in any event. Could anything as offbeat as this occur in practice? It already has!

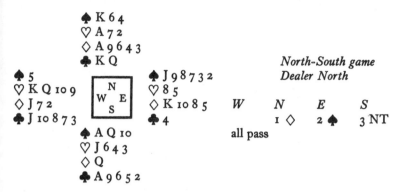

```
            ♠ K 6 4
            ♡ A 7 2
            ◊ A 9 6 4 3
            ♣ K Q                    North-South game
♠ 5              ♠ J 9 8 7 3 2        Dealer North
♡ K Q 10 9   N   ♡ 8 5
◊ J 7 2    W   E ◊ K 10 8 5       W    N    E    S
♣ J 10 8 7 3  S  ♣ 4                   1 ◊  2 ♠  3 NT
            ♠ A Q 10                all pass
            ♡ J 6 4 3
            ◊ Q
            ♣ A 9 6 5 2
```

West led the queen of hearts, which required East to drop the jack if he had it. The queen was allowed to win, and West switched to the two of diamonds. When dummy played low, East won with the king and returned his heart to knock out the ace. The play of the king and queen of clubs revealed the distribution, and declarer, after some thought, led a spade to his ten. (Even the fourth-dimensional defence of the jack of spades would not have helped East, for South would have confined the conflict to mere Newtonian space by winning with the queen.)

Now the spade queen was led in this position:

West had no answer. When he chose to throw a diamond, the play concluded: spade king from dummy, diamond ace for a club discard, a spade to the ace, forcing a club discard from West, then ace and another club to effect the throw-in.

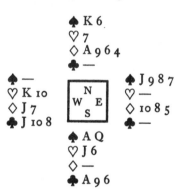

```
            ♠ K 6
            ♡ 7
            ◊ A 9 6 4
            ♣ —
♠ —              ♠ J 9 8 7
♡ K 10      N    ♡ —
◊ J 7     W   E  ◊ 10 8 5
♣ J 10 8    S    ♣ —
            ♠ A Q
            ♡ J 6
            ◊ —
            ♣ A 9 6
```

It is natural to wonder whether these disconnected positions can ever lead to a progessive squeeze in which more than one trick is gained.

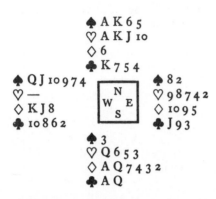

♠ A K 6 5
♡ A K J 10
◇ 6
♣ K 7 5 4

♠ Q J 10 9 7 4
♡ —
◇ K J 8
♣ 10 8 6 2

♠ 8 2
♡ 9 8 7 4 2
◇ 10 9 5
♣ J 9 3

♠ 3
♡ Q 6 5 3
◇ A Q 7 4 3 2
♣ A Q

After a weak jump overcall in spades, a double of six diamonds by West, a double of six hearts by East, and a retreat to six no trumps by South, West leads the queen of spades.

Since East presumably holds all five hearts, it is not unreasonable to hope to find West with a 6–0–3–4 shape. If this is the case, he can be squeezed on the third heart. Declarer wins the king of spades, king and ten of hearts, and two clubs in the closed hand. (If South does not 'unblock' two rounds of hearts he will end up in the wrong hand, and although a squeeze will mature it will not be progressive.) This leaves the following position:

West knew there was some reason why he didn't want to get up today, and when South leads the six of hearts he realizes that this was it. He cannot throw a diamond without allowing South to set up the whole suit, with the heart queen as an entry when dummy wins with the ace. If West parts with a club he gives up one trick at once, and he is strip-squeezed in spades and diamonds after the play of the two winning clubs and the last heart.

♠ A 6 5
♡ A J
◇ 6
♣ K 7

♠ J 10 9
♡ —
◇ K J 8
♣ 10 8

♠ 2
♡ 9 8 7
◇ 10 9 5
♣ J

♠ —
♡ Q 6
◇ A Q 7 4 3 2
♣ —

If West discards a spade on the six of hearts, dummy wins with the jack in order to preserve the later entry on the table. The play of the ace and another spade then sets up a spade winner. West cannot return a diamond without giving South his twelfth trick. And if he leads a club, the play of the heart and spade winners in the North hand effect a simple minor-suit squeeze to finish him off.

Unbalanced Positions

We have seen that an unbalanced trump position can, under certain conditions, be used to operate a positional trump squeeze. In the same way, an unbalanced entry-shifting suit can sometimes be used at no trumps, although the conditions are even more stringent.

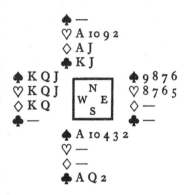

♠ —
♡ A 10 9 2
◇ A J
♣ K J

♠ K Q J
♡ K Q J
◇ K Q
♣ —

♠ 9 8 7 6
♡ 8 7 6 5
◇ —
♣ —

♠ A 10 4 3 2
♡ —
◇ —
♣ A Q 2

There are no trumps and South needs seven of the last eight tricks. When he leads the queen of clubs, West cannot hold the position.

A diamond discard concedes the seventh trick at once. A spade? South remains in hand and plays the ace and a low spade. A heart? South overtakes with the king of clubs and plays the ace and a low heart.

The key element in the squeeze is the two way double-entry position in clubs. Declarer can not only cross or stay on the squeeze trick, he can also decide which hand needs a club entry later on.

It is worth while taking the trouble to verify for yourself that seven tricks cannot be made against best defence if the ace of clubs or the two of clubs is led.

Opportunities for this sort of play usually go undetected at the table. You may think it unlikely that you will ever have enough information to give you a chance of recognizing the position. Still, it is handy to know about such things in advance, so that if one does make an unexpected appearance you won't need to work out your entry-shifting manoeuvre on the spot. Consider this deal from a match-point pairs event.

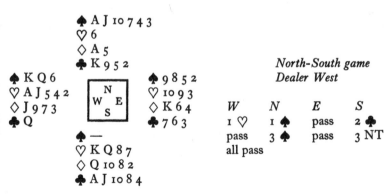

♠ A J 10 7 4 3
♡ 6
◇ A 5
♣ K 9 5 2

♠ K Q 6
♡ A J 5 4 2
◇ J 9 7 3
♣ Q

♠ 9 8 5 2
♡ 10 9 3
◇ K 6 4
♣ 7 6 3

♠ —
♡ K Q 8 7
◇ Q 10 8 2
♣ A J 10 8 4

North-South game
Dealer West

W	N	E	S
1 ♡	1 ♠	pass	2 ♣
pass	3 ♠	pass	3 NT
all pass			

West leads the three of diamonds to his partner's king. East returns the ten of hearts, your king is captured by the ace, and West exits with a diamond to dummy's ace. You play the club king, unblocking the ten from your hand, and reflect on the result. Now you are safe for nine tricks, but those who play in five clubs will certainly make eleven tricks and some may be allowed to make twelve. It looks as though you will need an overtrick to be sure of a good score. You continue with the two of clubs to your jack, West throwing a heart, and suddenly the full deal becomes crystal clear. West would surely have led a heart from a six-card suit, and East would have returned a low heart from 10 x x, so the position must be like this:

Knowing the layout, you still seem to be facing a hopeless task since all three of your menaces are disconnected. But you remember the squeeze which, because of the suppleness of the entry-shifting suit itself, practically takes over and performs the duties of a whole communications network. You have only to lead your eight of clubs and the defence crumbles.

If West discards a spade, you overtake with the nine of clubs, establish the spades, and later re-enter dummy with the five of clubs. If West throws a diamond, you overtake, discard a heart on the ace of spades, and return to hand with a club to cash the rest of your winners. If West throws a heart, you play the five of clubs from dummy and cash the queen of hearts. Then (a) if West unblocks the jack of hearts, you cash the queen of diamonds, put East in with the nine of hearts, and collect dummy's ace of spades on the forced return; or (b) if West keeps his jack of hearts, you can put him in with it at once.

The triple threat against West was necessary to make up for the entry misery, the complete disconnection, in all three menace suits. The squeeze had to mature two tricks earlier than usual – that is, while you still had two winners outside of the menace suits – because of the need for extra communication in the squeeze suit itself.

There are also unbalanced entry-shifting squeezes at no trumps in which the squeeze matures as declarer severs the last link between the hands.

This ending comes from a hand played in the United States by the distinguished friend of a friend of yours:

```
        ♠ —
        ♡ —
        ◇ K
        ♣ A x
♠ A   ┌─────┐  ♠ x
♡ A   │  N  │  ♡ —
◇ A   │W   E│  ◇ —
♣ —   │  S  │  ♣ Q x
      └─────┘
        ♠ 6
        ♡ K
        ◇ —
        ♣ K
```

Declarer was in a no trump contract, needing two more tricks, and he knew that West had three aces left. He was just about to lead the club king to squeeze West when somebody rushed into the room to announce that he had just been elected President.

Pandemonium broke out. What with the excitement, confusion, 'phone calls, bonfires, impromptu press conferences, dazzling television lights and swarms of lynx-eyed security men, South completely forgot whether East's small spade was the five or the seven.

But did it really matter? Not at all. The 'New President's Squeeze' functions whether East guards the spade or not.

When West threw the spade ace (other plays are clearly hopeless), South played the low club from dummy and continued with the six of spades, and he was bound to make a further trick whether the six of spades was a winner or not. If East's spade is high, it acts as a 'stepping-stone', enabling South to reach the stranded ace of clubs.

This position is one trick 'tighter' than the unbalanced entry-shifting no trump squeezes we have encountered so far. That is why West is squeezed although he appears to be menaced in only two suits. His value in the third suit (spades) is strategically, not materially, necessary to a successful defence.

Here is a similar position in which strategic values are threatened:

Needing three tricks at no trumps, South leads the king of clubs.

West is at liberty to choose his own way of going under. He can unguard a winner directly by throwing one of his red aces, in which case South overtakes with the ace of clubs, cashes the established red king, and puts either opponent on lead to gain access to his disjointed ace of spades.

Alternatively, West can force his partner into a standard stepping-stone position by discarding a spade. Now South lets the king of clubs win and

```
             ♠ —
             ♡ K
             ◇ K
             ♣ A x
♠ K J     ┌─────┐  ♠ Q 10
♡ A       │  N  │  ♡ —
◇ A       │W   E│  ◇ —
♣ —       │  S  │  ♣ Q x
          └─────┘
             ♠ A x x
             ♡ —
             ◇ —
             ♣ K
```

plays the ace and another spade to retrieve his disconnected ace of clubs.

An interesting point is that the retention by declarer of the ace of spades is not relevant to the squeeze or to the stepping-stone as far as West, East and South are concerned. But North, who is not privileged to hold one card more than the other players, would not like it at all if the ace of spades were led before the king of clubs.

Let us have a look at one or two of these endings in the setting of a complete deal. You might be surprised at how easily these odd-looking positions can be recognized when they make an appearance. By the time the fateful moment arrives, declarer is often facing a double-dummy situation with only a few cards left in each hand.

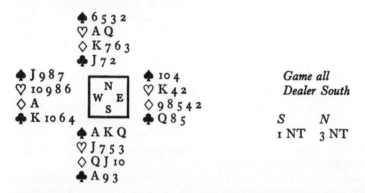

♠ 6 5 3 2
♡ A Q
◇ K 7 6 3
♣ J 7 2

♠ J 9 8 7
♡ 10 9 8 6
◇ A
♣ K 10 6 4

♠ 10 4
♡ K 4 2
◇ 9 8 5 4 2
♣ Q 8 5

♠ A K Q
♡ J 7 5 3
◇ Q J 10
♣ A 9 3

Game all
Dealer South

S	N
1 NT	3 NT

West leads the ten of hearts to the queen and king. East, thinking that this may be his only chance to make a damaging return, tries a shift to the ten of spades. You win the trick and lead the ten of diamonds to West's ace. Seeing his partner's two on this trick, West blocks you out of the king of diamonds by playing a second round of hearts. Now you have only eight tricks if neither spades nor diamonds break favourably, so, to prepare the ground for a squeeze, you concede a third trick to the defence by ducking a club. Whatever the return, you cash winners and come down to a three card ending akin to the New President's Squeeze.

When you lead the queen of diamonds, West cannot prevent you from making two of the last three tricks. A major-suit discard enables you to score either the seven of hearts or the six of spades, while a club discard exposes his partner to the stepping-stone ending.

On that deal, with the one-card menaces

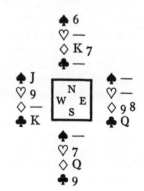

♠ 6
♡ —
◇ K 7
♣ —

♠ J
♡ 9
◇ —
♣ K

♠ —
♡ —
◇ 9 8
♣ Q

♠ —
♡ 7
◇ Q
♣ 9

divided between the two hands, there was no question of squeezing dummy. But when both menaces are on the table you have to be careful.

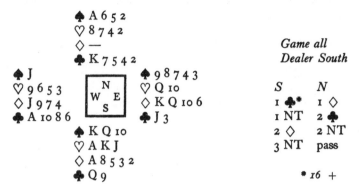

```
        ♠ A 6 5 2
        ♡ 8 7 4 2
        ◇ —
        ♣ K 7 5 4 2
♠ J                    ♠ 9 8 7 4 3
♡ 9 6 5 3      N       ♡ Q 10
◇ J 9 7 4   W   E      ◇ K Q 10 6
♣ A 10 8 6     S       ♣ J 3
        ♠ K Q 10
        ♡ A K J
        ◇ A 8 5 3 2
        ♣ Q 9
```

Game all
Dealer South

S	N
1 ♣*	1 ◇
1 NT	2 ♣
2 ◇	2 NT
3 NT	pass

*16 +

West leads the four of diamonds, you discard a club from dummy, and East plays the queen. When you allow this to hold, East continues with the king of diamonds. Whether you duck again or win with the ace and play a third diamond, East will learn that you have five diamonds and the tempo of the suit will be the same. But holding up the ace leaves you better placed strategically, so you allow the king to win and throw a second club from dummy. East now switches to the jack of clubs. Your queen loses to the ace, and West continues with the ten of clubs to dummy's king. You finesse in hearts, cash the king and queen of spades and the ace and king of hearts. When East discards on the third heart the position is virtually double-dummy.

On the lead of the spade ten West has no good card to play.

Note the difference it would have made if you had won the second diamond and played a third round of the suit. Dummy would have been squeezed out of an indispensable card. The ending would have been reduced to three cards in each hand instead of four, and any card taken away from dummy ruins the position. The needed 'elbow room' is missing.

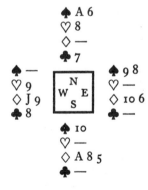

```
        ♠ A 6
        ♡ 8
        ◇ —
        ♣ 7
♠ —                ♠ 9 8
♡ 9      N         ♡ —
◇ J 9  W   E       ◇ 10 6
♣ 8      S         ♣ —
        ♠ 10
        ♡ —
        ◇ A 8 5
        ♣ —
```

All these manoeuvres are what might be called 'rescue' squeezes. They compensate partly or entirely for the damage caused by blocked suits and lack of entries, enabling declarer to reach the tricks that are rightfully his. The last two – the stepping stones –

have a hint of sacrifice about them, for in overtaking a winner declarer sets up a trick for an opponent.

The element of sacrifice is more marked on the next hand, where there are three disconnected suits.

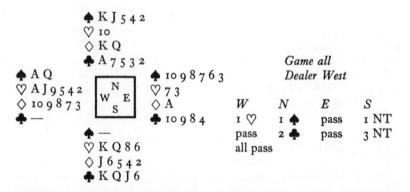

♠ K J 5 4 2
♡ 10
◇ K Q
♣ A 7 5 3 2

♠ A Q
♡ A J 9 5 4 2
◇ 10 9 8 7 3
♣ —

♠ 10 9 8 7 6 3
♡ 7 3
◇ A
♣ 10 9 8 4

♠ —
♡ K Q 8 6
◇ J 6 5 4 2
♣ K Q J 6

Game all
Dealer West

W	N	E	S
1 ♡	1 ♠	pass	1 NT
pass	2 ♣	pass	3 NT
all pass			

West leads the ten of diamonds to his partner's ace, and East returns the seven of hearts. Your king is captured by the ace, and West switches back to diamonds. You appear to have precisely eight tricks with little prospect of a ninth. West cannot be end-played in hearts, for after running the clubs you will have no way back to hand. Still, you have no option but to play on your long suit. And a funny thing happens on the third round of clubs – West is entry-shift-squeezed in three suits.

If West plays a red card on the jack of clubs, you play low in dummy and concede a trick in the suit he discarded, throwing spades from the table.

If West parts with the queen of spades, you overtake with the ace of clubs and return a low spade, discarding a red loser from your hand. You win the return, cash

♠ K J 5 4 2
♡ —
◇ —
♣ A 7 5

♠ A Q
♡ J 9 5
◇ 9 8 7
♣ —

♠ 10 9 8 7 6
♡ 3
◇ —
♣ 10 4

♠ —
♡ Q 8 6
◇ J 6 5
♣ J 6

your other red winner and exit with your club, using East as a stepping stone to reach dummy's spades. The annoying thing from East's point of view is that he cannot escape by unblocking in clubs; that merely gives you an overtrick.

Finally, here is a non-sacrificial but even more unbalanced entry-shifting

[174]

squeeze, in which the flexibility of the entry-shifting lead supplies a vital extra option.

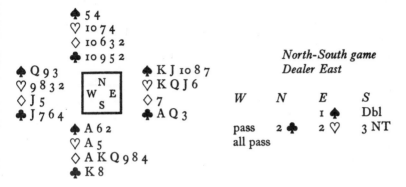

```
                  ♠ 5 4
                  ♡ 10 7 4
                  ◇ 10 6 3 2
                  ♣ 10 9 5 2
♠ Q 9 3                          ♠ K J 10 8 7         North-South game
♡ 9 8 3 2        N               ♡ K Q J 6            Dealer East
◇ J 5         W     E            ◇ 7
♣ J 7 6 4        S               ♣ A Q 3           W      N      E      S
                  ♠ A 6 2                                        1 ♠    Dbl
                  ♡ A 5                             pass   2 ♣   2 ♡    3 NT
                  ◇ A K Q 9 8 4                     all pass
                  ♣ K 8
```

West leads the three of spades and East plays the king. If you could afford to duck just one round of spades, you could pulverize East by running the diamonds. Suppose you duck the first trick and East continues spades. You win and play six rounds of diamonds, reducing East to five cards. Two of these must be hearts (because of the threat of dummy's ten), and two more must be clubs (otherwise you can lead your low club). Regardless of which fifth card East keeps and of which cards *West* keeps, you can exit successfully and wait for your ninth trick.

The most fascinating variations are those in which East keeps three hearts (not necessarily all honours), and two clubs (not necessarily the queen). If you work them all out you will see that *each* defender is squeezed in three suits, although there is no entry to dummy.

Now perhaps East cannot quite see all this coming, but it will be obvious to him that he can hardly lose by shifting to the king of hearts at trick two. This switch allows the defenders to hold the position. If you run the diamonds, West can throw clubs and East spades. The setting trick in hearts is kept on ice until needed.

So you cannot afford to duck the first trick, but when you win the ace of spades your count is wrong. If you run the diamonds, careful discarding by the defenders will beat the contract.

With six tricks to go, for instance, the defenders can come down to this position, leaving you helpless.

Can anything be done? Yes. The squeeze against East must be made to act earlier, when you still retain the option of leading up to your club king. You can take up this option if East reduces his number of quick winners.

After winning the spade ace, therefore, you cash the ace and king of diamonds and continue with the eight of diamonds to dummy's ten. This is the position:

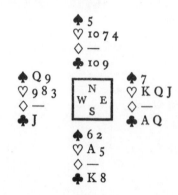

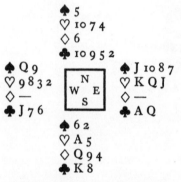

When the six of diamonds is led from dummy, East is entry-shift-squeezed in an unfamiliar way. If he throws a spade, you underplay with the four of diamonds and lead a club towards your king.

If East keeps all his spades, you overtake and finish the diamonds, throwing clubs from dummy. Then (a) if East threw the club queen on the six of diamonds, his last six cards must be the club ace, plus at least two hearts, and at most three spades. You lead your low club, setting up the club king while you still hold the ace of hearts. Or, (b) if East threw a heart on the six of diamonds, his last six cards must include two hearts, the ace and queen of clubs (to avoid the first variation), and only two spades. You simply play the ace and a low heart, setting up dummy's ten. The defenders cannot cash more than four tricks, and eventually they must let you score either the heart ten or the club king.

If you had been inflexible on the fourth round of diamonds, playing ace, king, queen, and then low to the ten, East could have defeated the contract by retaining all his spade winners, for the use of the heart ace (your sole re-entry) would relieve him of any further squeeze pressure. (Had there been another re-entry – a fifth small diamond in dummy, for instance – there would have been no need for the entry-shifting play. Nor would there have been this need if you could have led from dummy at trick eight.)

This is an unusual form of entry-shifting squeeze in which a defender is squeezed out of . . . Well, what was East squeezed out of? Nothing material – he did not set up a winner for you. Was he squeezed into a premature commitment? Perhaps, although he did not truly commit himself. All he gave away was information. He was forced to reveal what his discarding strategy would be. This could be called a reconnaissance squeeze. East was squeezed out of the secrecy of his strategy.

You didn't know there could be squeezes against this sort of nothingness? Then it is time we took a closer look at 'non-material' values.

10

Non-Material Squeezes

The whole concept of non-material values in the play of the cards is strangely linked in your mind with a particular piece of music. That is because you were deeply immersed in non-material studies some years ago when you attended a performance by your favourite pianist of Rachmaninov's piano concerto in C minor. George interpreted the music with passionate intensity, and the haunting, recurrent themes seemed to provide an eloquent counterpoint to your central idea, suggesting the presence of factors that were invisible, intangible, perhaps even supernatural, in the situations that you were thinking about.

For a while you were lost in clouds of uncertainty, but reassurance came with the shift to the major key in the third movement. The majestic and triumphant ending served as a reminder that the power of a non-material squeeze is no less than that of a material one and its conclusion no less inevitable. You left the concert hall with a keener appreciation of Rachmaninov's music and with a new perspective on bridge.

A non-material squeeze is one that does not result in immediate material gain. The defender does not have to discard a winner or unguard a stopper, he feels little pain, and he may not even realize that he has been squeezed at all. The squeeze is 'invisible' in the sense that it operates against strategic rather than material values. In the end, of course, there must always be a material gain, otherwise there would be no point in the play. The squeeze may appear to operate against idle cards, but this is an illusion. In reality the 'idle' cards are busy cards in disguise, cards that have some vital function to perform. The hidden tasks of these pseudo-idle cards are various, and we can classify our non-material squeezes as follows:

(a) Squeezes against cards that deny an extra entry.
(b) Squeezes against 'idle' trump cards.
(c) Squeezes against exit cards that prevent a throw-in.
(d) Squeezes against link cards vital to enemy communication.
(e) Squeezes against cards essential to opponents' strategy.

Group (a) comprises the entry squeezes. We have already seen something of these in Chapter 3, and we shall be returning for a further look at the subject.

In group (b) we studied one variety, the backwash squeeze, in Chapter 4, and in a later chapter we shall meet a different type of squeeze against 'idle' trump cards.

In this chapter we shall concentrate on the remaining three groups of non-material squeezes.

Squeezes Against Exit Cards

This is the best known of our five groups, and it is the one that straddles the boundary between 'material' and 'strategic' territory. You are familiar, of course, with the many types of strip-squeeze in which a defender is squeezed out of his surplus winners and/or exit cards before being thrown in to make a fatal lead. If he has to part with a surplus winner he may be conscious of material loss. But if he gives up an exit card, the loss does not seem so material although it is certainly just as grave.

We are not going to spend any time on these routine plays. In less familiar situations, however, the strip-squeeze may take the form of an 'information' squeeze, where your purpose is to compel an opponent to tell you which line of play to adopt.

♠ Q J 5 4 3
♡ K Q 6
◇ 7
♣ A Q J 10

```
    N
 W     E
    S
```

♠ K 9 7 2
♡ A J 7 4
◇ A Q J
♣ K 6

North wanted to play this hand in six spades, but you knew better and converted to six no trumps.

West leads the ten of hearts and you take a moment to consider the position. There will be no problem unless spades are 4–0, and you can pick up four spades in the East hand with a finesse, provided that you tackle the suit the safe way.

What if West holds four spades? If he has the king of diamonds as well, you can squeeze him; and if he hasn't, a simple finesse in diamonds will do. Telling the opponents as much, you lay down your hand and claim the contract.

West is taken aback and stammers out a protest.

'But . . . but . . . look here, now, you can't see where the king of diamonds is.'

'But I shall know,' you reply. 'If you are mulish enough not to tell me right now, I shall have to give you a long and dull explanation.'

Well, West remains mulish and your explanation goes something like this: You win the heart king, come to hand with the king of clubs and lead a spade to the jack. When East shows out (no problem otherwise), you cash the queen of hearts. If East shows out again, West started with five hearts and so cannot have more than four clubs. You run the clubs, discarding the queen and jack of diamonds. If West retains one heart more than you, you force him to part with it by cashing the diamond ace. Then finish the hearts and lead the spade king to end-play West. In effect, you strip West down to your shape to enforce the end-play.

If East follows to the second heart, you finish the suit, throwing a spade from dummy. Next come two more rounds of clubs. If the count shows that West still has one club more than dummy, he cannot have any diamonds left and the finesse is sure to succeed. If West does not have more clubs than dummy, you finish as before: last club, diamond ace, spade king.

Thus your contract is 100% secure irrespective of the position of the king of diamonds.

Although exit cards in strip-squeezes can be plainly visible, there are times when they are not quite so obvious – times when the discard looks harmless enough. We saw some examples in Chapter 8 when we were considering balanced three-suit trump squeezes. Here is a reminder.

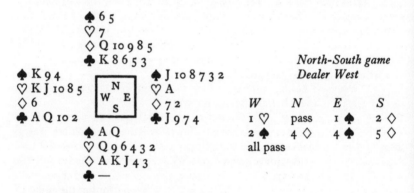

♠ 6 5
♡ 7
◇ Q 10 9 8 5
♣ K 8 6 5 3

♠ K 9 4   ♠ J 10 8 7 3 2
♡ K J 10 8 5   ♡ A
◇ 6   ◇ 7 2
♣ A Q 10 2   ♣ J 9 7 4

♠ A Q
♡ Q 9 6 4 3 2
◇ A K J 4 3
♣ —

North-South game
Dealer West

W	N	E	S
1 ♡	pass	1 ♠	2 ◇
2 ♠	4 ◇	4 ♠	5 ◇
all pass			

West leads the six of diamonds and you win in hand with the king. A heart goes to East's ace, a second trump comes back, and when you play the *jack* West is squeezed.

A discard of the small spade may not seem to involve a conspicuous material loss, but the strategic loss is decisive. You continue with the ace and queen of spades, and West has to give you two tricks in either hearts or clubs.

If West had somehow been able to retain the third spade, he could have used it as an exit card, for the ruff and discard would have done you no good at all. But there was no profitable way for West to keep that third spade. Even if East had returned a spade instead of his trump, you would have gone up with the ace and played the jack of diamonds yourself to achieve the same position.

Squeezes Against Link Cards

Of particular importance to the defenders are the small cards which permit them to cross freely from hand to hand. Like any other cards that have hidden value, these link cards are subject to the pressure of a squeeze. It may be possible to cut the defenders' communications completely, or, at least, to ensure that the dangerous defender cannot gain the lead at a vital stage.

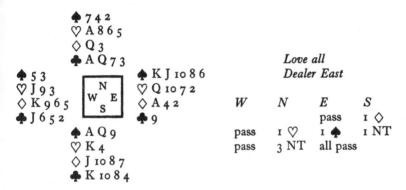

```
              ♠ 7 4 2
              ♡ A 8 6 5
              ◇ Q 3                    Love all
              ♣ A Q 7 3                Dealer East
♠ 5 3              ♠ K J 10 8 6
♡ J 9 3      N     ♡ Q 10 7 2
◇ K 9 6 5  W   E   ◇ A 4 2          W     N      E      S
♣ J 6 5 2      S   ♣ 9                                pass   1 ◇
              ♠ A Q 9             pass   1 ♡    1 ♠    1 NT
              ♡ K 4              pass   3 NT   all pass
              ◇ J 10 8 7
              ♣ K 10 8 4
```

West leads the five of spades to his partner's king, and you recognize what might be a deal from a standard textbook on defence. East is likely to have five spades headed by K J 10, but he passed originally so he probably has only one of the diamond honours. If you win the first spade and play on diamonds, West will win and clear the spades – curtain! And if you hold up the ace of spades, East will realize the futility of continuing the suit and shift to hearts. You may hold up, but the defenders will win the first diamond in the appropriate hand and clear the hearts – curtain!

Do you shrug your shoulders in despair? Not a bit of it. Knowing something about 'invisible' squeezes, you realize that if East has length in hearts along with his spades you may be able to bring pressure to bear on him by playing on clubs. One snag is that East cannot be forced to keep four hearts unless you preserve a late re-entry in dummy. So the clubs have to be tackled in such a way that you can play three rounds and later reach dummy with the fourth.

You win the first spade and lead the eight of clubs to dummy's ace. The appearance of East's nine is good news, and when you continue with the three of clubs to your king, East discards a diamond. This is the position:

Now you lead the ten of clubs.
There is no way for West to deny
you a fourth-round club entry to
dummy. And East is squeezed. If
he parts with a spade, that threat is
neutralized and you can go about
your business of establishing a
diamond trick. If East throws a
heart, you play three rounds of
hearts, setting up your game-going
trick in that suit (with a club entry
to cash it). Finally, if East gives up
the four of diamonds, the little card
with the big invisible value, he

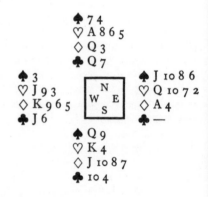

♠ 7 4
♡ A 8 6 5
◇ Q 3
♣ Q 7

♠ 3
♡ J 9 3
◇ K 9 6 5
♣ J 6

♠ J 10 8 6
♡ Q 10 7 2
◇ A 4
♣ —

♠ Q 9
♡ K 4
◇ J 10 8 7
♣ 10 4

breaks the defensive link in diamonds. East will be forced to win the first
diamond, after which no successful defence is possible.

Try the next one as a single-dummy problem.

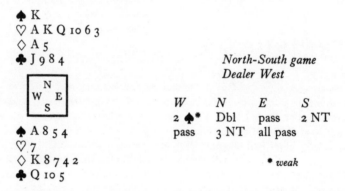

♠ K
♡ A K Q 10 6 3
◇ A 5
♣ J 9 8 4

♠ A 8 5 4
♡ 7
◇ K 8 7 4 2
♣ Q 10 5

North-South game
Dealer West

W	N	E	S
2 ♠*	Dbl	pass	2 NT
pass	3 NT	all pass	

* *weak*

West leads the queen of spades to dummy's king, and you test the hearts.
When you discard a spade on the second round so does West. How should
you continue?

That spade discard is very revealing. With 6–1–3–3 or 6–1–2–4 distribution, West would surely have discarded a club. Unless he is playing a
subtle game, therefore, his shape must be 6–1–4–2, and the position at the
moment must be something like this:

With only seven top tricks, you need to establish two more. But if you play clubs at this point, East will win and clear the spades and the defenders will make five tricks.

First you must cash the queen of hearts, discarding the eight of spades from hand. This will force West to weaken his hand in some way. If he parts with another spade, that suit is no longer a threat and you can tackle the clubs. If West throws a diamond, you can

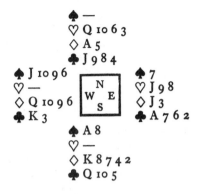

set up the extra tricks you need in diamonds by playing the ace, king and another. And if West abandons his link card, the three of clubs, it is again safe for you to play on clubs.

The need for this sort of play is easiest to spot when an opponent has been active in the bidding.

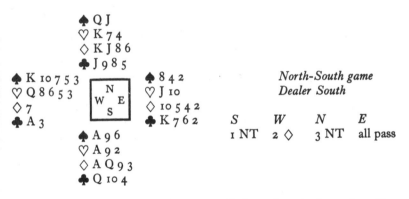

		North-South game
		Dealer South

S	W	N	E
1 NT	2 ◇	3 NT	all pass

On enquiry you learn that West's overcall showed 5–5 in the majors. How helpful! If only you could meet more opponents like this.

West leads the five of hearts to his partner's ten. You can't afford to hold up since a spade switch would be fatal. So you win the first trick with the ace, hoping for a blockage in hearts such as does, in fact, exist. But by now you know better than to go for the clubs straight away. East would win and return the jack of hearts, and when you held up the king he would switch to spades. You would have to play low, and when West won with the king he would shift back to hearts to establish a setting trick for the defence.

[183]

First you must cash the diamonds to force some discards from West. Here is the position:

This hand differs from the two previous ones in that you do not have an alternative threat. You are going to play clubs next no matter what West discards on the fourth diamond.

If West throws another spade and East wins the first club, you let the jack of hearts hold the next trick. But now, when the spade switch comes, you can afford to go up with the ace and clear the clubs.

If West gives up a heart and East wins the first club, you simply win the heart return and knock out the ace of clubs.

And if West parts with the three of clubs, he is forced on lead with the ace of clubs at the next trick. You play low from dummy on the heart continuation and let the spade switch run to the king, and the defenders can make no more than four tricks.

Suppose the opening lead had been a spade instead of a heart. Then four rounds of diamonds would squeeze West immediately. But all is not lost if you pull the wrong card and find yourself playing a club at trick two. When East wins with the king and returns a spade, you can put up the ace and run the diamonds to squeeze West out of one of his spade winners.

It is as well to realize, however, that the immediate application of pressure against the defenders' link cards is not always the right answer on hands of this type. Try shuffling the North-South spades in the previous deal.

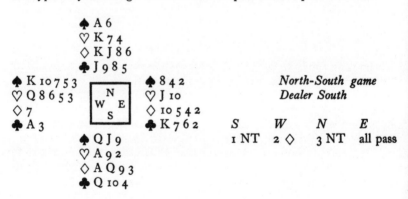

```
          ♠ A 6
          ♡ K 7 4
          ◇ K J 8 6
          ♣ J 9 8 5
♠ K 10 7 5 3          ♠ 8 4 2          North-South game
♡ Q 8 6 5 3          ♡ J 10           Dealer South
◇ 7                  ◇ 10 5 4 2
♣ A 3                ♣ K 7 6 2
          ♠ Q J 9                   S    W    N    E
          ♡ A 9 2                   1 NT 2 ◇ 3 NT all pass
          ◇ A Q 9 3
          ♣ Q 10 4
```

West leads the five of spades and you win the trick with the nine. If you hopefully play out four rounds of diamonds, you will be disconcerted to find that there is no squeeze. West will discard two hearts and his small club, and you will have no play for the contract. The essential difference is that this time you are unable to hold up the ace of spades. West can be sure of knocking out your ace on the second round of the suit, hence he does not need to retain his link card in clubs.

On this hand your only chance is to lead a low club at trick two, hoping to slip past the ace. What's that? You'd always play the ace in West's position? Then you are a truly fine player. If West plays low – and there are many experienced players who would – you are home. East wins and returns a spade to the ace, but then the run of diamonds forces West to part with a spade winner.

An initial heart lead gives you fewer problems this time. You win with the ace, play a club to East's king, hold off the second heart, and end up with ten tricks.

You may be in a position to threaten both opponents.

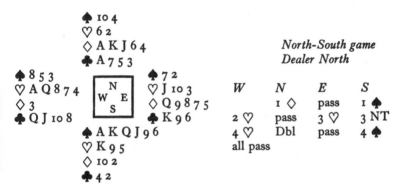

```
              ♠ 10 4
              ♡ 6 2
              ◇ A K J 6 4          North-South game
              ♣ A 7 5 3            Dealer North
♠ 8 5 3              ♠ 7 2
♡ A Q 8 7 4    N     ♡ J 10 3       W      N      E      S
◇ 3          W   E   ◇ Q 9 8 7 5          1 ◇   pass   1 ♠
♣ Q J 10 8      S    ♣ K 9 6       2 ♡    pass   3 ♡    3 NT
              ♠ A K Q J 9 6        4 ♡    Dbl    pass   4 ♠
              ♡ K 9 5              all pass
              ◇ 10 2
              ♣ 4 2
```

West leads the three of diamonds, and at first glance it looks like a defensive problem. If East is allowed to win the first trick with the queen of diamonds, he must switch to the heart jack, making sure of two heart tricks before giving his partner a ruff. Otherwise you will be able to discard three losers on the diamonds, using the ten of spades as a second-round trump entry.

But you don't see why you should give the defenders a sporting chance, so you go up with the ace of diamonds and play out your trumps.

West throws a heart and dummy a club on the fifth trump – and East feels the pinch. If he parts with his link card, the three of hearts, your next move is to run the diamond ten to his queen. With hearts blocked the defenders cannot cash more than two tricks in the suit, and your remaining losers go away on dummy's diamonds. Nor does it help East to discard the jack or ten of hearts instead of the three – again the defenders are restricted to two heart tricks.

Clearly East cannot gain by discarding a diamond on the fifth trump; you would simply ruff out the queen

```
                  ♠ —
                  ♡ 6
                  ◇ K J 6
                  ♣ A 7 3 5
    ♠ —          ┌─────────┐        ♠ —
    ♡ A Q 8 7    │   N     │        ♡ J 10 3
    ◇ —          │ W   E   │        ◇ Q 9 8
    ♣ Q J 10 8   │   S     │        ♣ K 9
                  └─────────┘
                  ♠ J 9
                  ♡ K 9 5
                  ◇ 10
                  ♣ 4 2
```

of diamonds to establish your tenth trick. So East will probably decide to come down to a singleton club.

Now the pressure switches to West. When you continue with your last trump (or the ten of diamonds, for that matter) West cannot afford to part with another heart. That would allow you to run the ten of diamonds with impunity. So West has to discard a club, after which it is a matter of routine to throw him in on the second round of clubs. He can cash two club tricks but then has to open up the hearts, and the king of hearts becomes your tenth trick.

'Lunar' Menaces

A different sort of invisibility arises when pressure is applied against material values through menaces that appear to be beyond reach. Such a situation changes a mundane, everyday squeeze to one in which we establish menaces on the moon.

```
              ♠ 8 7 5 4 2
              ♡ 10 3
              ◇ Q 6 3
              ♣ A 7 5                      Game all
    ♠ A K Q 10 3  ┌─────────┐  ♠ J 9 6      Dealer West
    ♡ J 9 8 7 5 2 │   N     │  ♡ 4
    ◇ A J         │ W   E   │  ◇ 10 8 7 5 4 2
    ♣ —           │   S     │  ♣ Q 4 2
                  └─────────┘
              ♠ —
              ♡ A K Q 6
              ◇ K 9
              ♣ K J 10 9 8 6 3
```

W	N	E	S
1 ♡	pass	pass	2 ♡
2 ♠	pass	pass	3 ♣
3 ♠	4 ♣	pass	4 ♡
pass	6 ♣	all pass	

You ruff the opening lead of the king of spades with the eight of clubs and take stock. Dummy has just about what you expected, except for the extra heart. If East has all three trumps, as seems probable, you will not be able to ruff a heart. However, there are other strings to your bow. You envisage a throw-in against West, forcing him to lead away from his jack of hearts. But there is a snag. If you execute the throw-in after playing your last trump, when you have no re-entry to your hand, West will exit with the heart *jack*, blocking the heart suit. The only way of overcoming this defence is to establish some winners in dummy.

Accordingly, you lead the nine of diamonds at trick two. West has to allow the queen to score, and the appearance of his jack tells you that his distribution is 5-6-2-0. You ruff a spade with the nine of clubs, lead the jack to dummy's ace, and continue with the five of clubs. Whether East covers or not he cannot deny you access to dummy to ruff a third spade. This is your objective because by removing all East's spades you have established the remaining spades in dummy as menace cards against West. They are visible, material menaces. The fact that they are stranded in dummy without an entry is a mere detail. What does this matter when you are reaching for the moon? This is the position:

You lead your last trump and West is squeezed. The only card he can throw to avoid immediate material loss is the ace of spades. Thus your 'menaces on the moon' become established. Dummy discards a diamond, and you throw West in with the diamond king. *Now* it does not help West to exit with the heart jack – you can win the second round with the ten and, having reached the moon, cash the spades that you worked so hard to establish.

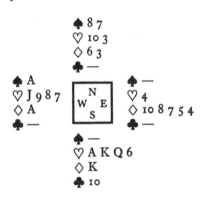

Note that having the right to make the opening lead did West no good on this hand. He was in the grip of an invisible throw-in because of his obligation to make the opening lead. This is our first encounter with a non-material throw-in, a theme we shall be examining fully in a later chapter. West's spade lead gave away nothing material, as a red-suit lead would have done, but in effect it provided dummy with an extra entry with which to ruff a spade, thus establishing the moon menaces and preparing the ground for the squeeze. If West could have given South the 'right' to make the opening lead, the contract would have been defeated.

Are you ready for the next moon shuttle?

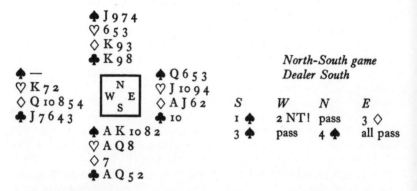

```
              ♠ J 9 7 4
              ♡ 6 5 3
              ◇ K 9 3
              ♣ K 9 8
♠ —                         ♠ Q 6 5 3        North-South game
♡ K 7 2        ┌─────┐      ♡ J 10 9 4        Dealer South
◇ Q 10 8 5 4   │  N  │      ◇ A J 6 2
♣ J 7 6 4 3    │ W E │      ♣ 10            S    W     N    E
               │  S  │                      1 ♠  2 NT! pass 3 ◇
              ♠ A K 10 8 2                   3 ♣  pass  4 ♠  all pass
              ♡ A Q 8
              ◇ 7
              ♣ A Q 5 2
```

West leads the five of diamonds and, having seen West's overcalls before, you play low from dummy. East wins with the jack and returns the jack of hearts. You play low from hand, and put up the ace of hearts on the second round. When you cash the ace of spades, West shows out, as expected. You cross to the king of clubs and run the seven of spades, then the nine of spades, East playing low each time. Now your problem is similar to that of the last hand. After finishing the trumps, you can throw West in with the heart, but he will exit with the jack of clubs to block the suit. First you must establish a moon menace against West. Play the king of diamonds and ruff out the ace, leaving this position:

```
                    ♠ J
                    ♡ 6
                    ◇ 9
                    ♣ 9 8
♠ —                          ♠ Q
♡ K          ┌─────┐         ♡ 9 4
◇ Q          │  N  │         ◇ 6 2
♣ J 7 6      │ W E │         ♣ —
             │  S  │
                    ♠ K
                    ♡ Q
                    ◇ —
                    ♣ A Q 5
```

Now the play of the king of spades squeezes West out of his master diamond. You exit with the heart, and West cannot prevent you from making the rest of the tricks.

A tenace position is not always needed for this type of squeeze. Here is a sort of lunar stepping stone.

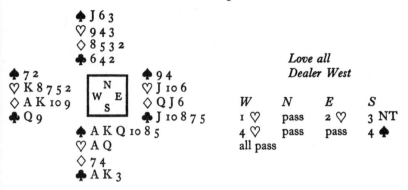

♠ J 6 3
♡ 9 4 3
◇ 8 5 3 2
♣ 6 4 2

Love all
Dealer West

W	N	E	S
1 ♡	pass	2 ♡	3 NT
4 ♡	pass	pass	4 ♠
all pass			

West leads the king of diamonds on which East drops the queen. Winning the second diamond with the jack, East returns the jack of hearts. That's annoying. They're defending too well. Anyway, the heart finesse is sure to be wrong, so you may as well play the ace. Now you appear to have nine tricks and no chance of a tenth. It is hard to imagine, looking at that featureless and entryless dummy, how there can be any sort of squeeze.

And yet in the nine of hearts you have a moon menace of sorts. If East has five clubs plus the ten of hearts, as seems quite likely, it may be possible to exert pressure on him. The first task is to eliminate the diamonds, so you cash the ace of spades, lead the eight of spades to the jack, ruff a diamond high, return to the six of spades and ruff the fourth diamond.

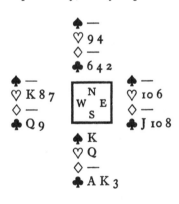

When you play the last trump, discarding a club from dummy, East is fixed. He cannot discard another club without giving you three tricks in the suit. When he parts with the six of hearts, you cash the top clubs and exit in hearts, using West's king to boost you across to the moon.

Squeezes Against Enemy Strategy

When the opponents hold cards that are potentially threatening, it is often a good idea to squeeze them out of those cards before starting on your own plans for establishing extra tricks. We saw an example of this technique in the entry-shifting squeeze at the end of the last chapter.

Many squeezes of this sort – they would be called pre-emptive strikes by the military – fall into an esoteric category in which all the values menaced by the squeeze are invisible; that is, they have strategic rather than material significance. You might say the squeeze isn't really there at all – just a sort of shadow squeeze.

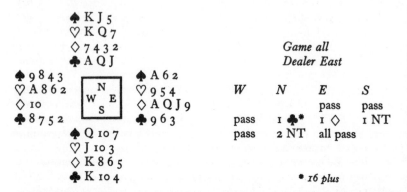

Your stop in two no trumps has less to do with your bidding style than with your part-score of 40. Don't worry, even eight tricks will be hard enough.

West leads the ten of diamonds to his partner's jack. Why should you have any trouble in making your contract? You have two spades, two hearts, one diamond and three clubs, a total of eight tricks. The defenders have three diamonds plus the major suit aces, a total of five tricks. What could be simpler?

But that is a superficial analysis. Your problem has to do with aces, those things that control suits. The opponents have three aces and they stand ready to make good use of them. The moment you play a second round of either major, the defenders will counter-attack in the same suit. If you attack spades, for instance, East will win the second round, cash his diamonds and play a third spade, setting up a long spade for West. If you go for hearts, West will hold up twice, and he will be in a position to score two heart tricks before you can set up your second spade.

In order to neutralize the counter-attack that will develop if you make a frontal assault on your target, you must first soften up the enemy with some long-range artillery. You must threaten West's thirteeners in the majors with a squeeze.

So you allow the jack of diamonds to win the first trick. East continues with the nine of diamonds to your king, and West. . . .

'Idle cards, my eye!' is what West is thinking as he broods over his discard. Eventually he lets go a club, his best choice for the moment. You immediately play a third diamond and West discards another club. In an attempt to avoid squeezing his partner, East switches to a club, but you win and play a fourth round of diamonds yourself. When you regain the lead you run the clubs and, sooner or later, West must part with a major suit card. As soon as he does, it becomes safe for you to attack that major.

With West holding 4–4–1–4 distribution, the squeeze is straightforward and automatic. In practice declarer does not know West's shape, but we can still formulate the best line of play on a single-dummy basis. After winning the second diamond declarer should play a third diamond. If West throws two clubs and East returns a club, declarer can lead a fourth diamond, putting maximum pressure on West. If East shifts to a major suit, however, declarer should play two club winners in order to clarify the club position. It will be safe to lead the other major once, and possibly the last round of clubs as well, before deciding how to continue.

If West throws a major-suit card on the third round of diamonds, declarer should attack that suit as soon as he regains the lead. With the aces split (as the bidding indicates), the defenders will not be able to set up the suit of West's discard, because the invisible squeeze will have operated. Consider this diagram:

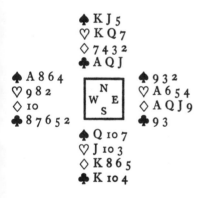

Here West has uneven major-suit distribution, but declarer can still succeed by attacking the major that West discards on the third diamond.

If West throws a spade, South attacks spades and there is no long card for the defenders to establish. If West throws a heart, a vital link card, declarer attacks hearts. Now the defenders may *establish* a long heart but they cannot cash it.

It remains only to consider the effect of a switch by East at trick two. On a club switch, declarer can win in dummy and return a diamond to start squeezing West as before. But if East shifts to a major suit the play is different. On this defence East is never going to make more than two diamond tricks, so declarer can afford to lose a long-card trick in a major suit, and his best plan is to knock out the ace of the suit that East attacks, retaining the double stopper in the other. With careful timing declarer can always prevail, although he may go astray if West has five to the ace in either major.

On this hand the invisible squeeze denied the defenders the elbow-room they needed to set up a long-card trick. You may recall that we saw a similar squeeze on page 46. Here is a reminder.

Against your contract of two no trumps West led the ten of spades to his partner's jack, and East continued with the queen of spades to knock out your ace. You cashed the king of hearts, forcing East to part with the king of spades, and then led your low diamond to dummy's ten. East could not afford to win, and you continued with the eight of spades, cutting the link between the defenders' hands. West had to choose between abandoning his fourth spade, or cashing it and squeezing East out of a potential long-card trick in the minors.

```
                    ♠ 8 5 4
                    ♡ 10 7 6 4 2
                    ◇ 10 4
                    ♣ J 6 3
      ♠ 10 9 7 6            ♠ K Q J 2
      ♡ Q J 8 3      N      ♡ —
      ◇ 7 3        W   E    ◇ A 9 8 5 2
      ♣ 8 5 2        S      ♣ A 10 9 4
                    ♠ A 3
                    ♡ A K 9 5
                    ◇ K Q J 6
                    ♣ K Q 7
```

Carrying the idea of neutralizing threatened enemy attacks one step further, we note that 'idle' cards sometimes have invisible value as part of a complex of squeeze menaces. When cards have value – any sort of value – the player holding them is susceptible to a squeeze. Thus it is perfectly possible to have a squeeze against a squeeze. This situation has been aptly named the 'nightmare squeeze'.

Here is a rather complicated nightmare to disturb your sleep.

```
              ♠ K 8 5 4 2           Love all
              ♡ A J                 Dealer East
              ◇ K 3
              ♣ A J 6 4
  ♠ A Q 10 7 3                  W      N      E       S
  ♡ Q 10 8 5        N                        pass   pass
  ◇ 8             W   E         1 ♠    pass   pass   2 ♡
  ♣ K 10 8          S          pass   2 NT   pass   3 ◇
                               pass   4 ♡    all pass
```

You try the lead of the eight of diamonds, dummy playing the three, East the five and South the jack. Declarer finesses the jack of hearts and cashes the ace, East following with the two and the six. The king of diamonds is then led from dummy. East takes the ace and you discard a

[192]

spade (safe since declarer can have no more than one spade; East would have grabbed the ace of diamonds at trick one to return a singleton spade if he had one). Now East plays the ten of diamonds to declarer's queen. It's your move.

Before deciding what to do, let us reconstruct the deal as far as we can. South clearly has the rest of the hearts. He must have exactly one spade, for with J 9 x in spades, a doubleton heart and the ace of diamonds, East would not have passed your opening bid. South is also marked with the queen of clubs and there must be a small club with it (with 1-5-6-1 distribution, South would have led the queen of clubs earlier to get a spade discard). So South started with 1-5-5-2. At most he has the spade jack and the club nine for his unknown black cards.

This is the position to think about:

First things first. If you fail to ruff South's queen of diamonds, declarer can get to dummy twice and ruff black cards, eloping with his low trumps for ten tricks (one spade, two diamonds, two clubs and five trumps). So you ruff with the queen of hearts and a spade is thrown from dummy. Now what?

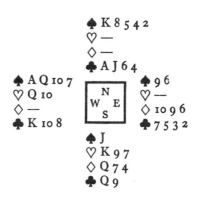

              ♠ K 8 5 4 2
              ♡ —
              ◇ —
              ♣ A J 6 4

♠ A Q 10 7   ♠ 9 6
♡ Q 10   ♡ —
◇ —   ◇ 10 9 6
♣ K 10 8   ♣ 7 5 3 2

              ♠ J
              ♡ K 9 7
              ◇ Q 7 4
              ♣ Q 9

Suppose you play the ace and another spade. Declarer will discard a diamond on the spade king, ruff a spade, cash the king of hearts and continue with his last trump, taking the rest of the tricks on a double squeeze. That's no good.

How about the king of clubs, blocking the suit? Not good enough. Declarer will win, come to hand with the club queen, draw your last trump and lead a spade. Then you will have to allow him access to the two winners in dummy.

Well, then, what about cashing the ace of spades and *then* shifting to the king of clubs? Better, but still not good enough. Declarer will simply unblock the club queen under the ace, cash the king of spades, ruff a spade, and proceed with his double squeeze as before.

Here's an idea: lead the *queen* of spades, preventing declarer from rectifying the count. He must take his king to have any chance, and if he tries to rectify the count by ducking the next spade, *East* will win and cash a diamond. Close, but no prize. The double squeeze is averted, but a different squeeze comes to declarer's rescue. He takes the queen of spades with the king and plays another spade, hoping to pass it to you. But when he sees

East's nine of spades, he ruffs and draws the last trump, discarding a spade from dummy. Now East is squeezed. If East throws a club, unguarding dummy's six, declarer leads the club queen and ducks when the king appears. If East throws a diamond, declarer simply sets up a further diamond trick and later takes the club finesse.

This is a nightmare indeed. You cannot find any plain suit attack that will break up the squeeze, so you decide to fall back on the old bromide: 'When in doubt, lead a trump.' And just look what happens when you return the ten of hearts in this position:

Now declarer is caught up in the nightmare because it is dummy that is squeezed. If dummy discards a club, the long club menace against East disappears. When declarer leads the jack of spades, therefore, you can cover with the queen – the defence that ruins the timing of the double squeeze.

```
                    ♠ K 8 5 4
                    ♡ —
                    ◇ —
                    ♣ A J 6 4
      ♠ A Q 10 7                   ♠ 9 6
      ♡ 10          ┌───────┐      ♡ —
      ◇ —           │   N   │      ◇ 9 6
      ♣ K 10 8      │ W   E │      ♣ 7 5 3 2
                    │   S   │
                    └───────┘
                    ♠ J
                    ♡ K 9 7
                    ◇ 7 4
                    ♣ Q 9
```

If dummy discards a spade on the ten of hearts, you capture the jack of spades with the ace and play another spade. After taking the spade king, South cannot return to hand except by ruffing the last spade, thereby destroying his own menace card.

Declarer has one other possible play. After winning the heart ten with the king, he may, instead of leading the jack of spades, continue with another trump. And he may do this after throwing either a spade or a club from dummy on the ten of hearts. It would take up too much space to probe these variations here, because for satisfying proof one always has to resort to the empirical method – what G. H. Hardy, referring to chess problems, called a 'proof by enumeration of cases'. But, as you will realize if you investigate the variations for yourself, the declarer cannot prevail if you and your partner are careful with your discards.

Your play of the heart ten forced declarer to commit himself before you could be faced with a fatal decision. This premature commitment is the essence of all squeeze play. In this case South had two strategies available. You could defeat either but you could not cope with the threat of both. The nightmare squeeze forced declarer to select his strategy prematurely, putting you in the commanding position.

Similar technique is needed to avert a strip-squeeze on the next hand.

```
              ♠ K Q 9
              ♡ 9 5 4 2
              ◇ K J 8
              ♣ J 10 5                        North-South game
♠ J 6                   ♠ 10 8 7 4 3          Dealer West
♡ A Q 8 6      ┌─────┐  ♡ 10 3
◇ A 7 6 3      │  N  │  ◇ Q 4
♣ Q 9 4        │W   E│  ♣ 8 6 3 2     W      N      E      S
               │  S  │                 1 ♡   pass   pass   1 NT
              └─────┘                  pass   2 ♣*  pass   2 NT†
              ♠ A 5 2                   pass   3 NT  all pass
              ♡ K J 7
              ◇ 10 9 5 2
              ♣ A K 7                 *range enquiry    † maximum
```

You lead the three of diamonds, the jack is played from the table and partner wins with the queen. East returns the ten of hearts to the jack and queen, and you switch to the jack of spades. Declarer wins with dummy's queen and leads the king of diamonds. Do you take it?

If you win with the ace of diamonds, the defence is finished. Declarer will win your spade or diamond return in hand and checkmate you by leading the heart seven. If you put up the ace, he will make two heart tricks (since you cannot attack dummy's spade entry); if you play low, declarer will win with the heart nine, finish the diamonds, and cross to the king of spades, squeezing you out of your surplus heart winner. At the end you will be thrown in with the heart and forced to lead away from your queen of clubs.

You therefore allow the diamond king to win. South cannot bring off his coup with the seven of hearts while you still have the ace of diamonds, so he plays another diamond to your ace. What now?

If you passively return a spade you will end up in the same sorry mess; but if in this position you play your last diamond, *dummy is squeezed.*

Both of the spades in dummy are needed to prevent you from knocking out the entry to the long heart if you take your ace of hearts on the second round, and dummy's heart holding is a necessary threat. If dummy throws a club, you can do the same on the third round of spades, trusting partner to hold the eight of clubs.

If you worked out all this at trick

```
              ♠ K 9
              ♡ 9 5 4
              ◇ —
              ♣ J 10 5
♠ 6                     ♠ 10 8 7
♡ A 8 6        ┌─────┐  ♡ 3
◇ 7            │  N  │  ◇ —
♣ Q 9 4        │W   E│  ♣ 8 6 3 2
               │  S  │
              └─────┘
              ♠ A 5
              ♡ K 7
              ◇ 10
              ♣ A K 7
```

three, you were indeed far-sighted, because your spade shift was as essential as the proper handling of the diamond suit. If instead of the spade you lead a low diamond at trick three, you can win the third diamond and play a fourth, but dummy will not be squeezed. Dummy can throw a spade, and the 'dilemma coup' will operate. It seems that invisible squeezes, like so many visible ones, may need an adjustment in the *idle* card count before they will function.

Many similar hands are played in three no trumps every day of the week – hands on which everything depends on the particular order in which the suits are played. Whoever can adjust the timing to his own advantage will carry the day. The successful defence here used an invisible squeeze only as an appropriate weapon at the end of a particular variation. The overall triumph was one of timing.

Take the East seat for the next hand and see if you can defeat a slam.

With both sides vulnerable, South deals and opens three diamonds. West overcalls three hearts, and North closes the auction with a jump to six diamonds.

West leads the king of hearts which declarer ruffs in hand. On the play of the ace of diamonds West throws a heart. Uncharacteristically, declarer goes into a trance lasting several minutes. Finally he plays a low diamond, giving you your trump trick while West discards another heart. What do you play now?

First let's work out what declarer *doesn't* have. Since he must have at least one spade (West would not bid hearts with 6–6 in the majors), he will have twelve tricks if he has either the spade king or the club queen. There is no chance of talking him out of the spade finesse if he needs it. If South is 1–0–7–5 (or, improbably, 5–0–7–1), a smart spade (or club) shift will cut his entry for a double squeeze. Clearly a spade is a better shot than a club.

But then a thought strikes you. You realize that declarer – a grand master and a superb dummy player – would have played differently with a black singleton. Far from conceding your trump trick in a hurry, he would have end-played you out of it.

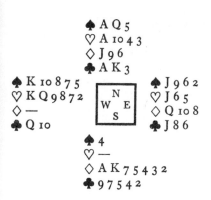

♠ A Q 5
♡ A 10 4 3
◇ J 9 6
♣ A K 3

♠ K 10 8 7 5   ♠ J 9 6 2
♡ K Q 9 8 7 2   ♡ J 6 5
◇ —   ◇ Q 10 8
♣ Q 10   ♣ J 8 6

♠ 4
♡ —
◇ A K 7 5 4 3 2
♣ 9 7 5 4 2

With this hand, for instance, South would have abandoned trumps when West showed out, taking the spade finesse and using dummy's three entries to ruff a spade and two hearts in hand. You would have been thrown in at trick eleven for a trump end-play. And you could not escape by ruffing the fourth heart ahead of declarer, for he would simply throw his last losing club.

So much for the smart spade shift. Let's think of something else. If declarer's shape is 4–0–7–2 you cannot beat the contract; West's inability to guard the spades will be fatal to the defence. For example, if you return a club to the king, declarer will continue ace of hearts, heart ruff, spade finesse, spade ace, diamonds, leading to a standard double squeeze position.

If declarer is 2–0–7–4, you can defeat the contract by returning any suit (except perhaps clubs), provided that partner does the right thing by guarding clubs while you hold the spades.

Only if declarer is 3–0–7–3 is your choice critical. That is why your correct lead at this point is the jack of hearts.

If you return anything but the jack of hearts, declarer can establish a compound squeeze. Suppose, for example, you lead a 'safe' trump. Declarer wins and plays another trump, and West must come down to two cards in one of the black suits. Declarer finesses the queen of spades, cashes the remaining top cards in the black suit that West unguarded, takes the ace of hearts, discarding from the *other* black suit in the closed hand, ruffs a heart, and leads his last trump to effect a double squeeze.

♠ A Q 5
♡ A 10 4
◇ J
♣ A K 3

♠ K 10 8   ♠ J 9 6 2
♡ Q 9 8   ♡ J 6
◇ —   ◇ Q
♣ Q 9 5 4   ♣ J 8 6

♠ 7 4 3
♡ —
◇ K 7 5 4
♣ 10 7 2

A black-suit return at trick four does not interfere with declarer's plans, but note the effect of returning the jack of hearts. South dares not ruff, for he needs the heart ruff to return to hand after the first phase of his compound squeeze is completed. But neither can he discard sensibly on this trick, because he does not yet know which black suit West will abandon. Your lead of the heart jack ruins declarer's timing, squeezing South before he can squeeze West. Your partner can shape his defence accordingly; on the fourth round of diamonds he gives up the same black suit as South did, and you can now guard both menaces *from behind*.

Not only do 'idle' cards have an assortment of functions that make them targets for a squeeze, they may assume different roles at different times during the play of a single deal.

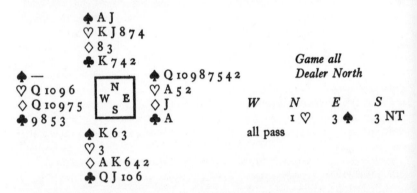

♠ A J
♡ K J 8 7 4
♢ 8 3
♣ K 7 4 2

Game all
Dealer North

♠ —
♡ Q 10 9 6
♢ Q 10 9 7 5
♣ 9 8 5 3

N
W E
S

♠ Q 10 9 8 7 5 4 2
♡ A 5 2
♢ J
♣ A

♠ K 6 3
♡ 3
♢ A K 6 4 2
♣ Q J 10 6

W	N	E	S
	1 ♡	3 ♠	3 NT
all pass			

West leads the ten of hearts to the jack and ace. East cashes the ace of clubs, South unblocking with the ten, and exits with the jack of diamonds. (You can verify that this is as good a line of defence as any.)

South wins with the king of diamonds, checks the club position by cashing the jack, and leads a spade to dummy's ace. On this trick West is entry-squeezed out of an 'idle' club. (If West throws a heart, dummy's hearts can be established. If he throws a diamond, declarer can come to an extra diamond trick, ducking a diamond at once so that if West switches to hearts declarer can shift his own attack to that suit.)

With West reduced to one club fewer than North and South, dummy has an extra potential entry, although the need for it is not immediately obvious. But declarer is now in sight of an entry-shifting squeeze against West. To adjust the loser count, he leads the jack of spades and lets East win with the queen. West can afford to throw a diamond on this trick, but when East returns a spade to declarer's king (a heart return allows declarer to establish the suit for the loss of one trick), West is squeezed again in this position:

A diamond discard is suicidal, and a heart pitch also loses because of the double entry to dummy squeezed out two tricks ago. What about the club nine? It doesn't guard the second entry to dummy any more and thus seems even more 'idle' than the eight of clubs was. Yet, if the club nine is discarded, a danger that it was guarding against suddenly appears. South discards a heart from dummy and leads the six of clubs to produce a standard entry-shifting squeeze

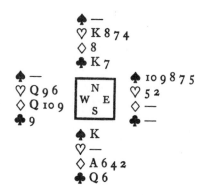

♠ —
♡ K 8 7 4
◇ 8
♣ K 7

♠ —   ♠ 10 9 8 7 5
♡ Q 9 6   ♡ 5 2
◇ Q 10 9   ◇ —
♣ 9   ♣ —

♠ K
♡ —
◇ A 6 4 2
♣ Q 6

against West. If West throws a heart, dummy wins with the seven; if he throws a diamond, dummy wins with the king. In either case, declarer then attacks the suit of West's discard.

So West was squeezed three times. First by an invisible squeeze that created an extra club entry in dummy, allowing declarer to reach a position where a second invisible squeeze operated. This in turn forced the victim into a third squeeze – at last a material squeeze of the entry-shifting type.

11

Non-Material Finesses

The boundary of non-material country extends far beyond the squeeze to encompass every known technique in the field of card play. A finesse, for example, is non-material in nature when it is taken not for the purpose of gaining an extra trick but in order to serve some strategic end. The trick gained, if indeed the finesse does gain a trick, is irrelevant to the success of the contract.

Thinking about finessing takes you back to those boyhood holidays at Great-Aunt Clara's. Among those who enjoyed the protection of the house were four dogs, a cat with a litter of five kittens, and Great-Uncle Timothy, whose room was a treasure house of ivory elephants, sun-helmets, jade carvings and similar objects. At breakfast Uncle Tim received letters from all over the world and allowed you to purloin the stamps. He was a retired professor, a great authority on – was it cuneiform writing? – symbolic logic? – palaeoasiatic linguistics? You never quite found out. At all events he was a bachelor and a happy man.

The liveliest of the kittens, a fearless tomcat called Fred or, more properly, Sir Frederick, Lord of Metzengerstein, was probably the best male dummy player in the house. When Uncle Tim was declarer, Fred was fond of jumping up on someone's knee and thence to the table, where he would sit and contemplate dummy with a knowing eye.

'Come, puss, that won't do,' Uncle Tim would say as Fred tried to claw a card from dummy. 'We must draw trumps first.' But, invariably, Fred's idea would have been the better shot. Whatever Uncle Tim was expert at, it certainly wasn't bridge. He was a keen player utterly lacking in card sense. Finessing towards him was a kind of safety play – either the finesse would win, or he would return the trick with interest by leading back into your tenace.

It was Aunt Clara who, after giving you a solid grounding in the more common finessing situations and waving aside Aunt Alice's renewed attempts to tell you about a hand where you can make a trick more if the finesse is wrong, first introduced you to non-material finesses.

The best-known of the non-material finesses are those concerned with creating extra entries. We have already seen some examples of these. Here is a familiar position:

Needing three entries to dummy, South leads a low card A Q 10 and finesses the ten. There is no material gain when the finesse wins, but the strategic gain may be decisive. The K x x same play may be made, as we have seen, in order to adjust the matrix for an entry-shifting squeeze. The 'queer finesses' that we studied in Chapter 5 were essentially non-material. There was no prospect of scoring an extra trick in the suit itself, but the finesse was needed in order to reach the correct entry-shifting matrix.

Here is a more orthodox entry finesse.

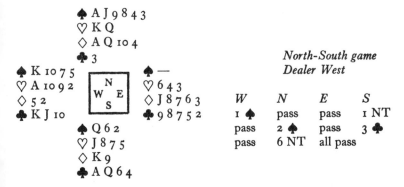

```
        ♠ A J 9 8 4 3
        ♡ K Q
        ◇ A Q 10 4
        ♣ 3
                                    North-South game
♠ K 10 7 5        ♠ —               Dealer West
♡ A 10 9 2    N   ♡ 6 4 3
◇ 5 2       W   E ◇ J 8 7 6 3       W     N     E      S
♣ K J 10      S   ♣ 9 8 7 5 2      1 ♠   pass  pass   1 NT
        ♠ Q 6 2                    pass  2 ♠   pass   3 ♣
        ♡ J 8 7 5                  pass  6 NT  all pass
        ◇ K 9
        ♣ A Q 6 4
```

After this unusual auction, West leads the ace and another heart. You appear to have six spades, two hearts, three diamonds and a club for a total of twelve tricks. But then the snag occurs to you. In order to pick up the spades you will need to lead three times from the South hand, and you have only two obvious entries. So, at trick three, you lead the four of diamonds for a finesse of the nine. It is not the extra diamond trick that you need – just the extra entry. When the nine of diamonds wins, you play the queen of spades to the king and ace, return to the king of diamonds and lead another spade for a finesse of the eight. After a club to the ace, you play your third spade to gather the rest of the tricks.

Is there any defence? What if East is bright enough to play the jack of diamonds on the first round? Well, that puts paid to your non-material finesse, but it does give you four diamond tricks and thus paves the way for a strictly material progressive squeeze against West. You win the king of diamonds, lead the queen of spades to the king and ace, and cash the rest of the diamonds.

On the last diamond you discard a spade or the small club, and West has no way of preventing you from making the rest of the tricks.

Nevertheless, the contract could have been defeated by a non-material defence. After cashing the ace of hearts, West had a good idea of the forces ranged against him. He could see that there was no hope for the defence if you had two entries in diamonds, and he might therefore have considered the merits of a club switch at trick two. This is a non-material

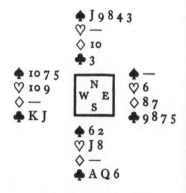

play if ever there was one. The club lead actually gives you an extra trick but, at the same time, by killing the squeeze, it denies you two tricks.

The effect of the club shift is to force you to use your minor-suit entries in the wrong order. You may continue by leading the queen of spades to the king and ace, unblocking the hearts and playing the four of diamonds. But now East can insert his jack to hold you to eleven tricks.

On certain hands the only way to maintain a satisfactory entry position is to take what may appear to be a frivolous finesse in trumps.

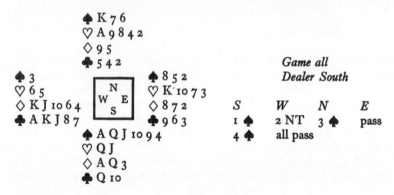

West starts with the ace and king of clubs and East follows with the three and the nine. Correctly interpreting the nine of clubs as a suit-preference signal, West switches to the six of hearts. When you play low from the table, East wins with the king and returns the three of hearts. To your relief West follows suit, and you are reaching for a small heart in dummy when you snatch your hand back, almost dislocating your wrist.

A thought has struck you. The bidding marks West with five cards in each of the minors, and he will surely have the king of diamonds for his vulnerable overcall. He has already shown up with two hearts, and therefore cannot have more than a singleton spade. Unless that spade is specifically the eight, you will lack the two entries that you need in dummy in order to develop the hearts.

Well, odds of three to one on are a big improvement on three to one against, so you overtake the queen of hearts with the ace and return the six of spades, running it when East plays low. West's three is a welcome sight and you switch promptly back to hearts, ruffing out East's ten and establishing two winners to take care of your losing diamonds. If East had covered the six of spades, of course, you would still have had the two entries you needed in dummy. Note that the trump finesse brought you no material gain; it simply enabled you to stay in dummy for the purpose of developing the hearts.

Why, you wonder, do the opponents so often find the optimum defence against you? If East had switched to a diamond at trick four, you would have had no real problem.

On some hands you have to take an 'unnecessary' finesse in order to prepare a safe re-entry to your hand.

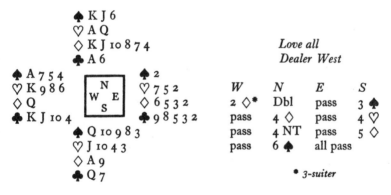

```
              ♠ K J 6
              ♡ A Q
              ◇ K J 10 8 7 4
              ♣ A 6
                                            Love all
                                            Dealer West
♠ A 7 5 4          ♠ 2
♡ K 9 8 6     N    ♡ 7 5 2        W      N      E      S
◇ Q        W    E  ◇ 6 5 3 2      2 ◇*   Dbl    pass   3 ♠
♣ K J 10 4    S    ♣ 9 8 5 3 2    pass   4 ◇    pass   4 ♡
              ♠ Q 10 9 8 3        pass   4 NT   pass   5 ◇
              ♡ J 10 4 3          pass   6 ♠    all pass
              ◇ A 9
              ♣ Q 7                      * 3-suiter
```

West leads the queen of diamonds which you win in hand with the ace. You can count twelve tricks without any finessing – four spades, six diamonds and two aces. But the warning flags are out and you will ignore them at your peril.

On the bidding, West is marked with 4-4-1-4 distribution. If you play trumps immediately, West will hold up his ace until the third round and exit with a heart, leaving you with no way back to hand to draw the last trump.

To avoid the indignity of being locked in dummy in this manner, you must take the non-material heart finesse at trick two. Continue with the ace of hearts and – careful, now – the six of spades to your eight. West is likely to hold off since he cannot gain by taking his ace, and you must continue with the jack of hearts. If West plays low, you discard a diamond from dummy, ruff the fourth heart with the king of spades, and lead the spade jack to your queen. West is no better off if he covers the jack of hearts. Again you ruff with the king and lead the jack of spades to your queen, and West has to yield the rest of the tricks whether he returns a trump, a heart or a club.

Sometimes it is possible, by means of a phantom finesse, to place a defender in a 're-entry or tempo' dilemma.

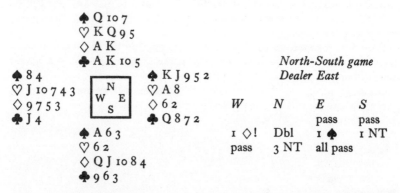

```
                ♠ Q 10 7
                ♡ K Q 9 5
                ◇ A K                    North-South game
                ♣ A K 10 5               Dealer East
  ♠ 8 4              ♠ K J 9 5 2
  ♡ J 10 7 4 3    N  ♡ A 8
  ◇ 9 7 5 3    W     E  ◇ 6 2           W      N      E      S
  ♣ J 4          S   ♣ Q 8 7 2                      pass   pass
                ♠ A 6 3                  1 ◇!    Dbl    1 ♠    1 NT
                ♡ 6 2
                ◇ Q J 10 8 4             pass   3 NT   all pass
                ♣ 9 6 3
```

The opening lead is the eight of spades, and when dummy goes down you see that you have been jockeyed into playing this contract the wrong way round. Three no trumps by North would have been a cinch. Well, you must do the best you can.

You cover with the ten of spades and allow East's jack to hold the trick. After some thought East returns the one card you did not wish to see – the king of spades. This takes out your only card of entry before you have had a chance to unblock the diamonds. Confound the fellow! He is defending too well.

Winning the ace of spades, you review your prospects. There is clearly little point in playing on hearts. Even if West has the ace (and you are aware that his bid may have been a complete psyche), you can lead the suit only once from your hand. There remains a slender chance that the nine of clubs could be a re-entry for the long diamonds. Either defender could have Q J doubleton, for instance. So at trick three you lead the three of clubs.

If West plays an honour, you intend to win with the king, unblock the diamonds, and lead the ten of clubs from dummy. If either opponent takes this, you will score nine tricks by way of two spades, two clubs and five diamonds. And if they refuse to take the ten of clubs, you may be able to score four club tricks, two diamonds, two spades and a heart.

But West plays the four of clubs on the first round and you put in dummy's ten. You do not really expect this finesse to win, for West would not have played low with both honour cards. You are still hoping to establish the nine of clubs as a re-entry. East sees the danger, however, and after a huddle he follows with the two of clubs. You continue with the ace and king of clubs, noting West's diamond discard on the third round, and cash the top diamonds to reach this position:

By this time you know East to have at most a doubleton heart, and your only remaining chance is that he has the ace without the jack or the ten. So you lead the nine of hearts from the table. West wins with the ten and returns a low heart, and when you play the five from dummy you are rewarded by the sight of East's ace. After cashing the queen of clubs, East has to yield the rest of the tricks.

Observe the dilemma that confronted East when you finessed the ten of clubs. By refusing to win he denied you the use of the nine of clubs as a re-entry. But he could do this only at the cost of allowing you to score three club tricks without losing the lead, and you made use of the extra tempo to develop your game-going tricks in the heart suit.

Here is a further example of the 'tempo or re-entry' finesse.

	♠ Q	
	♡ K Q 9 5	
	◇ —	
	♣ 5	
♠ —		♠ 9 5 2
♡ J 10 7 4 3	N W E S	♡ A 8
◇ 9		◇ —
♣ —		♣ Q
	♠ 6	
	♡ 6 2	
	◇ Q J 10	
	♣ —	

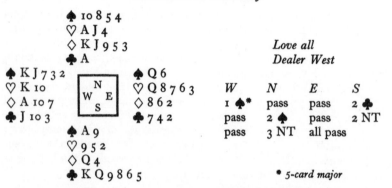

♠ 10 8 5 4
♡ A J 4
◇ K J 9 5 3
♣ A

Love all
Dealer West

♠ K J 7 3 2   ♠ Q 6
♡ K 10   ♡ Q 8 7 6 3
◇ A 10 7   ◇ 8 6 2
♣ J 10 3   ♣ 7 4 2

♠ A 9
♡ 9 5 2
◇ Q 4
♣ K Q 9 8 6 5

W	N	E	S
1 ♠*	pass	pass	2 ♣
pass	2 ♠	pass	2 NT
pass	3 NT	all pass	

* *5-card major*

West leads the three of spades to his partner's queen, and you win reluctantly with the ace. The lead assures you of two spade tricks but it gives you little joy, for the blockage in clubs spells trouble, even if the suit breaks 3–3. There can be no point in crossing to the ace of clubs and returning a diamond, hoping to find the ace with East. Without the diamond ace West would not have an opening bid, and with it East would have a response. Yet if you play on diamonds immediately you will make no more than eight tricks. West will win and clear the spades, limiting you to four diamonds, two spades and two aces.

Your only chance of success lies with the heart suit. If you can find West with K 10 or Q 10 doubleton, an instant finesse will work. You play a low heart at trick two and cover West's ten with the jack. Now East faces the familiar dilemma. He can win and return a spade to clear his partner's suit, but, with a third-round heart re-entry in your hand, you score ten tricks without touching the diamonds. Alternatively, East can allow dummy's jack of hearts to win. Having snatched an extra heart trick, you then switch your attack to diamonds, and West is powerless to defeat you.

What if West plays the king on the first round of hearts? You win with the ace, unblock the ace of clubs, and continue with the jack of hearts to give East the same problem.

Sometimes a finesse should be taken, not in a serious attempt to win a trick but as a safety measure to ensure the success of the contract. Try this hand as a single-dummy problem.

♠ A Q 6 4
♡ J
◇ A J 5
♣ K 8 5 4 2

```
      N
  W       E
      S
```

♠ K 7 3
♡ A K Q 10
◇ K 10 6
♣ A 10 9

With no interference from the opponents, you reach a contract of six no trumps and the nine of hearts is led.

There are eleven top tricks and it certainly looks as though you should be able to avoid a guess in diamonds. Suppose you cash the top clubs and discover that someone started with Q J x x. You can then test the spades, ending in hand. If spades fail to break you can run the hearts, throwing clubs from dummy, to reach this four-card ending:

♠ 6
♡ —
◇ A J 5
♣ —

```
      N
  W       E
      S
```

♠ —
♡ —
◇ K 10 6
♣ 9

Now, if the black-suit winners are split between the defenders, there are intriguing throw-in possibilities. At least one defender must have kept three diamonds, otherwise your troubles are over. If West has reduced to the queen of clubs and three diamonds, you simply throw him in with the club. If West has the spade winner and three diamonds, you cross to the ace of diamonds and exit with the spade. If East has the queen of clubs and three diamonds, he can be thrown in just as easily.

But if East controls spades and West has kept two club winners, you are reduced to guessing the diamond position. This is also the case if either defender has a winner in both black suits.

Well, it would have been amusing to let the defenders take the diamond finesse for you, but the chances of success are not really good enough. Let's think of something else – a squeeze, perhaps. Suppose you cash the ace of clubs and then run the ten, taking a safety finesse through West. If West follows to the second club you are home; and if he shows out you can run the ten anyway, letting East have the trick. Now, in the end-game, only East can hold the clubs, and if West controls the spades you will have a sure double squeeze. And what if East controls the spades? Alas, no squeeze, for East is sitting behind your black menace cards. That's a pity. You seem to be on the right track, yet you are unable to cope with the case where East has length in both black suits without giving up some other chances. If West has length in both black suits there is no difficulty.

At last you see it. You must take your safety finesse in clubs the other way round in order to exclude the possibility of *East* keeping high clubs in

[207]

the end game. Play the king of clubs at trick two and continue with a low club, inserting the ten whether East plays low or shows out. In the latter case, you win the club return, play three rounds of spades, ending in hand, and cash two more hearts, discarding a club and the jack of diamonds from dummy. This is the position when you play the last heart:

Since West is known to hold the club winner, you have a double squeeze if the master spade is with East.

And if West controls both black suits, he is forced to part with a diamond on the play of the last heart. You throw a black card from dummy, lead the six of diamonds to the ace and, if the queen does not appear, take the marked finesse against East on the way back.

This line of play guarantees the contract against any distribution of the cards.

There is one situation where, in preparation for a strip-squeeze, a non-material finesse may have to be taken for reasons of control. We

♠ 6
♡ —
◇ A 5
♣ 8

```
   N
 W   E
   S
```

♠ —
♡ Q
◇ K 10 6
♣ —

may call this play a Rio de Janeiro finesse, because the manoeuvre was first reported from that city.

♠ Q 10 7 3
♡ K 9 3
◇ J 8 7 4 2
♣ 9

♠ —   ♠ A J 9 8 4 2
♡ 8 6 4 2   ```   ♡ —
◇ K Q 9 3   N   ◇ 10 6 5
♣ J 10 6 5 2 W   E   ♣ K 8 7 3
             S```

♠ K 6 5
♡ A Q J 10 7 5
◇ A
♣ A Q 4

North-South game
Dealer East

W	N	E	S
		2 ♠	Dbl
pass	3 ◇	pass	4 ♡
pass	5 ♡	pass	6 ♡
all pass			

West leads the two of hearts, and when dummy goes down you see that the slam is by no means a lay-down. Still, even on the trump lead, you can ruff your club losers in dummy to give you a total of ten top tricks. An eleventh trick can be developed in spades, and the twelfth may come from an end-play against East, who will be under pressure when you run the trumps.

However, a closer look convinces you that it would be dangerous to relinquish control in the minor suits. This might enable East to keep a club or a diamond winner, which he would cash after scoring the ace of spades. Reluctantly, you decide that you must risk a 'superfluous' finesse in clubs. You put in the nine of hearts from dummy, lead the singleton club to your queen, ruff the four of clubs with the king of hearts and run your trumps. This is the position when you lead the last trump:

East will no doubt discard his diamond on your last trump, but when you continue with the ace of diamonds he is forced to part with a club. Now the ace of clubs extracts his last exit card, and a spade to the queen completes the end-play.

Of course, by varying his earlier discards, East might have arrived at the diagram position with two diamonds and one club instead of the other way round. But it should not be too hard to read the position and make the contract.

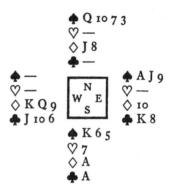

Note the importance of keeping both minor-suit aces for the ending. Does this mean that an initial diamond lead would have defeated you? Not in this particular case, for you can strip East of his diamonds by ruffing twice in your hand – diamond ace, heart to nine, club finesse, club ruffed small, diamond ruff, heart to king, diamond ruff, and the last two trumps put the screws on East as before. But if East had started with four diamonds and three clubs, a diamond lead would indeed have been a killer.

Here is another 'January River' finesse.

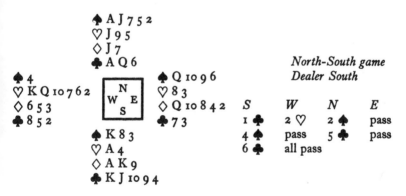

[209]

You manage to reach the right slam, but West makes a nuisance of himself by leading the four of spades. To test the position you put in the jack. East covers with the queen and you win with the king. Now it looks as though the lead was a singleton, but if the clubs are 3–2 there may still be a chance of setting up a long spade to take care of your losing heart. The trouble is that you would need to take the double diamond finesse, and the entry problems are insoluble.

Suppose you cash the king of clubs and continue with a spade to the ace, West discarding a diamond. At this point you would have to tackle diamonds, leading the jack to the queen and king. But when you concede a spade to East at the next trick, West will discard his last diamond and score a diamond ruff to defeat the contract.

So you decide upon a straight end-play against East. To retain strategic control you must still take the 'superfluous' double finesse in diamonds. You play a club to the queen, return the jack of diamonds to the queen and king, cross back to dummy with the club ace, and play the seven of diamonds for a finesse of your nine. Three more rounds of trumps produce this ending:

East has postponed the moment of truth by discarding hearts, but when you cash the ace of hearts he has to part with a diamond. Now you cash the diamond ace and run the eight of spades to achieve your throw-in.

Note that in this case the extended menace in spades is necessary.

```
                    ♠ A 7 5 2
                    ♡ J
                    ◇ —
                    ♣ —
         ♠ —                      ♠ 10 9 6
         ♡ K Q 10 7    N          ♡ —
         ◇ 6         W   E        ◇ 10 8
         ♣ —           S          ♣ —
                    ♠ 8 3
                    ♡ A 4
                    ◇ A
                    ♣ —
```

If dummy had a spade less and a heart more in the diagram, East could defeat you by discarding a spade on the ace of hearts.

A further example:

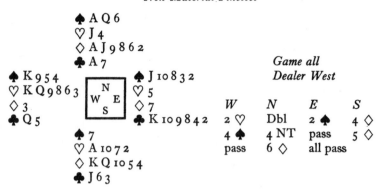

```
              ♠ A Q 6
              ♡ J 4
              ◇ A J 9 8 6 2
              ♣ A 7                        Game all
♠ K 9 5 4        ┌─────┐  ♠ J 10 8 3 2     Dealer West
♡ K Q 9 8 6 3    │  N  │  ♡ 5
◇ 3            W │     │ E◇ 7              W    N    E    S
♣ Q 5            │  S  │  ♣ K 10 9 8 4 2   2♡   Dbl  2♠   4◇
              ┌──┴─────┴──┐                4♠   4NT  pass 5◇
              ♠ 7          pass 6◇  all pass
              ♡ A 10 7 2
              ◇ K Q 10 5 4
              ♣ J 6 3
```

West leads the four of spades and by now you know you have to finesse the queen, not for the sake of an extra trick (indeed, the finesse does not produce an extra trick) but because it is the only way to trim West down to size in the end-game. Let the kibitzers cackle if they will. You continue by ruffing the six of spades in hand, and then run the trumps to produce this ending:

On the last trump you are careful to discard a club, not a heart, from hand. There is no ambiguity since you have a good count of the hand, and West can do nothing to escape the eventual end-play.

These Rio-finesses might be thought to be beyond the scope of a palooka, but nothing is impossible at this game. You remember a hand on which Uncle Tim brought home a

```
              ♠ A
              ♡ J 4
              ◇ 8
              ♣ A 7
♠ K 9     ┌─────┐  ♠ J 10
♡ K Q 9   │  N  │  ♡ 5
◇ —      W│     │E ◇ —
♣ Q       │  S  │  ♣ K 10 9
          └─────┘
              ♠ —
              ♡ A 10 7 2
              ◇ —
              ♣ J 6
```

contract of five clubs by means of a *losing* Rio-finesse. Mind you, he had a little help.

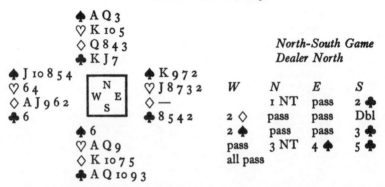

Sitting West, you led the jack of spades. When Aunt Clara laid down her dummy and went off to make coffee, Uncle Tim did not give the hand his immediate attention as he was engaged in an earnest discussion with Aunt Alice on his right about the influence of Seneca on Marcus Aurelius. The Lord of Metzengerstein was not distracted, however. Sizing up the situation at a glance, Fred stalked across the table and settled upon the ace of spades, obscuring it completely.

Thus when Uncle Tim returned his attention to the game, only twelve cards were visible in dummy. The jack of spades was covered by the queen and king. Tim ruffed the spade return, drew trumps, cashed the ace and queen of hearts, and led the nine of hearts to dummy's king in this position:

♠ Fred
♡ K
◇ Q 6 4
♣ —

♠ 10 8   ♠ 9 7
♡ —   N   ♡ J 8 7
◇ A J 9 W   E ◇ —
♣ —   S   ♣ —

♠ —
♡ 9
◇ K 10 7 5
♣ —

You had to discard a spade, of course. And Fred, displaying a nice sense of timing, chose that moment to rise and stretch. Uncle Tim gratefully cashed the ace of spades before leading a diamond to his king.

That's why you considered Fred to be your best dummy player.

12

Non-Material Throw-Ins

Having eaten, you went out on deck for a last smoke before turning in. The *Cormorant* was safely anchored for the night in a natural harbour sheltered by a rocky promontory. You listened to the slap of water against the hull and the gentle creaking of the timbers, and you tried to identify the stars as they made brief appearances between the scudding clouds.

Alec was in one of his rare talkative moods. When his pipe was drawing well, he began to tell you a little more about his prison experiences. Solitary confinement was apparently the standard punishment for minor breaches of discipline, the theory being that the lack of human companionship would soon bring a man to heel. But for Alec this was no punishment at all. The 'solitary' cells were situated high in the fortress and had small barred windows overlooking the bay. Alec could ask for nothing better than solitude to contemplate a beautiful seascape while he let his mind roam free. His thoughts turned to music, literature, mathematics, navigation, and, inevitably, bridge.

It was always a profound disappointment when the period of solitary confinement came to an end, and Alec soon learned to judge the exact degree of impertinence needed to return him to his private cell.

'When they pitched me back in and slammed the door,' he joked, 'I suppose you might call it a non-material throw-in.'

That was one of the subjects that Alec had analysed in his lonely cell. He discovered that the technique of the throw-in could often be brought to bear against 'invisible' values. In the commonest type of non-material throw-in, declarer is concerned with winning an extra entry in one way or another.

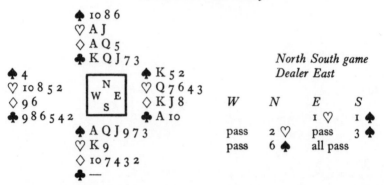

♠ 10 8 6
♡ A J
◇ A Q 5
♣ K Q J 7 3

North South game
Dealer East

W	N	E	S
		1 ♡	1 ♠
pass	2 ♡	pass	3 ♠
pass	6 ♠	all pass	

Not fancying the chances of establishing tricks in hearts, West tries the lead of the nine of diamonds. Dummy's queen is captured by the king, and East suffers from an instant throw-in. This is not a material throw-in, for East does not have to concede a trick on his return. He can play either a heart or a spade without material loss, but the result is fatal to the defence. The major suit return gives you an extra entry to dummy, which you use to good effect by ruffing two small clubs in hand and setting up club winners to take care of your losing diamonds.

It is hard to find fault with the initial diamond lead, attacking the only suit in which the defenders can expect to win tricks. And yet, a heart lead would have defeated the contract. Suppose you win the ace, run the six of spades, ruff a small club, cash the king of hearts, and lead a diamond for a finesse of the queen. Isn't East thrown in now, as he was on the original diamond lead? No, he is not, and it seems rather mysterious that the same diamond finesse should not work several tricks later. Once the heart entry has gone from dummy, East can afford to exit with the ace of clubs. You ruff and cross to dummy with the ace of diamonds, but East does not cover the ten of spades and you are unable to enjoy all three club tricks.

'Next time try leading your partner's suit,' says East grumpily.

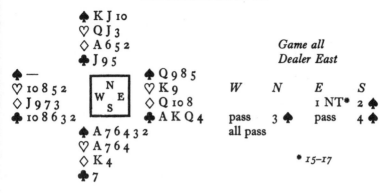

```
              ♠ K J 10
              ♡ Q J 3
              ♢ A 6 5 2            Game all
              ♣ J 9 5              Dealer East
♠ —                    ♠ Q 9 8 5
♡ 10 8 5 2      N      ♡ K 9         W      N      E      S
♢ J 9 7 3    W   E    ♢ Q 10 8                     1 NT*   2 ♠
♣ 10 8 6 3 2    S      ♣ A K Q 4   pass   3 ♠    pass    4 ♠
              ♠ A 7 6 4 3 2        all pass
              ♡ A 7 6 4
              ♢ K 4                    * 15–17
              ♣ 7
```

West leads the three of diamonds to the queen and king. You play a low spade to the king and return the queen of hearts, which is covered by the king and ace. Now, unless the hearts break evenly, you are in danger of losing four tricks, for you cannot ruff a heart in dummy except at the cost of a trump trick.

Any chance of a red-suit squeeze? Only against a friendly defence. If you concede a trump to East and he tries to cash two club tricks, you may be able to negotiate a ruffing squeeze against West. The need for East's co-operation would not deter you if there were nothing better to try. But here there is an excellent chance of making ten tricks by elopement play.

Don't make the mistake of conceding the club at this point. There are only two entries to dummy and you need three. You must plan to throw East in with the club at a stage when he must either concede a third entry to dummy or (the same thing) assist your elopement with a club return. So you play a diamond to the ace, ruff a diamond, cross to the heart jack and lead the fourth diamond. If East ruffs with the eight of spades it costs him a trump trick, for you simply discard your club. You can then afford to ruff the fourth heart in dummy; whether East over-ruffs or not, the defenders will make only three tricks.

East therefore discards a club, letting you ruff the fourth diamond. Now you exit in clubs, catching East in the invisible throw-in (fortunately you can be sure from the bidding that only East can win the club trick). If he returns a club, you ruff and exit in hearts. If he returns the queen of spades, you win, cross to the jack of spades, and ruff a club for your tenth trick.

When an entry to dummy is worth more than one trick, a gambit may be in order.

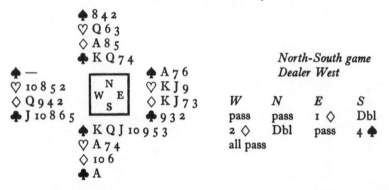

```
        ♠ 8 4 2
        ♡ Q 6 3
        ◊ A 8 5
        ♣ K Q 7 4
                                    North-South game
♠ —              ♠ A 7 6            Dealer West
♡ 10 8 5 2       ♡ K J 9
◊ Q 9 4 2        ◊ K J 7 3      W      N      E      S
♣ J 10 8 6 5     ♣ 9 3 2       pass   pass   1 ◊    Dbl
        ♠ K Q J 10 9 5 3        2 ◊    Dbl    pass   4 ♠
        ♡ A 7 4               all pass
        ◊ 10 6
        ♣ A
```

West leads the two of diamonds to his partner's king, and East continues with the jack of diamonds. You plan to duck this trick as well, which would leave East poorly placed, but West thoughtfully overtakes with the queen and you have to win with dummy's ace. When you continue with the eight of diamonds East plays low. It looks as though the nine is with West, so you ruff high, unblock the ace of clubs, and lead . . . what?

A high trump is not good enough; East will hold up his ace until the third round and exit with his diamond. No, you must lead the five of spades at this point. If West plays the six or seven you can cover with dummy's eight, and eventually you will gain access to the table with the four of spades.

When West shows out on the first round of spades, you resort to the trump gambit, playing low from dummy. East gains an unexpected second trick in trumps, but the invisible throw-in yields two tricks in return. There is no way for East to prevent dummy from gaining the lead, and your two heart losers go away on the winning clubs.

Here is a similar trump gambit, but this time the defensive options are rather different.

```
            ♠ 5
            ♡ J 10 9 8 7 6 2
            ◇ A 4 2
            ♣ A K
♠ K J 7 2        ┌─────┐      ♠ Q 10 9 6 4 3
♡ K 5 4          │  N  │      ♡ —
◇ K J 9          │W   E│      ◇ 10 6 5 3
♣ Q 10 3         │  S  │      ♣ 9 7 4
                 └─────┘
            ♠ A 8
            ♡ A Q 3
            ◇ Q 8 7
            ♣ J 8 6 5 2
```

Love all
Dealer South

S	W	N	E
1 NT	pass	2 ◇*	pass
2 ♡	Dbl	4 ♡	4 ♠
pass	pass	5 ♡	all pass

* *transfer to hearts*

West leads the two of spades to the queen and ace. You ruff your second spade with the six of hearts and cash the top clubs. Now if you run the jack of hearts West will hold off, while if you play a heart to your queen he will win and return a heart.

In order to cater for a possible 3–0 break, therefore, you play the two of hearts from dummy, intending to play the three from your hand regardless of East's card. When East shows out, your three of hearts puts West on lead with no satisfactory return.

Suppose West returns the queen of clubs for dummy to ruff. You can either play a trump to the ace and continue with winning clubs, or play a trump to the queen and king. A low diamond return you can run to your queen, and if West chooses instead to exit with the king of diamonds, you can play a trump to your ace, ruff out the queen of clubs, and play another trump. Finally, if West returns a spade, you discard a diamond from dummy and ruff with the queen of hearts. A club ruff is followed by a trump to your ace, and dummy's remaining diamond loser disappears on an established club.

It is not only in suit contracts that an invisible throw-in can be used to create extra entries. Here is a no trump slam.

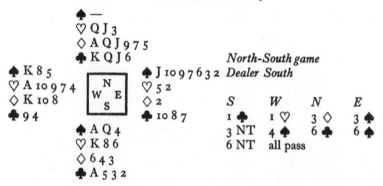

♠ —
♡ Q J 3
◇ A Q J 9 7 5
♣ K Q J 6

♠ K 8 5   ♠ J 10 9 7 6 3 2   *North-South game*
♡ A 10 9 7 4   N   ♡ 5 2   *Dealer South*
◇ K 10 8   W   E   ◇ 2
♣ 9 4   S   ♣ 10 8 7

♠ A Q 4
♡ K 8 6
◇ 6 4 3
♣ A 5 3 2

S	W	N	E
1 ♣	1 ♡	3 ◇	3 ♠
3 NT	4 ♠	6 ♣	6 ♠
6 NT	all pass		

In a pairs game you give up the chance of a sizeable penalty in order to
try for the maximum. When West leads the nine of clubs and dummy goes
down, you can't be sure if you have done the right thing.

To make the contract you will have to bring in the diamonds without loss.
That may require two entries in the closed hand, but your only sure entry
is the ace of clubs. Where did West find this awkward lead? On a heart or
a spade lead you would have had no problem.

Well, perhaps he can be persuaded to take the first or the second heart.
You win in dummy with the king of clubs and play the queen of hearts
followed by the jack. No joy! West holds up his ace. Now you continue
with the queen of clubs, then the six of clubs, on which East plays the ten.
Seizing your last chance, you play low from hand, catching East in the non-
material throw-in. East must either lead a diamond himself or allow you to
gain the lead with the ace of spades. In either case you wrap up twelve
tricks with the aid of two diamond finesses.

It is interesting to note that your entry threat in hearts was enough to
kill West's ace. Little did you think, when dummy first went down, that
your only loser would be a club.

Gambit plays that involve conceding a trick in a no-loser suit are comparatively rare, but opportunities do come along from time to time. Try
the next hand as a single-dummy problem.

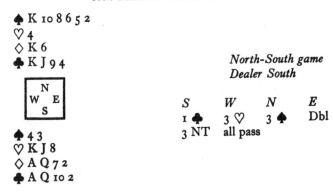

♠ K 10 8 6 5 2
♡ 4
◇ K 6
♣ K J 9 4

North-South game
Dealer South

S	W	N	E
1 ♣	3 ♡	3 ♠	Dbl
3 NT	all pass		

♠ 4 3
♡ K J 8
◇ A Q 7 2
♣ A Q 10 2

West leads the seven of hearts to East's nine and your jack. That gives you eight tricks, but it is not immediately clear where the ninth trick might come from. Still, there are throw-in possibilities and it might seem a good idea to start by running the clubs. That is not the strongest line, however. To preserve all your options, you must cash the top diamonds first.

Suppose you play off the king, ace and queen of diamonds, both opponents following suit while you discard a spade from dummy. Then you play the ten of clubs, unblocking the nine from dummy, and on the next trick overtake your queen of clubs with the king. On these two tricks West follows, let us say, with the five and six, East with the three and seven. Now you can be fairly confident of success. It looks as though West started with no spades, seven hearts, three or four diamonds and three or two clubs. You lead the four of clubs from dummy, and if East plays the eight you overtake and exit with the diamond to West, who must give you a further heart trick on his return.

If East shows out on the third club, you play the two, conceding the trick to West. Again West must give you a second heart trick, and after scoring this you exit with the diamond to East, collecting the king of spades as your ninth trick. If either defender throws the master diamond on the third club, of course you have nine tricks anyway.

A different type of non-material throw-in gains not an extra entry but a strategic advantage in a squeeze ending. As is the case with squeezes, the invisible throw-in may come in two stages – a preliminary throw-in that weakens an opponent by removing some of his flexibility, and a final throw-in that seals his doom.

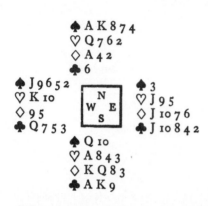

♠ A K 8 7 4
♡ Q 7 6 2
♢ A 4 2
♣ 6

♠ J 9 6 5 2   ♠ 3
♡ K 10   ♡ J 9 5
♢ 9 5   ♢ J 10 7 6
♣ Q 7 5 3   ♣ J 10 8 4 2

♠ Q 10
♡ A 8 4 3
♢ K Q 8 3
♣ A K 9

North-South game
Dealer South

You open one no trump (16–18) as South. West, trailing in the match, decides to mess up your bidding with an Astro two-diamond overcall (showing spades and another suit). You should be grateful to him, for after a series of doubles, during which it transpires that his second suit is clubs, you pass up the chance of a moderate penalty to try for six no trumps (instead of six hearts down one or a spade ruff, as happened in the other room).

West leads a low club to the ten and king. Since West is marked with five spades, you have only eleven tricks even if the hearts are distributed favourably. Hoping to get some help with your squeeze chances after a second lead from West, you play the ace and another heart. As expected, West is forced in with the king. (If West had thrown his heart king under the ace, you could have led the queen and ten of spades to establish an eleventh trick, then squeezed East in the red suits for your twelfth – all clearly marked by West's foolish bidding.)

Let's help West with his problem at trick four. A spade, or a diamond lead (assuming you guess correctly – and how could you not, after the bidding) results in a material loss. A further club lead involves no material loss yet results in a strategic defeat. Why? Because, if West leads another club, both defenders cannot retain club guards. West has to commit the defence one way or the other. If he leads the queen of clubs, leaving East's jack as the only guard against your nine, you finish the hearts, cash ace and king of diamonds, and then play three rounds of spades to squeeze East in the minors. Alternatively, if West leads a low club, forcing out the jack and leaving his queen as the only guard, you play the hearts and continue with three rounds of diamonds to squeeze West in the black suits.

Note that there were *two* strategic throw-ins on this deal. West had to give away something on the opening lead. A spade or a diamond would give you a twelfth trick at once in a material, visible way. A heart lead would allow you to win two fast heart tricks, play on spades, then squeeze East in the red suits. The club lead seemed to give little away, but by removing one of East's club honours West set the stage for the second strategic throw-in which forced him to destroy the flexibility of the defensive club position.

From the defenders' point of view, one club lead was always necessary to cut the link for your threatened double squeeze, but their club suit was not solid enough to stand two leads. If you had held the eight of clubs instead of the nine (or, for that matter, the seven of diamonds instead of the eight) your contract could have been defeated.

An invisible throw-in that enforces a defensive commitment of this sort may lead not to alternative squeezes but to alternative material throw-ins.

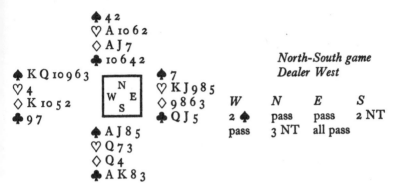

♠ 4 2
♡ A 10 6 2
◇ A J 7
♣ 10 6 4 2

North-South game
Dealer West

♠ K Q 10 9 6 3
♡ 4
◇ K 10 5 2
♣ 9 7

♠ 7
♡ K J 9 8 5
◇ 9 8 6 3
♣ Q J 5

♠ A J 8 5
♡ Q 7 3
◇ Q 4
♣ A K 8 3

W	N	E	S
2 ♠	pass	pass	2 NT
pass	3 NT	all pass	

West leads the king of spades and you allow him to hold the first trick. Already in the grip of a throw-in of sorts, West has only one safe card to lead at trick two – the singleton heart. When he finds the heart switch you play low from dummy, allowing East to win with the king. Now it is East who feels the pressure of the strategic throw-in. A heart continuation or a club switch leads to material loss, so East is forced to open up the diamonds. His nine is covered by the queen and king, and dummy's ace wins the trick.

You play a low club to your ace, and West makes a nuisance of himself by dropping the nine. Now you may be tempted to make the safety play of a low club from hand on the second round. But if you do, East will have a safe exit in clubs, and you will be left with eight tricks and no squeeze or throw-in for the ninth. So, spurning the unsafe 'safety play', you play the king and another club, placing East on lead in this position:

This is the third strategic throw-in of the deal, and it leads directly to a fourth throw-in – a material one.

East is forced to make a fatal commitment in diamonds. He has the

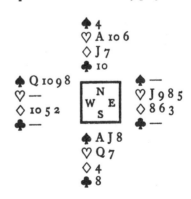

♠ 4
♡ A 10 6
◇ J 7
♣ 10

♠ Q 10 9 8
♡ —
◇ 10 5 2
♣ —

♠ —
♡ J 9 8 5
◇ 8 6 3
♣ —

♠ A J 8
♡ Q 7
◇ 4
♣ 8

choice of leading the eight of diamonds, in which case West will eventually be thrown in to lead away from his queen of spades, or a small diamond, in which case he himself will be thrown in to yield the ninth trick in hearts.

Even when an effective defence is possible in these situations, it is seldom easy to find.

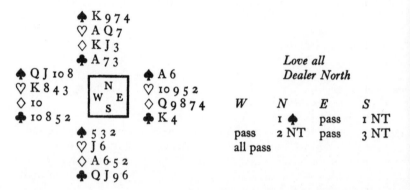

```
              ♠ K 9 7 4
              ♡ A Q 7
              ◇ K J 3
              ♣ A 7 3
                                         Love all
♠ Q J 10 8        ♠ A 6                   Dealer North
♡ K 8 4 3    N    ♡ 10 9 5 2
◇ 10      W     E ◇ Q 9 8 7 4      W    N     E      S
♣ 10 8 5 2    S   ♣ K 4                  1 ♠   pass   1 NT
                                   pass  2 NT  pass   3 NT
              ♠ 5 3 2                all pass
              ♡ J 6
              ◇ A 6 5 2
              ♣ Q J 9 6
```

West leads the queen of spades which is allowed to win the first trick. His switch to the ten of diamonds brings the three from dummy, the nine from East and the two from you. Now West tries a third suit, leading the two of clubs to his partner's king.

East is not thrown in materially at this point, for he has an exit card in clubs. Nevertheless, this can be regarded as a strategic throw-in, for East is compelled to attack hearts in order to break up the entries for the impending double squeeze. He leads the ten of hearts to the jack, king and ace. You cash the ace of clubs and exit with the seven of spades, leaving East on lead again in this position:

Now another heart cuts the link for the double squeeze but – alas for the defenders – it enforces the commitment in hearts. According to whether East returns the nine of hearts or a low heart, you will either squeeze West in the majors or East in the red suits.

Where did the defenders go wrong? The slip occurred at trick two, when the diamond switch had the effect of

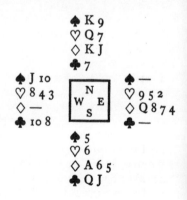

```
              ♠ K 9
              ♡ Q 7
              ◇ K J
              ♣ 7
♠ J 10            ♠ —
♡ 8 4 3    N      ♡ 9 5 2
◇ —     W     E   ◇ Q 8 7 4
♣ 10 8     S      ♣ —
              ♠ 5
              ♡ 6
              ◇ A 6 5
              ♣ Q J
```

rectifying the count for your squeeze. If West just continues with the eight of spades, East can return the ten of hearts to the jack, king and ace. When in with the club king, East continues with the nine of hearts to leave this subtly different position:

Now the timing is wrong for a squeeze against West, and you cannot duck a diamond to rectify the count because the defenders have hearts to cash. One down.

It takes a special brand of alertness to guard against early invisible throw-ins. An experienced player can usually see a material throw-in coming and is sometimes able to take steps to avoid it. An invisible throw-in, by its very nature, is harder to anticipate. One's attention is seldom drawn to strategic or invisible values. One imagines them rather than sees them. Would you, for example, have defended correctly on this deal?

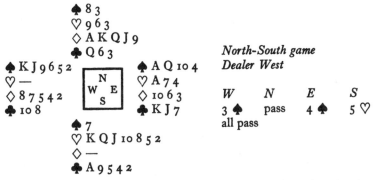

     ♠ K 9
     ♡ 7
     ◇ K J 3
     ♣ 7

♠ J 10   ♠ —
♡ 8 4   ♡ 5 2
◇ 10   ◇ Q 9 8 7 4
♣ 10 8   ♣ —

     ♠ 5
     ♡ —
     ◇ A 6 5 2
     ♣ Q J

     ♠ 8 3
     ♡ 9 6 3
     ◇ A K Q J 9
     ♣ Q 6 3

♠ K J 9 6 5 2   ♠ A Q 10 4
♡ —   ♡ A 7 4
◇ 8 7 5 4 2   ◇ 10 6 3
♣ 10 8   ♣ K J 7

     ♠ 7
     ♡ K Q J 10 8 5 2
     ◇ —
     ♣ A 9 5 4 2

North-South game
Dealer West

W	N	E	S
3 ♠	pass	4 ♠	5 ♡
all pass			

Suppose that you are East. Partner leads the six of spades, the three is played from dummy and you win with the ace. What now?

Clearly declarer has no more spades, and he is likely to have all the missing hearts since he came in, vulnerable, at the five-level, with no more than one ace on the side. There can be no chance of defeating the contract if declarer has a diamond, so assume that he hasn't. All you have to do is keep him out of dummy. Then, if partner has a couple of strong middle clubs. . . .

So what do you lead now? Not a club or a diamond, certainly. And a heart lead will give dummy an entry with the nine. You return a spade, therefore, forcing declarer to ruff in his hand.

But even this defence proves to be inadequate. Seeing no problem if trumps are 2–1, South prepares against the possibility that you have all three. He ruffs your spade return with the king and leads the eight of hearts to dummy's nine. You can't leave him on the table (you will be over-ruffed on the fourth diamond and then put in with the heart ace), so you win the trick with the ace. Now you are the victim of a throw-in. If you return the seven of hearts, declarer can draw trumps ending in dummy. If you lead the four of hearts, South plays the five and overtakes in dummy with the six. When you ruff the fourth diamond, he over-ruffs and reaches the last diamond by leading the two of hearts to dummy's three. If you try a spade return, conceding a ruff and discard, South needs only three diamond tricks. There is no defence.

Wait a minute! You now realize that you were invisibly thrown in at trick one. Your harmless-looking spade continuation helped declarer to eliminate that suit, which was an essential preparation for the second, visible throw-in. Wait another minute! You could have escaped this first-trick throw-in by a gallant gambit. All you had to do was play the four of spades at trick one. Declarer wins with the seven but now has no way of reaching dummy's diamonds. In exchange for the spade trick he has to give up two club tricks. If he still tries a lead of the eight of hearts to dummy's nine, you can win with the ace and get off lead with the queen or ten of spades (to be overtaken by West if declarer discards). You remain with the 7 4 of trumps poised over dummy's 6 3, and there is nothing that South can do (naturally, you play low if South leads the five of hearts and plays the three from dummy).

Wait still another minute! Declarer made a mistake too. He could have ensured the success of the contract by rising with dummy's eight of spades at trick one, forcing you to overtake and thus transferring the disastrous necessity of winning the first trick to you.

Even the most hard-boiled of players is unlikely to escape a moment of dizziness when contemplating gambit plays of this sort. Are you wondering whether the game is played with aces and kings any more?

Well, the invisible throw-in caught you unawares on that hand, but surely you will see it coming this time.

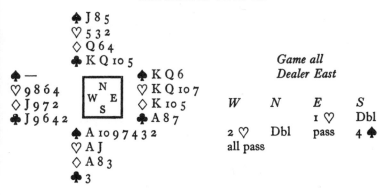

```
          ♠ J 8 5
          ♡ 5 3 2
          ◇ Q 6 4
          ♣ K Q 10 5                    Game all
♠ —                  ♠ K Q 6            Dealer East
♡ 9 8 6 4    ┌─────┐ ♡ K Q 10 7
◇ J 9 7 2    │  N  │ ◇ K 10 5
♣ J 9 6 4 2  │W   E│ ♣ A 8 7           W      N      E      S
             │  S  │                                  1 ♡    Dbl
          ┌──└─────┘─┐
          ♠ A 10 9 7 4 3 2             2 ♡    Dbl    pass   4 ♠
          ♡ A J                        all pass
          ◇ A 8 3
          ♣ 3
```

West leads the nine of hearts to your queen and declarer's ace. South immediately leads the three of clubs, on which partner plays the two and dummy the ten. You take your ace, of course, for partner is more likely to have five clubs than three. And if he *has* three clubs, the chances of defeating the contract are distinctly poor.

It is clear that partner started with four hearts without the jack (with the jack he would have led small). You finger the king of hearts, and then suddenly you realize that if you cash that card you will be caught in an invisible throw-in similar to that of the previous deal. South will ruff the third heart and play a low spade to dummy's eight – curtains!

The seven of hearts, then? Steady! Put it back in your hand, for even that is not good enough. South will win, lead a spade to the eight and queen, and discard a diamond on your heart return. Whatever you play next, he will make the rest of the tricks.

Finally you see that the only card to kill the contract at trick three is the *ten* of hearts. Now you can lead the seven on the third round, and if declarer discards, partner can overtake and lead a diamond.

13

Adjusting the Hand Pattern

The *Cormorant* ran eagerly before a stiff breeze as you sat at the helm, watching the ever-changing patterns of water and sky. Alec was making coffee, which was sorely needed. You were both a little bleary-eyed after discussing non-material throw-ins until the small hours of the morning.

The wind veered slightly and you compensated with a small adjustment of the tiller. How vital it was for the yachtsman, you reflected, to make allowance for shifting patterns of wind, tide and current – in fact, not just to make allowance for but to make use of such changes, to turn them to his own advantage.

It was not long before the bridge analogy occurred to you. The bridge player sometimes finds himself in a position to benefit from a change in hand pattern. This may come about by accident. More often, however, it takes careful preparation to create an opportunity for adjusting the hand pattern.

We are still concerned with throw-ins, but only with throw-ins of a particular kind – those in which a defender is forced to lead a suit in which both you and dummy are void, conceding a ruff and discard. The resulting gain is often non-material in nature – merely a strategic advantage conferred by the re-arrangement of your hand pattern. Here is an example.

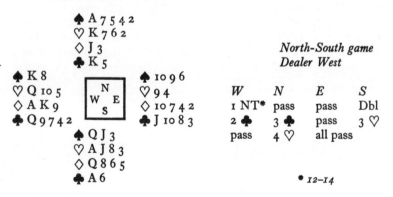

	♠ A 7 5 4 2					
	♡ K 7 6 2					
	◇ J 3			*North-South game*		
	♣ K 5			*Dealer West*		

♠ K 8		♠ 10 9 6				
♡ Q 10 5	N	♡ 9 4				
◇ A K 9	W E	◇ 10 7 4 2	*W*	*N*	*E*	*S*
♣ Q 9 7 4 2	S	♣ J 10 8 3	1 NT*	pass	pass	Dbl
	♠ Q J 3		2 ♣	3 ♣	pass	3 ♡
	♡ A J 8 3		pass	4 ♡	all pass	
	◇ Q 8 6 5					
	♣ A 6		* *12–14*			

West leads the ace of diamonds and promptly switches to a low club. You win in dummy and lead the jack of diamonds to knock out the king. Winning the club return, you play a trump to the king and return a small trump. The finesse is against the odds and there are good chances even if the queen does not drop, so you play the ace of hearts, cash the queen of diamonds, and continue with a third trump to put West on lead in this position:

Unable to touch spades, West has to lead another club. You throw a spade from dummy, ruff in hand, and lead the spade queen to the king and ace.

What have you gained from the forced club lead? Nothing material, for you could always make your trumps separately. What's the difference whether you ruff a club in hand or ruff a diamond in dummy? Strategically, the difference is vital because you are now in a position to *lead*

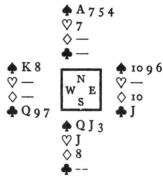

dummy's trump with a choice of discarding your spade or your diamond loser. Since East happens to guard both suits, he succumbs to the squeeze.

If dummy had held a third club instead of a fifth spade (a 4–4–2–3 pattern instead of 5–4–2–2), you could have executed this squeeze without the help of the throw-in manoeuvre. What you gained from the ruff and discard was really a shift of hand pattern that enabled you to interchange the roles of your last two trumps, thus turning the diamond loser into a menace card.

Well, any lead into your double void effects a change in your distributional pattern which is usually favourable, although sometimes irrelevant and occasionally damaging. Normally you gain a trick by ruffing in one hand while discarding a loser from the other. But the gain is not necessarily limited to one trick. A single shift in your hand pattern may produce a gain of several tricks, which opens up intriguing possibilities in the field of gambit play.

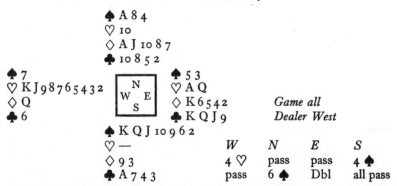

♠ A 8 4
♡ 10
◇ A J 10 8 7
♣ 10 8 5 2

♠ 7   ♠ 5 3
♡ K J 9 8 7 6 5 4 3 2   ♡ A Q
◇ Q   ◇ K 6 5 4 2   *Game all*
♣ 6   ♣ K Q J 9   *Dealer West*

♠ K Q J 10 9 6 2
♡ —
◇ 9 3
♣ A 7 4 3

W	N	E	S
4 ♡	pass	pass	4 ♠
pass	6 ♠	Dbl	all pass

East doubled in the hope that his partner could find the club lead, and, sure enough, West leads the six of clubs against your shaky slam.

Well, there is only one chance now. You win with the ace, cross to the ace of diamonds, ruff dummy's heart, and lead a low spade, playing the four from dummy when West produces the seven. The trick lost in trumps returns four-fold when West has to lead a heart. Six spades, doubled and made.

But you are not compelled to ruff and discard – you may choose to 'discard and discard' instead. This well-known device illustrates clearly that what you gain from a lead into your double void is a favourable adjustment of your hand pattern.

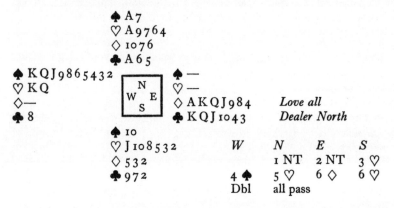

♠ A 7
♡ A 9 7 6 4
◇ 10 7 6
♣ A 6 5

♠ K Q J 9 8 6 5 4 3 2   ♠ —
♡ K Q   ♡ —
◇ —   ◇ A K Q J 9 8 4   *Love all*
♣ 8   ♣ K Q J 10 4 3   *Dealer North*

♠ 10
♡ J 10 8 5 3 2
◇ 5 3 2
♣ 9 7 2

W	N	E	S
	1 NT	2 NT	3 ♡
4 ♠	5 ♡	6 ◇	6 ♡
Dbl	all pass		

West leads the king of spades and the sight of dummy is a disappointment. For one thing you appear to have six losers, and also this looks suspiciously like a phantom sacrifice. However, when East shows out on the

[228]

ace of spades you begin to feel more cheerful. You cash the ace of hearts, ruff the seven of spades in hand, play a club to dummy's ace, and concede a trump to put West on lead.

On the forced spade return you discard a diamond from dummy and a club from hand. Now that awful mirror distribution in the minor suits is beginning to look better. On the next spade another diamond goes from dummy and a further club from your hand. The pattern is improving trick by trick. The next spade lead permits you to throw the last diamond from the table as you ruff in hand and claim the rest of the tricks.

So, in the end you escape for two down, not five down, and the loss of 300 is a mere flea-bite compared with the 920 you would have lost defending against six diamonds.

Now for some more of the non-material ruff and discard situations.

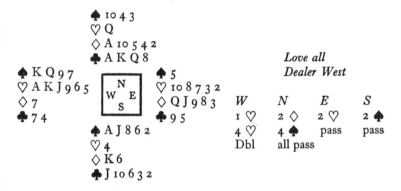

	♠ 10 4 3				
	♡ Q				
	◇ A 10 5 4 2			*Love all*	
	♣ A K Q 8			*Dealer West*	

♠ K Q 9 7		♠ 5					
♡ A K J 9 6 5	N	♡ 10 8 7 3 2					
◇ 7	W E	◇ Q J 9 8 3	W	N	E	S
♣ 7 4	S	♣ 9 5	1 ♡	2 ◇	2 ♡	2 ♠
	♠ A J 8 6 2		4 ♡	4 ♠	pass	pass
	♡ 4		Dbl	all pass		
	◇ K 6					
	♣ J 10 6 3 2					

West leads the king of hearts and continues with the ace. What do you do?

Hmm! It looks as though the lead into your double void is a good move for the defence. If you ruff in dummy, enter hand with the king of diamonds, and lead a low trump, West will play the queen and kill you with a further heart lead.

So you try it the other way round, discarding a club honour from dummy and ruffing in hand. When you continue with a low spade to the queen, West is not so well placed. A switch to a minor suit gives you an easy time; you ruff and run the ten of spades to the king, and since dummy is able to ruff a further heart lead there is nothing West can do. So West is forced to lead another heart at trick four. Again you discard a high club from dummy and ruff in hand, reaching this position:

You see what has happened? The double ruff and discard has enabled you to transform the club suit from an awkward 5–4 into a winning 5–2 pattern. You cash the ace and jack of clubs and the king of diamonds, then continue clubs and enjoy the music of West gnashing his teeth.

The power (and the danger for the defence) of this sort of pattern-shifting is clearly seen in the next example.

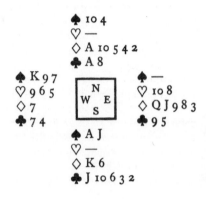

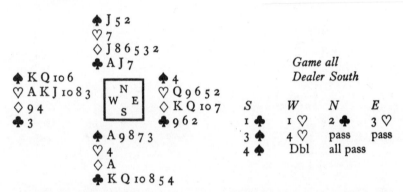

		Game all	
		Dealer South	
S	W	N	E
1 ♣	1 ♡	2 ♣	3 ♡
3 ♠	4 ♡	pass	pass
4 ♠	Dbl	all pass	

Again West begins with two top hearts. You discard the seven of clubs from dummy, ruff in hand, and play a low spade to West's queen. If West sees no danger and continues with the heart force, you discard the ace of clubs from dummy, ruff in hand and cash the king of clubs. As the cards lie, you will not be punished for cashing the ace of diamonds at this point, but West might be 4–6–0–3 and there is no need to take chances. With five clubs as trump-substitutes, you are in control. Just continue clubs and let West discard diamonds if he will. He may choose to discard his diamonds, then ruff the fourth club with the king of spades and play a fourth heart in this position:

It makes no difference. You ruff in hand with the nine of spades, even though this leaves you with the singleton ace, and continue to draw West's trumps by playing clubs.

How could West have defeated the contract? Simply by making a neutral club or diamond lead at trick four, refusing to allow you the deadly pattern-shift in clubs. The defender can always prevail in such situations when his third-best trump is higher than declarer's second-best.

The pattern of a side suit may be adjusted dramatically to achieve a *coup en passant.*

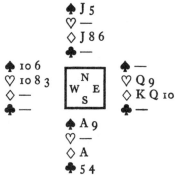

♠ J 5
♡ —
◇ J 8 6
♣ —

♠ 10 6   ♠ —
♡ 10 8 3   ♡ Q 9
◇ —   ◇ K Q 10
♣ —   ♣ —

♠ A 9
♡ —
◇ A
♣ 5 4

♠ 5 2
♡ K
◇ 10 8 6 5 4 2
♣ J 10 9 6

♠ 9 7 6   ♠ 3
♡ 3   ♡ Q J 9 8 7 4 2
◇ A Q J 7 3   ◇ K 9
♣ A Q 8 2   ♣ 7 5 3

♠ A K Q J 10 8 4
♡ A 10 6 5
◇ —
♣ K 4

North-South Game
Dealer West

W	N	E	S
1 ◇	pass	3 ♡	4 ♠
all pass			

On the natural lead of the singleton heart you are home. Just ruff a diamond and continue with the six of hearts, discarding a club from dummy when West ruffs. West will probably switch to a trump at this point. If instead he leads a diamond for you to ruff, you should cash one high trump yourself, just in case the trumps are 2–2. (It's not often you have to guard against a 2–2 trump break, but if East had a 2–7–2–2 shape and you failed to take a round of trumps, West would ruff the ten of hearts and play a third diamond, on which East would discard a club.)

Now when you lead the ten of hearts, West is caught in the *coup en passant.* If he discards, you score your tenth trick by ruffing in dummy. If he ruffs, you discard another club from the table. A third club goes away on the ace of hearts, altering the club pattern from 4–2 to 1–2, and your tenth trick comes from a club ruff in dummy.

An initial trump lead is needed to defeat four spades.

It is clear that a lead into a double void will usually be to declarer's advantage when he can ruff in one hand and discard a loser from the other. But what about those situations where declarer has no obvious loser to discard – where the only discard available is that of a potential winner? Is the ruff and discard then irrelevant? Not necessarily. Declarer will be delighted to accept the ruff and discard if he can dispose of a potential winner which he would not otherwise have time to establish. The ruff and discard may work to declarer's advantage by giving him an extra tempo. This is a point for the defenders to bear in mind on hands like the following:

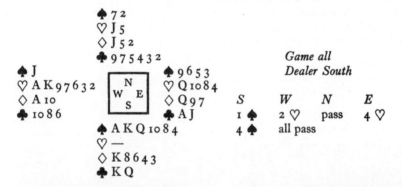

```
        ♠ 7 2
        ♡ J 5
        ◊ J 5 2
        ♣ 9 7 5 4 3 2                Game all
♠ J              ♠ 9 6 5 3           Dealer South
♡ A K 9 7 6 3 2  ♡ Q 10 8 4
◊ A 10    N      ◊ Q 9 7
♣ 10 8 6  W E    ♣ A J          S      W       N      E
           S                    1 ♠    2 ♡     pass   4 ♡
        ♠ A K Q 10 8 4           4 ♠    all pass
        ♡ —
        ◊ K 8 6 4 3
        ♣ K Q
```

You ruff the heart lead, cash the ace of spades, and lead a small diamond, playing low from dummy when West produces the ten. In order to defeat the contract East must overtake with the queen of diamonds and return a trump. Then the 4–1 trump break prevents you from establishing the diamonds *and* setting up a club trick.

If East allows his partner to win the third trick with the ten of diamonds, your troubles are over. You can ruff the next heart and lead a low diamond to knock out the ace. Now dummy can ruff the third heart while you discard a useless club honour from hand. You return to hand with the king of diamonds, draw the outstanding trumps and cash two more diamonds to make your contract.

And that will be a double game swing, for your team-mates in the other room are likely to bid five hearts and make it when North understandably fails to find the killing club lead.

On certain hands, a ruff and discard alone may not be enough to see you home, but it may be a necessary preliminary to a squeeze.

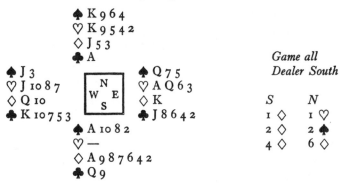

♠ K 9 6 4
♡ K 9 5 4 2
◇ J 5 3
♣ A

Game all
Dealer South

S	N
1 ◇	1 ♡
2 ◇	2 ♠
4 ◇	6 ◇

West leads the jack of hearts, and when dummy goes down you are thankful that you avoided the trap of playing in six spades. Not that six diamonds is going to be easy. You play low from dummy and ruff the jack of hearts. Crossing to the ace of clubs, you lead the four of hearts on which East plays the queen. You ruff and play the queen of clubs, covered by West and ruffed in dummy.

Now you resist the temptation to play another heart, partly because you cannot be sure that East's queen was a true card, and partly because there is no hurry with the hearts anyway. Instead you lead the small diamond, hoping to be able to duck the trick to a singleton honour – either the king or queen with West or the king with East. If the partial elimination succeeds, a spade return may allow you to pick up the suit by playing for split honours, and a heart return may give you two tricks in that suit. At worst, a club return will give you a ruff and discard, leaving you with squeeze chances. So when East produces the king of diamonds you allow him to hold the trick. This is the position:

You might, of course, have ruffed another heart and led a small trump from hand to throw East in. But then he would have been able to defeat you by returning the blank ace of hearts, yielding only one trick. As it is, a heart return from East gives you two tricks, as does a spade. So East returns the jack of clubs, giving you a sterile spade discard in hand as you ruff in dummy. But you return to hand by

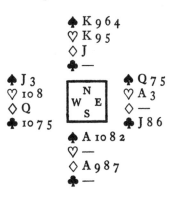

♠ K 9 6 4
♡ K 9 5
◇ J
♣ —

♠ J 3
♡ 10 8
◇ Q
♣ 10 7 5

♠ Q 7 5
♡ A 3
◇ —
♣ J 8 6

♠ A 10 8 2
♡ —
◇ A 9 8 7
♣ —

ruffing a small heart, and when you play the rest of your trumps from the top East is squeezed in the majors.

We have seen some deals where you were able to counter a forcing attack by adjusting the hand pattern of dummy, so that you were eventually able to bring off a trump end-play against your left-hand opponent. There are also times when, in order to achieve the trump end-play, you have to adjust your own hand to the exact shape of your left-hand opponent's.

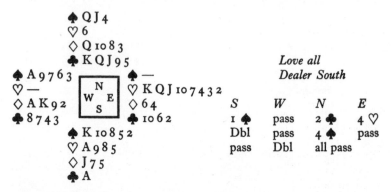

```
              ♠ Q J 4
              ♡ 6
              ◊ Q 10 8 3
              ♣ K Q J 9 5                    Love all
♠ A 9 7 6 3        ♠ —                        Dealer South
♡ —         N      ♡ K Q J 10 7 4 3 2
◊ A K 9 2 W   E    ◊ 6 4        S      W      N      E
♣ 8 7 4 3     S    ♣ 10 6 2     1 ♠    pass   2 ♣    4 ♡
              ♠ K 10 8 5 2      Dbl    pass   4 ♠    pass
              ♡ A 9 8 5         pass   Dbl    N 4 ♠  all pass
              ◊ J 7 5
              ♣ A
```

Partner has played his part by removing your double of the cold four hearts. The rest is up to you.

West begins with the ace, king and another diamond. Naturally you play the queen from dummy on the third round, and when East discards a heart the distribution of the whole hand becomes crystal clear, West is marked with a 5–0–4–4 shape, and you have a chance only if you can discard all your hearts on dummy's minor-suit winners. Furthermore, since both spade honours are needed in dummy for the ending, you must rely on the ten of clubs dropping from the East hand.

You therefore jettison the ace of clubs on the fourth round of diamonds and start running the clubs. Your luck holds when the ten appears, and you are able to discard your last heart – the ace – on the nine of clubs. The following cards are left:

Now you play the heart or the club from dummy and ruff with the ten of spades. If West over-ruffs, he has to concede the rest on his return. And if West plays low, you lead the two of spades to dummy's jack and repeat the

```
              ♠ Q J 4
              ♡ 6
              ◊ —
              ♣ 5
♠ A 9 7 6 3        ♠ —
♡ —         N      ♡ Q J 10 7 4
◊ —       W   E    ◊ —
♣ —           S    ♣ —
              ♠ K 10 8 5 2
              ♡ —
              ◊ —
              ♣ —
```

manoeuvre, ruffing the other plain card with the king of spades. No matter what West does, he can make only one trump trick.

Be sure that you appreciate the need to unblock the ace of clubs. The end-play does not work if you play a club to the ace at trick four and return to dummy with a trump. This is the four-card ending:

Now, when you ruff the heart or the club with the ten of spades, West under-ruffs and you are beaten.

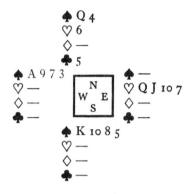

The occasions when a ruff and discard will be damaging to the declarer can often be recognized from the bidding. When declarer has a side suit to establish, either in dummy or in the closed hand, his trumps will be working hard and he may not be able to spare one for an 'unproductive' ruff. A lead into his double void may then prove to be a killing move.

Here is an example.

```
            ♠ A K                Game all
            ♡ 5 4                Dealer North
            ◇ A K 6 5
            ♣ A 8 5 4 2    W     N       E       S
♠ Q 10 7 4                       1 ♣*    pass    1 ◇†
♡ A K 8 6 2     N                1 ♡     2 ♣     pass    2 ♠‡
◇ 10 4        W   E       pass    3 ◇     pass    4 ◇
♣ K Q           S         pass    5 ◇     all pass
                              * 16 +    † negative
                              ‡ 5-card suit
```

You lead the ace of hearts, on which partner plays the jack and declarer the three. Needing more information, you continue with the king of hearts. If South's queen does not drop, you intend to switch to a trump. The contract will be unbeatable if South's shape is 5–3–5–0, but the trump lead will win against 5–3–4–1 by denying South any chance of setting up his spades.

But in practice South plays the queen of hearts on the second round. Now you have an extra chance. The defence can prevail, not only when South is 5–2–4–2, but also when he is 5–2–5–1 without the queen of diamonds, if you continue with a third round of hearts, offering South an unwanted ruff and discard. Whatever declarer does, he will be unable to negotiate two spade ruffs in dummy and still return to hand to enjoy the fifth spade.

The full hand:

Note that a third round of hearts does not give away the contract even if South has two clubs and four strong diamonds.

There are certain hands on which the normal techniques – ruffing in one hand and discarding in the other, or taking a double discard – are of no use to declarer. What then is left?

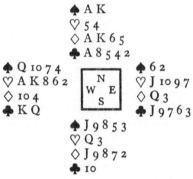

♠ A K
♡ 5 4
◇ A K 6 5
♣ A 8 5 4 2

♠ Q 10 7 4
♡ A K 8 6 2
◇ 10 4
♣ K Q

♠ 6 2
♡ J 10 9 7
◇ Q 3
♣ J 9 7 6 3

♠ J 9 8 5 3
♡ Q 3
◇ J 9 8 7 2
♣ 10

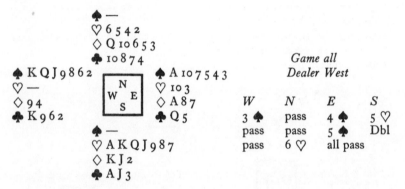

♠ —
♡ 6 5 4 2
◇ Q 10 6 5 3
♣ 10 8 7 4

♠ K Q J 9 8 6 2
♡ —
◇ 9 4
♣ K 9 6 2

♠ A 10 7 5 4 3
♡ 10 3
◇ A 8 7
♣ Q 5

♠ —
♡ A K Q J 9 8 7
◇ K J 2
♣ A J 3

Game all
Dealer West

W	N	E	S
3 ♠	pass	4 ♠	5 ♡
pass	pass	5 ♠	Dbl
pass	6 ♡	all pass	

West leads the king of spades, offering you an immediate ruff and discard. It seems natural to ruff in dummy and discard a club from hand, but this play destroys one of your options. On the bidding, East is likely to have the ace of diamonds and he may well be able to hold it up until the third round. Lacking a trump entry in dummy, you will then be held to two diamond tricks. However, there will still be a chance of establishing three club tricks, provided that you do not make the mistake of discarding a club at trick one.

Well, if you can't spare a discard from your hand, what about ruffing in hand and discarding from dummy? No, that doesn't work either. Any discard from dummy destroys your long-card threat in that suit. Your hand pattern on this deal is perfect as it is; you do not want to make any adjustment. So you are forced to the conclusion that the only way to preserve all your options is to ruff in both hands!

The double ruff brings the solution of the problem within your grasp. After drawing trumps you lead the king of diamonds and continue with the jack of diamonds to dummy's queen. East may hold up again, but the ace of diamonds is dead if he does. You switch to clubs, leading low to your jack. If West takes his king, you will find a parking place for your diamond loser by taking a third-round finesse against the nine of clubs. If West holds up, he will be thrown in on the third round of clubs, forced either to yield a further club to dummy or to concede a ruff and discard.

There are interesting possibilities for the defence in this type of situation. Move round to the East seat for this hand.

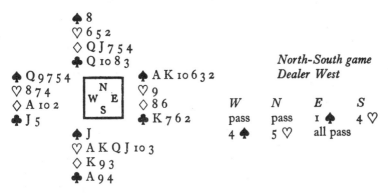

```
                ♠ 8
                ♡ 6 5 2
                ◇ Q J 7 5 4
                ♣ Q 10 8 3                    North-South game
  ♠ Q 9 7 5 4    ┌─────┐   ♠ A K 10 6 3 2     Dealer West
  ♡ 8 7 4        │  N  │   ♡ 9
  ◇ A 10 2       │ W E │   ◇ 8 6           W      N      E      S
  ♣ J 5          │  S  │   ♣ K 7 6 2       pass   pass   1 ♠    4 ♡
                └─────┘                    4 ♠    5 ♡    all pass
                ♠ J
                ♡ A K Q J 10 3
                ◇ K 9 3
                ♣ A 9 4
```

West leads the five of spades to your king. On any switch, declarer will draw trumps, play a diamond to the queen and a diamond back to his king. When West holds off, South will change his tack, leading the nine of clubs to dummy's ten, and you will have no way of preventing him from making eleven tricks.

The winning defence – far from easy to see at the table – is a spade continuation. A double ruff doesn't help declarer this time. If a trump is left outstanding, West can win the second diamond and play a third diamond, while if South draws three rounds of trumps first he squeezes dummy out of one of his options.

Why is that second round of spades so deadly? There are three ways of looking at it. (1) It forcibly alters the good hand pattern that declarer started with. A double ruff would have countered this had the trumps been 2–2. (2) It reduces declarer's playing margin by one vital trick. To be effective, the attack-shifting manoeuvre in the minor suits has to be started when there are nine cards in dummy; but, after two rounds of spades and three rounds of trumps, only eight cards are left. Thus South is denied the precious 'elbow-room' that he needs. (3) Declarer is caught in a compound strategic squeeze at trick two. He can find momentary relief in a double ruff, but this merely postpones the agony. Perhaps this is the most accurate explanation. It is a delayed-action non-material squeeze.

The double ruff is more commonly associated with trump end-plays. This device sometimes enables you to gain the equivalent of two entries at the one stroke.

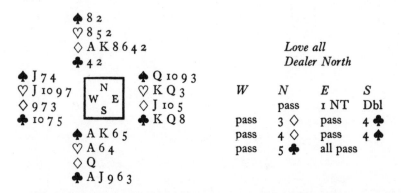

Love all
Dealer North

W	N	E	S
	pass	1 NT	Dbl
pass	3 ◇	pass	4 ♣
pass	4 ◇	pass	4 ♠
pass	5 ♣	all pass	

West leads the jack of hearts, luckily for you (a trump would have made things too difficult), and you win with the ace. After unblocking the queen of diamonds, you cash the top spades, ruff a third spade with the two of clubs, and discard your heart losers on the ace and king of diamonds.

You ruff a heart with the six of clubs, bringing your tally up to eight tricks, and lead your fourth spade. West has to ruff this, and you discard the last heart from dummy. Since West cannot afford to lead from his weakened trump holding, he returns a heart in this position:

It looks as though you need two entries in dummy – one to shorten your trumps, and the other to bring off the final trump coup. But West's lead into your double void has the effect of giving you both entries at once. You ruff in dummy with the four of clubs and under-ruff with your three, and the lead is in the right place for you to pick up East's trumps for the loss of one trick.

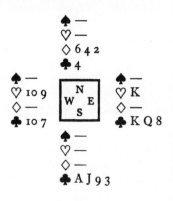

Sometimes a defender will have an opportunity of leading into a *triple*

void. Such a lead may be needed to produce the optimum result for the defence. Take the East seat again for the next hand.

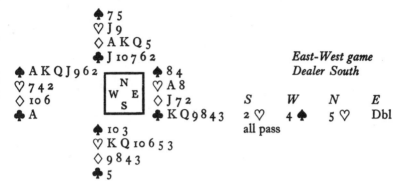

♠ 7 5
♡ J 9
◇ A K Q 5
♣ J 10 7 6 2

♠ A K Q J 9 6 2   ♠ 8 4
♡ 7 4 2   ♡ A 8
◇ 10 6   ◇ J 7 2
♣ A   ♣ K Q 9 8 4 3

♠ 10 3
♡ K Q 10 6 5 3
◇ 9 8 4 3
♣ 5

East-West game
Dealer South

S	W	N	E
2 ♡	4 ♠	5 ♡	Dbl
all pass			

West cashes the ace of clubs and two top spades. It looks as though you are going to receive a penalty of only 300 in compensation for your lost vulnerable game, but partner finds the way to give you a chance of 500. He continues with a third round of spades.

Now it is up to you. If dummy ruffs, you must over-ruff and return a club. Owing to the blockage in trumps, South will be unable to avoid the loss of a trick to partner's seven of hearts. And if dummy discards on the third round of spades, you must 'finesse' against the trumps on the table by ruffing with the eight of hearts. When you gain the lead with the ace of hearts you can return a club, and again partner's seven of hearts becomes a winner.

However, the classic case of the triple void lead is the smother play. Here the enforced lead helps the declarer to achieve a favourable shift in trump pattern.

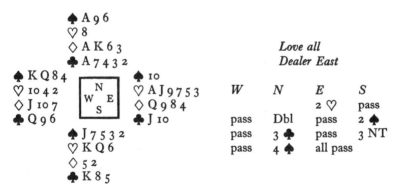

♠ A 9 6
♡ 8
◇ A K 6 3
♣ A 7 4 3 2

♠ K Q 8 4   ♠ 10
♡ 10 4 2   ♡ A J 9 7 5 3
◇ J 10 7   ◇ Q 9 8 4
♣ Q 9 6   ♣ J 10

♠ J 7 5 3 2
♡ K Q 6
◇ 5 2
♣ K 8 5

Love all
Dealer East

W	N	E	S
		2 ♡	pass
pass	Dbl	pass	2 ♠
pass	3 ♣	pass	3 NT
pass	4 ♠	all pass	

You would have been happier in three no trumps, but partner has propelled you into four spades, where you are in danger of losing a heart, a club and two trumps.

West leads the jack of diamonds to dummy's king, and you play the singleton heart which East wins (he cannot gain by ducking). You win the club return with the king and lead the jack of spades, hoping to pin something in the East hand – queen, ace, ten. Fine! Now you try an elopement, playing the ace and another diamond.

When East plays the queen you ruff, cash the king and queen of hearts, throwing clubs from dummy, cross to the ace of clubs, and lead the fourth diamond in this position:

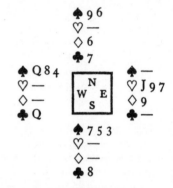

```
              ♠ 9 6
              ♡ —
              ◇ 6
              ♣ 7
♠ Q 8 4              ♠ —
♡ —       N         ♡ J 9 7
◇ —    W     E      ◇ 9
♣ Q       S         ♣ —
              ♠ 7 5 3
              ♡ —
              ◇ —
              ♣ 8
```

You cannot be sure who holds the nine of diamonds and who the queen of clubs. If West has the diamond, you intend to ruff this trick and score a further trump in dummy.

But when East produces the diamond nine you make a quick shift to the smother-tack, discarding the eight of clubs. East has to return a heart, and when you ruff with the five of spades West is powerless to make more than one trump trick.

14

Non-Material Dummy Reversals

Reversing the dummy is an expression that can be interpreted in more ways than one. When partnering Uncle Timothy in those far-off days, for instance, you all 'reversed the dummy' by arranging to play as many hands as possible yourselves, trying to anticipate the final contract and to get in first with the no trump bid on all sorts of unlikely shapes.

This was rather frustrating for Sir Frederick, the kitten, who was happiest when Uncle Tim was playing the hand. While prepared to sit on the corner of the table with half-closed eyes and sneer at *anyone's* dummy play, Fred reserved his expression of greatest disdain for Uncle Tim's performances.

The normal purpose of reversing the dummy is to gain an extra trump trick. The idea is to ruff losers in the long trump hand until eventually it becomes the shorter trump hand. Thus with five trumps opposite three, you may score six trump tricks instead of five. In effect, you achieve a beneficial adjustment of your trump pattern.

The technique of dummy reversal can be helpful in many situations, not all of which are well known.

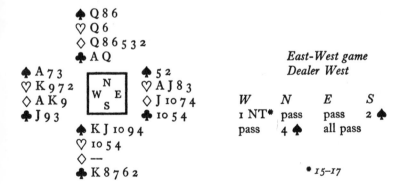

```
            ♠ Q 8 6
            ♡ Q 6
            ◇ Q 8 6 5 3 2
            ♣ A Q
  ♠ A 7 3              ♠ 5 2
  ♡ K 9 7 2    N       ♡ A J 8 3
  ◇ A K 9    W   E     ◇ J 10 7 4
  ♣ J 9 3      S       ♣ 10 5 4
            ♠ K J 10 9 4
            ♡ 10 5 4
            ◇ --
            ♣ K 8 7 6 2
```

East-West game
Dealer West

W	N	E	S
1 NT*	pass	pass	2 ♠
pass	4 ♠	all pass	

* 15–17

[241]

West starts aggressively with the ace and another spade, making it clear that he has no intention of allowing you to ruff a heart in dummy. This sets you an awkward problem. To make the contract you must somehow score five club tricks *and* five trumps. It seems impossible, even if clubs break 3–3, but you decide to play on reverse dummy lines and hope for the best.

Winning the second trump in dummy, you ruff a diamond, lead a club to the queen, ruff another diamond, cross to the ace of clubs, and ruff a third diamond with your last trump, establishing three diamond winners in dummy. You cash the king of clubs, leaving this position:

Although you have no re-entry in the closed hand, West cannot afford to ruff when you continue clubs, for you would over-ruff in dummy and score an overtrick with the help of the diamonds. So West has to let you make five club tricks after all, and dummy's trump provides the tenth trick.

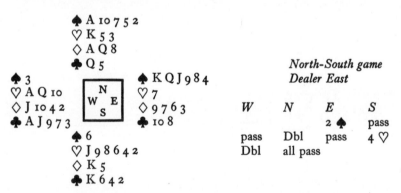

This was a material dummy reversal (it gained an extra trump trick) which led to a non-material suit establishment. You could not expect to cash the established diamonds, but the threat was enough to blackmail West into allowing you to make your clubs.

Dummy reversal technique may offer the only means of escape from a threatened trump promotion.

♠ A 10 7 5 2
♡ K 5 3
◇ A Q 8
♣ Q 5

♠ 3
♡ A Q 10
◇ J 10 4 2
♣ A J 9 7 3

♠ K Q J 9 8 4
♡ 7
◇ 9 7 6 3
♣ 10 8

♠ 6
♡ J 9 8 6 4 2
◇ K 5
♣ K 6 4 2

North-South game
Dealer East

W	N	E	S
		2 ♠	pass
pass	Dbl	pass	4 ♡
Dbl	all pass		

West leads the three of spades to dummy's ace. The location of the outstanding high cards is clearly marked by the bidding. You can afford to lose two trumps and a club, and there should be a play for the contract if trumps are not 4–0. The problem is that if you come to hand with the king of diamonds and lead a trump, West will play low; then, when in with the ace of clubs, he will cash two rounds of trumps, preventing you from ruffing a club in dummy. And if you try for the club ruff before touching trumps you may run into an over-ruff.

So you decide to reverse the dummy, leading a spade and ruffing at trick two. West discards a club (if he over-ruffs, you will be able to ruff a club in dummy after all). Careful with your entries now. Not a club to the queen at this point, for West would over-ruff the next spade and play ace and another club, promoting a third trump trick for the defence. First you must use the trump entry, leading a heart to the king and ruffing another spade. Now is the time to use the club entry. A club to the queen is followed by another spade ruff, three rounds of diamonds, and a fourth spade ruff. Surprise, surprise! You have ten tricks. And if West ruffs or over-ruffs at any stage it merely simplifies the play for you.

The key feature of the play was the timing of the club lead, which had to be made neither too early nor too late. If you had kept the club entry until last, West would have defeated you by playing the ace, drawing trumps, and returning a club.

Precise and demanding as your play may have been, it was still a material dummy reversal yielding an extra trump trick. By the time you ruffed the last spade, you had managed to reduce your trumps to one fewer than dummy's. *Three* ruffs in hand, reducing to parity with dummy, would not have been worth a brass farthing.

But this is not always the case. The non-material dummy reversals are those that do not produce an extra trump trick.

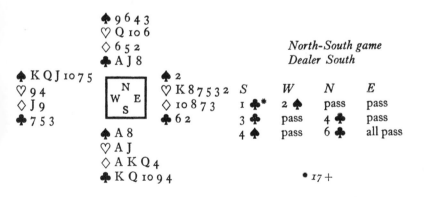

West leads the king of spades to your ace, and you return the eight of spades to keep the position flexible. East discards a heart and West switches to the three of clubs. You win in dummy with the eight and play the queen of hearts, running it when East plays low.

So far, so good. Now, if East has four diamonds and three trumps you might manoeuvre to ruff the fourth diamond in dummy. But that is surely unnecessary, for if East has four diamonds it must be possible to squeeze him in the red suits. No entries, did someone say? What's wrong with the trumps?

You ruff a spade with the nine of clubs and lead the ten to dummy's jack.

When both defenders follow suit, you can continue with a further spade ruff. Then you unblock the ace of hearts and lead your last trump in this position:

The outstanding trump is drawn and East is squeezed on the same trick.

Well, this time the dummy reversal did not result in the gain of a trump trick. You scored just five tricks in trumps and you had five trump winners from the start. All that you gained from the dummy reversal was a re-alignment of the entry position which enabled you to win the last trump in dummy and thus bring pressure to bear upon East.

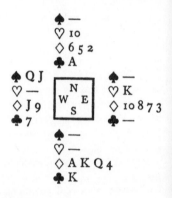

It is worth noting that six no trumps has no chance.

Here is a case for similar treatment.

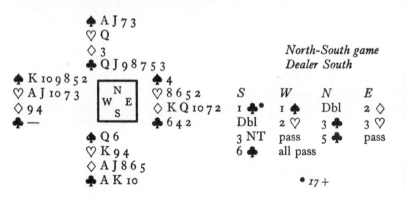

	S	W	N	E
	1 ♣*	1 ♠	Dbl	2 ◇
	Dbl	2 ♡	3 ♣	3 ♡
	3 NT	pass	5 ♣	pass
	6 ♣	all pass		

North-South game
Dealer South

* 17 +

West leads the nine of diamonds to the queen and ace. You ruff a diamond in dummy and return a club to your king. When West shows out it is clear that you cannot hope to ruff a spade in hand, so you ruff a second diamond in dummy and lead the queen of hearts. West cannot gain by holding off (this gives you a choice of two different ways of making the contract), so he takes his ace and returns the jack of hearts to your king. You discard a spade from dummy on this trick, ruff another diamond, lead a trump to your ten, and ruff the last diamond in dummy. Now you are in a position to win the last round of trumps in the closed hand, squeezing West in the process.

♠ A J 7
♡ —
◇ —
♣ Q

♠ K 10 9   ♠ 4
♡ 10   ♡ 8 6
◇ —   ◇ —
♣ —   ♣ 6

♠ Q 6
♡ 9
◇ —
♣ A

The dummy reversal would have been unnecessary if West had started with the ace and jack of hearts, leaving your diamond entry intact. You could then have made six clubs (or six no trumps, for that matter) simply by running the clubs and returning to hand with the ace of diamonds to squeeze West. However, West could have defeated you by leading the ace of hearts and switching to diamonds, for that would have left you short of an entry to ruff all four diamonds in dummy.

This kind of play can be used to alleviate entry problems in just about any type of squeeze ending. On the next hand the non-material dummy reversal sets the scene for a progressive squeeze.

♠ 7 4 3
♡ J 9 5
◇ A Q 7 3
♣ K 10 8

♠ A K Q 5 2
♡ A K
◇ 6
♣ A Q J 9 6

Knowing that the 'reversibility' of a solid trump suit can give you small but valuable extra chances, you choose to play your grand slam not in spades nor in no trumps but in your best suit – clubs.

West leads the five of diamonds to dummy's ace. There will be no problem if the spades behave, and if they don't, you may be able to do something about it in spite of the lack of entries in dummy. First you test the clubs by cashing the eight. When all follow, you ruff a diamond with the jack of clubs and return the queen to dummy's king. If both defenders follow suit, it is safe to ruff another diamond with the ace of clubs. After cashing the ace and king of hearts, you lead the nine of clubs to dummy's ten. Now, if either defender started with four spades, the queen of hearts and the king of diamonds, he is in the grip of a progressive squeeze. Alternatively, if one of red honours has already dropped, you may have a simple squeeze when you cash the established winner.

On the next hand a partial dummy reversal is needed to enforce a ruffing squeeze without the count.

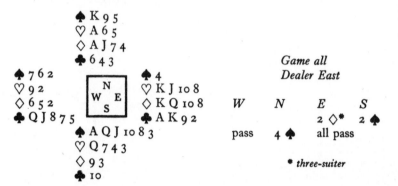

The opening lead is the six of diamonds. When you play low from dummy, East wins with the ten, cashes the king of clubs, and switches back to the king of diamonds. The bidding tells you that neither trumps nor hearts will break, so a red-suit squeeze against East is the only chance. The ruffing squeeze will work if the second last trump is won in dummy. It will therefore suffice to ruff two clubs in hand.

You win the ace of diamonds, ruff a club with the jack of spades, cash the spade ace and continue with a spade to the nine. After another club ruff, you lead a spade to the king in this position:

East has already been forced to part with his clubs, and whatever he discards now he can make only one trick.

Note that pressure can be applied only by ruffing two clubs in hand. If, at trick four, you had led a low heart from dummy, for instance, East's heart return would have killed all squeeze chances, whether you won in dummy or in the closed hand.

There is also an instructive point for the defence in this hand. East had no good reason for cashing the king of clubs at trick two. If he had just continued with the king of diamonds you would have had no play for the contract.

In defence, it takes a high degree of mental alertness to appreciate the dangers of such situations. You remember a recent hand on which a defender failed to recognize his problem. You had been discussing partial dummy reversals with a group of acquaintances at the club prior to an evening of rubber bridge. One of those present was sceptical.

'Oh, yes, these devices are cute enough, but they never crop up in practice.'

'Never,' you replied, 'until you learn of their existence.'

As if to prove the point, the Goddess Brigida favoured you with the following hand.

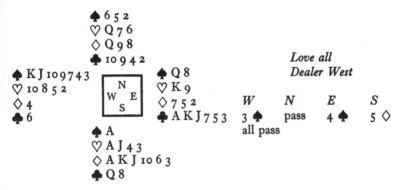

```
              ♠ 6 5 2
              ♡ Q 7 6
              ♢ Q 9 8
              ♣ 10 9 4 2                Love all
♠ K J 10 9 7 4 3   ┌─────┐  ♠ Q 8       Dealer West
♡ 10 8 5 2         │  N  │  ♡ K 9
♢ 4              W │     │ E ♢ 7 5 2     W      N      E      S
♣ 6                │  S  │  ♣ A K J 7 5 3  3 ♠   pass  4 ♠   5 ♢
              ♠ A        └─────┘         all pass
              ♡ A J 4 3
              ♢ A K J 10 6 3
              ♣ Q 8
```

West led the six of clubs to his partner's king. You dropped the queen, but East, the scornful one, was not fooled. He continued with the ace of clubs – and you were home!

East had to play a third round of clubs to prevent the establishment of a club winner in dummy. You ruffed with the ten of diamonds, led a trump to dummy's eight, and returned a heart for a finesse of the jack. After a trump to the nine, you ruffed dummy's last club with the king of diamonds, cashed the aces of spades and hearts, and led the jack of diamonds in this position:

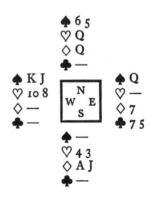

```
        ♠ 6 5
        ♡ Q
        ♢ Q
        ♣ —
♠ K J  ┌─────┐  ♠ Q
♡ 10 8 │  N  │  ♡ —
♢ —   W│     │E ♢ 7
♣ —    │  S  │  ♣ 7 5
        └─────┘
        ♠ —
        ♡ 4 3
        ♢ A J
        ♣ —
```

Caught in a criss-cross ruffing squeeze, West had to surrender.

By cashing the ace of clubs at trick two East played himself into a position where he had to help with your partial dummy reversal.

A player more alive to the danger of allowing you to shorten your trumps might have led a low club for his partner to ruff at trick two. A spade switch by West would then have ensured your defeat.

Do you remember about re-entry squeezes? Then you should have no difficulty with the next hand.

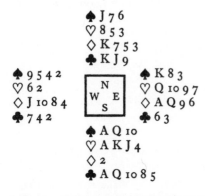

Game all
Dealer West

East opens third in hand with a bid of one heart, and eventually you land in six clubs.

West leads the six of hearts to the three, seven and jack. You have to assume the spade finesse is right, but the twelfth trick is not immediately visible. Since you are not likely to be able to ruff a heart on the table, you have to try reversing the dummy. On your diamond lead West plays the eight, dummy the three and East the nine. You win the trump shift in dummy, ruff a diamond, lead a trump to dummy's jack, ruff the seven of diamonds with the club ace, and lead your last trump to dummy's king.

East is squeezed into parting with a spade, giving you the required re-entry in dummy. Now you finesse the queen of spades, cash the ace, and play the ten of spades to dummy's jack to inflict the red-suit squeeze.

Yes, of course, an initial trump lead would have defeated the contract.

The next example shows clearly that these strategic dummy reversals act as emergency timing devices for squeeze purposes.

Non-Material Dummy Reversals

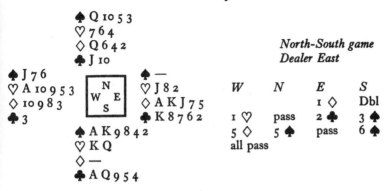

```
              ♠ Q 10 5 3
              ♡ 7 6 4
              ◇ Q 6 4 2            North-South game
              ♣ J 10               Dealer East

♠ J 7 6              ♠ —
♡ A 10 9 5 3   N     ♡ J 8 2       W     N     E     S
◇ 10 9 8 3  W   E    ◇ A K J 7 5                1 ◇   Dbl
♣ 3            S     ♣ K 8 7 6 2   1 ♡   pass  2 ♣   3 ♠
              ♠ A K 9 8 4 2        5 ◇   5 ♠   pass  6 ♠
              ♡ K Q               all pass
              ◇ —
              ♣ A Q 9 5 4
```

West leads the three of clubs and dummy's ten holds the trick. The distribution is clearly marked, so you ruff a diamond, cash the ace of spades, and exit with the king of hearts to West's ace. Winning the spade return in dummy with the ten, you ruff a diamond with the king of spades and cash the queen of hearts. Now the lead of a spade to the queen squeezes East in this position:

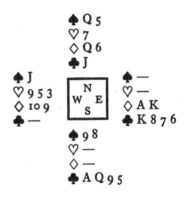

```
              ♠ Q 5
              ♡ 7
              ◇ Q 6
              ♣ J
♠ J              ♠ —
♡ 9 5 3    N     ♡ —
◇ 10 9  W   E    ◇ A K
♣ —        S     ♣ K 8 7 6
              ♠ 9 8
              ♡ —
              ◇ —
              ♣ A Q 9 5
```

If East parts with a diamond honour, you lead the jack of clubs, which he must duck, then ruff out the diamond and discard dummy's heart on the ace of clubs.

This ending, unlike the others we have seen, required you to keep precisely one trump in each hand for post-squeeze operations. If you had ruffed one diamond only in your hand, the count for the squeeze would not have been rectified.

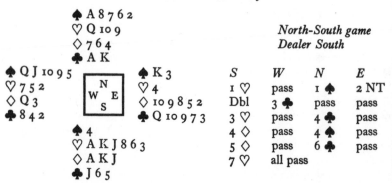

```
              ♠ A 8 7 6 2
              ♡ Q 10 9                    North-South game
              ◇ 7 6 4                     Dealer South
              ♣ A K
  ♠ Q J 10 9 5      ┌─────┐    ♠ K 3        S      W      N      E
  ♡ 7 5 2           │  N  │    ♡ 4          1 ♡    pass   1 ♠    2 NT
  ◇ Q 3           W │     │ E  ◇ 10 9 8 5 2  Dbl    3 ♣    pass   pass
  ♣ 8 4 2           │  S  │    ♣ Q 10 9 7 3  3 ♡    pass   4 ♣    pass
                    └─────┘                 4 ◇    pass   4 ♠    pass
              ♠ 4                           5 ◇    pass   6 ♣    pass
              ♡ A K J 8 6 3                 7 ♡    all pass
              ◇ A K J
              ♣ J 6 5
```

West leads the queen of spades against your grand slam. You win the ace, ruff a spade high, enter dummy with the nine of trumps, and ruff another spade high. East's discard shows that he is certainly 5–5 in the minors. (Long may you be blessed with opponents who go out of their way to reveal their distribution!)

It is clear that you can safely ruff a club in dummy, but then you would have to take the diamond finesse for your thirteenth trick. Having little faith in finesses, you opt for a dummy reversal and a count squeeze instead.

You enter dummy twice in clubs in order to ruff the last two spades high. Then your last trump to dummy's ten produces this position:

The play of the queen of hearts forces East to reveal all. When he comes down to a doubleton diamond, you discard the club jack and play for the drop in diamonds.

East might well have had both minor-suit queens, but as long as he had one of them you were never going to lose your grand slam.

That was a non-material dummy reversal of a different type. By ruffing four spades in your hand you merely recouped the trick lost by your failure to ruff a club in dummy. The gain came from the release of the jack of clubs to act as a menace card.

This final example combines the themes of dummy reversal and strategic throw-in.

```
              ♠ —
              ♡ Q
              ◇ 7 6 4
              ♣ —
  ♠ —              ┌─────┐    ♠ —
  ♡ 7              │  N  │    ♡ —
  ◇ Q 3          W │     │ E  ◇ 10 9 8
  ♣ 8              │  S  │    ♣ Q
                   └─────┘
              ♠ —
              ♡ —
              ◇ A K J
              ♣ J
```

```
          ♠9653
          ♡J 10 3
          ◇7 5 4                    North-South game
          ♣K 7 6                    Dealer East
♠K 10 7         ♠—
♡7 4       N    ♡Q 9 8 6       W      N      E      S
◇Q 8 6 2  W  E  ◇K J 10 9 3                 1 ◇   Dbl
♣Q 9 8 2   S    ♣A 10 5 3      2 ◇   pass   pass   3 ♠
          ♠A Q J 8 4 2         pass  4 ♠    pass   pass
          ♡A K 5 2             Dbl   all pass
          ◇A
          ♣J 4
```

West leads the two of diamonds to the king and ace. Clearly West will have the outstanding trumps, and even if he has a couple of queens as well he doesn't have much of a double. Still, East must surely have the ace of clubs for his opening bid. Obviously, you need to find the heart queen with East. The fourth round of spades will give you access to dummy to take the finesse, but, if the hearts fail to break, you will need to end-play East and force him to lead away from the ace of clubs.

Suppose you start with the ace and queen of spades. West will win and make the least helpful return of the ten of spades. You may then play a fourth spade to reach this position:

You can run the jack of hearts and then ruff a diamond, but the throw-in doesn't work because East has been able to retain an exit card in diamonds.

The problem has to be tackled in a subtler way. Try the effect of leading the *queen* of spades at trick two. Whether West wins immediately or keeps his king for the third round, he is caught in the toils of an invisible

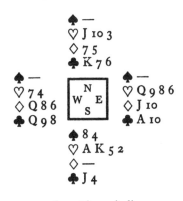

throw-in. A spade return gives you quick access to the table and allows you to ruff the fourth heart in dummy. A heart or a club switch is equally fatal for the defence, so West is forced to help shorten your trumps by returning a diamond. One ruff is all that is needed to adjust the timing of the strip-squeeze.

This is the position when you have entered dummy on the fourth round of trumps.

Now you play the jack of hearts, and it makes no difference whether East covers or not. In either case you can ruff out his last diamond before throwing him in with the fourth heart to lead away from his ace of clubs.

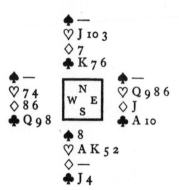

```
            ♠ —
            ♡ J 10 3
            ◇ 7
            ♣ K 7 6
♠ —                    ♠ —
♡ 7 4    ┌───────┐     ♡ Q 9 8 6
◇ 8 6    │   N   │     ◇ J
♣ Q 9 8  │ W   E │     ♣ A 10
         │   S   │
         └───────┘
            ♠ 8
            ♡ A K 5 2
            ◇ —
            ♣ J 4
```

15

It's a Knockout

It soon becomes a matter of routine to consider the possibility of reversing the dummy. Looking at the playing potential of each hand from dummy's viewpoint as well as your own is certainly a useful habit to acquire. You remember a deal where this habit led you to make an exciting discovery.

George was your partner at the time, and George had a lifelong interest which, for a musician, was somewhat unusual. He was a passionate follower of the boxing scene. Whenever there was a fight that did not clash with his concert schedule, he would make reservations and drag you along for a ringside view of the contest. Anyone less accustomed to George's eccentricities would have found it embarrassing to sit beside him as he ducked and weaved in his seat, shouting encouragement or abuse to the gladiators, with his artistic hands (said to be insured for a fabulous sum) balled into fists.

When the fight was over, George would mop his brow and sigh with contentment. 'That feels better,' he would say. 'Now for a quiet game of bridge.'

Not that George's brand of bridge was any less gory. He supported the blood-donor service by having his personal calling cards imprinted with the legend 'Give blood – play bridge.'

Anyway, it was George's obsession with boxing that suggested an apt name for your play on the following hand.

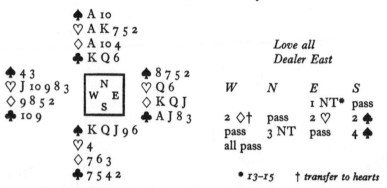

When West led the nine of diamonds and dummy went down, you saw that your cheeky bid of two spades had cut right across partner's intentions. George would have doubled two hearts for a worth-while penalty. Worse, although you had not fancied the trick-taking potential of your hand at no trumps, three no trumps was virtually lay-down.

What about four spades? There were only nine obvious tricks, since the ace of clubs was marked in the East hand. The long club might provide your tenth trick, but there was no guarantee that the suit would break 3–3. Anyway, the first task was to dispose of a diamond loser, so you went up with the ace of diamonds and cashed the top hearts, discarding a diamond from your hand. Then, because you were a dedicated reverser of dummies, you continued with a small heart from the table.

East frowned, hesitated, and finally, to your surprise, played a trump. That made it seem likely that his shape was 4–2–3–4. You over-ruffed and led a club, and your view of the distribution was confirmed when West played the ten. East captured the queen with his ace and returned a trump (he must, to prevent a club ruff in dummy). Keeping the position flexible, you played the king from hand and the ace from dummy. And, since East didn't seem to enjoy the heart lead last time, you tried another heart.

It worked again! East reluctantly discarded another trump. By now you knew beyond doubt that you had East groggy. You over-ruffed with the queen of spades, crossed to the king of clubs, and led dummy's last heart in this position:

What could East do? If he discarded a

```
            ♠ 10
            ♡ 7
            ◇ 10 4
            ♣ 6
♠ 4                      ♠ 8
♡ J          N          ♡ —
◇ 8 5 2   W     E       ◇ K Q
♣ —          S          ♣ J 8
            ♠ J 9
            ♡ —
            ◇ 7
            ♣ 7 5
```

diamond, you would ruff with the jack of spades and duck a diamond. He would have to return his spade to stop you making your trumps separately, but you would score the ten of diamonds as your tenth trick.

If East discarded a club, you would ruff the heart with the nine of spades and exit in clubs. Again East would be unable to defeat you.

In practice East chose to be consistent, discarding his last trump, but that didn't help him. You could then ruff with either trump and exit in either diamonds or clubs. The defenders had no way of preventing you from scoring two further trump tricks.

Well, that was a funny sort of squeeze – a non-material squeeze against 'idle' trump cards, acting through a partial dummy reversal. You hadn't actually the tempo to set up and cash a long club even if East had given up his third guard, but the constant threat of a club ruff in dummy was worth a tempo. East could not have saved himself by discarding differently. If he had let go a club or a diamond at an earlier stage, you would have been able to establish an extra trick in the suit he abandoned.

Would it have worked without the dummy reversal? It looks as though it ought to be all the same whether you *ruff* three hearts or *discard* them on your trumps, but it is not. The threat of completing the dummy reversal is an integral part of your complex of menaces.

George had been watching the play with mounting interest, and at the end he could hardly contain himself.

'It's a knockout! It's a knockout!' he cried excitedly.

Yes, George had a point. By leading hearts three times from dummy you managed, in effect, to hit East three times on the same spot with a left hook. The first blow shook him up, the second turned his legs to jelly and the third knocked him out. It could truly be called a knockout squeeze.

The trumps that East discarded were not really idle cards, of course. They were needed for leading – to extract dummy's trumps and deny you the chance of scoring six trump tricks. When, at the end, East found himself on lead with no trump left, he was powerless to prevent you finishing with a high cross-ruff.

Note, in the diagram position, the neat (and essential) entry-shift facility in trumps. By ruffing high or low according to East's choice of discard you could arrange to have a trump entry in the appropriate hand. If you had left yourself with Q J of trumps instead of J 9, East could have defeated you by throwing a diamond.

Any hint of an entry-shift is a sure sign of a positional squeeze, but these squeezes do not always involve entry-shifting and therefore do not have to be positional. The KO squeeze is, in fact, the general form of the strategic squeeze against 'idle' trump cards, of which the backwash (always, by its very character, anti-positional) is a particular case. We shall see shortly the close relationship that exists between the two types.

We should not leave the last deal without taking a quick look at alternative lines of defence. An initial heart or club lead does not affect the outcome, nor does it make any difference if East holds up his ace on the first round of clubs. An initial trump lead holds you to nine tricks, however. If you play on hearts, East can discard a trump on the third round and, when in with the ace of clubs, play a second trump to neutralize your threats. Well, who would have considered a trump lead on the bidding?

Let us see the knockout squeeze in a more basic form.

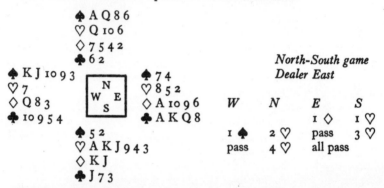

♠ A Q 8 6
♡ Q 10 6
◇ 7 5 4 2
♣ 6 2

♠ K J 10 9 3
♡ 7
◇ Q 8 3
♣ 10 9 5 4

♠ 7 4
♡ 8 5 2
◇ A 10 9 6
♣ A K Q 8

♠ 5 2
♡ A K J 9 4 3
◇ K J
♣ J 7 3

North-South game
Dealer East

W	N	E	S
		1 ◇	1 ♡
1 ♠	2 ♡	pass	3 ♡
pass	4 ♡	all pass	

West misses the killing trump lead, choosing instead to lead the three of diamonds to his partner's ace. It looks as though it doesn't matter, for East returns a trump at trick two and he has the tempo to lead trumps twice more, denying you a club ruff in dummy.

However, the need to return trumps each time puts East in a defensive straitjacket and his chin becomes vulnerable. You win with the ace of hearts, cash the diamond king, lead a spade for a finesse of the queen, ruff a diamond, play a spade to the ace, ruff a spade and concede a club. East cannot afford to play his diamond to wipe out dummy's menace; he has to return a trump. You let this run to the ten, and lead dummy's fourth spade to administer the knockout.

If East discards his diamond, you ruff with the king of hearts, lead the jack to dummy's queen, and enjoy the seven of diamonds. If he parts with a club, you ruff with the jack of hearts and set up a club trick.

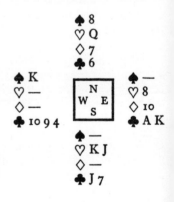

♠ 8
♡ Q
◇ 7
♣ 6

♠ K
♡ —
◇ —
♣ 10 9 4

♠ —
♡ 8
◇ 10
♣ A K

♠ —
♡ K J
◇ —
♣ J 7

And, of course, if East discards his trump on the eight of spades, you are in a position to ruff a club in dummy after all.

It is possible to floor an opponent with this sort of squeeze even when you lack first-round control in trumps.

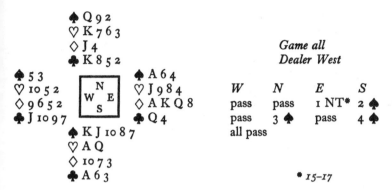

```
            ♠ Q 9 2
            ♡ K 7 6 3
            ◇ J 4                        Game all
            ♣ K 8 5 2                    Dealer West
♠ 5 3              ♠ A 6 4
♡ 10 5 2    ┌─────┐ ♡ J 9 8 4     W     N     E      S
◇ 9 6 5 2   │ N   │ ◇ A K Q 8     pass  pass  1 NT*  2 ♠
♣ J 10 9 7  │W  E │ ♣ Q 4         pass  3 ♣   pass   4 ♠
            │  S  │                pass
            └─────┘                all pass
            ♠ K J 10 8 7
            ♡ A Q
            ◇ 10 7 3
            ♣ A 6 3                       * 15–17
```

West attacks with the jack of clubs, thinking that this may be the winning lead. It isn't. You win with the ace, unblock the heart honours, cross to the king of clubs, discard your club loser on the king of hearts, and then play a small club, hoping for a 3–3 split. No luck! East discards a diamond. So you ruff with the ten of spades and play a diamond to the jack and queen.

East has no option but to return a trump in order to prevent the diamond ruff in dummy. He tries the effect of leading a small trump to dummy's nine, but the play of the fourth club from dummy stretches him on the canvas.

If East discards a trump, he cannot hope to prevent the diamond ruff. If he parts with anything else, you ruff low and exit in diamonds. When East continues with the ace of spades, you can unblock or not depending on where your winner lies

Instead of leading a low trump when in with the queen of diamonds, East might have played the ace and another, but it would have made no difference.

```
                    ♠ Q 2
                    ♡ 7
                    ◇ 4
                    ♣ 8
♠ 5              ┌─────┐  ♠ A 6
♡ —             │ N   │  ♡ J
◇ 9 6 5         │W  E │  ◇ A K
♣ 10            │  S  │  ♣ —
                └─────┘
                    ♠ K J 8
                    ♡ —
                    ◇ 10 7
                    ♣ —
```

He would still have been flattened by the lead of the eight of clubs from dummy.

However, we shall return to that point of defence in a moment. For the meantime it suffices to note that, once again, a trump lead, whether ducked or taken and continued, would have defeated you.

Now watch out for the curve – hairpin bends ahead.

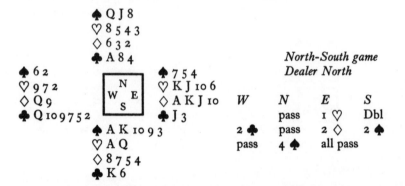

Determined not to muff the defence yet again, West leads a trump this time. Now it seems that the defenders have all the time in the world – even a spare tempo – to prevent the ruff of your fourth diamond in dummy. But you win with dummy's eight of spades, lead a heart for a finesse of the queen, and play the king, ace and another club. Result: an instant knock-out!

Irrespective of East's discard, you plan to ruff the eight of clubs with the king of spades. If East lets go a trump, he cannot prevent the diamond ruff. If he throws a heart, you can easily develop your tenth trick in hearts. And if he parts with a diamond, the play turns into a 'tempo or cross-ruff' dilemma for the defence. East must either let you set up a diamond trick or allow a high cross-ruff.

So it is clear that it does not always take a combination of punches to effect the knockout. A single well-timed blow may suffice.

All right, but where is the bend, the curve? Well, since no entry-adjusting play was needed on this hand, the squeeze ought to work automatically, against West as well as against East. Apparently it does.

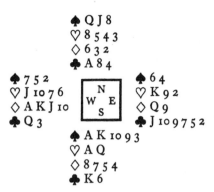

```
            ♠ Q J 8
            ♡ 8 5 4 3
            ◇ 6 3 2
            ♣ A 8 4
♠ 7 5 2              ♠ 6 4
♡ J 10 7 6     N     ♡ K 9 2
◇ A K J 10   W   E   ◇ Q 9
♣ Q 3          S     ♣ J 10 9 7 5 2
            ♠ A K 10 9 3
            ♡ A Q
            ◇ 8 7 5 4
            ♣ K 6
```

Now back to the four spades on page 257. That was a positional squeeze, involving an entry-adjustment or unblocking manoeuvre in trumps, so the squeeze ought to fail if the East and West hands are interchanged. That is correct, but in these situations the defenders can never afford to be careless. Let us see what might happen.

West fails to find the trump lead against your four spades, leading the jack of clubs instead. You win with the ace, unblock the hearts, cross to the club king, discard your losing club

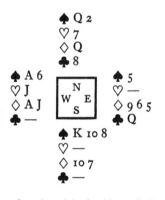

```
          ♠ Q 2
          ♡ 7
          ◇ Q
          ♣ 8
♠ A 6            ♠ 5
♡ J        N    ♡ —
◇ A J   W   E   ◇ 9 6 5
♣ —        S    ♣ Q
          ♠ K 10 8
          ♡ —
          ◇ 10 7
          ♣ —
```

Again you are in four spades instead of the easier three no trumps.

Winning the trump lead with dummy's eight, you take a successful heart finesse and continue with three rounds of clubs, ruffing the third club with the king of spades.

West is squeezed, backwash-wise, because you still haven't committed yourself about the late re-entry in spades.

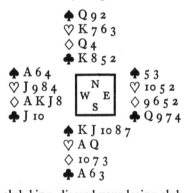

```
            ♠ Q 9 2
            ♡ K 7 6 3
            ◇ Q 4
            ♣ K 8 5 2
♠ A 6 4              ♠ 5 3
♡ J 9 8 4      N     ♡ 10 5 2
◇ A K J 8    W   E   ◇ 9 6 5 2
♣ J 10         S     ♣ Q 9 7 4
            ♠ K J 10 8 7
            ♡ A Q
            ◇ 10 7 3
            ♣ A 6 3
```

on the king of hearts, and ruff a club with the jack of spades. West discards the eight of diamonds, and you concede a diamond to his king.

At this point West must attack trumps to stop your diamond ruff. Suppose he thinks it safe to lead a small trump. You win in dummy with the nine and lead the eight of clubs, and when you ruff with the ten of spades West feels the waters of the backwash swirling around him. However hard he looks, he can find no discard to defeat the contract.

The only successful defence for West, when in with the king of diamonds, is to play the ace and another spade, reducing the position to four cards.

The play of two rounds of spades has the dramatic effect of transforming the squeeze into a positional one. The attempted knockout fails because you have to commit yourself, before West plays, as to which trump you will use to ruff the eight of clubs.

So it is sometimes possible to escape a threatened knockout by attacking the automatic functioning of the squeeze. An understanding of this point can bring rich rewards. The basic defence against the knockout is to take out as many rounds of trumps as possible. This applies even when the only squeeze in sight is a positional one.

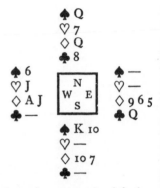

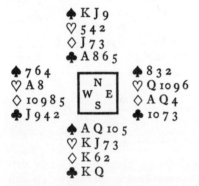

It is not necessary to have great length in trumps before you can set up an opponent for the knockout. The fewer trumps you have, in fact, the less work is needed in the way of reversing the dummy. Try your hand at a 4–3 trump fit.

Three no trumps might have been more sensible but, in a pairs contest, you try for a top by playing in four spades.

West leads the ten of diamonds to the three, four and king. Your first task is to dispose of one of your losing diamonds, so you cash the king and queen of clubs, lead your low spade to the nine, discard a diamond on the ace of clubs, and then lead a heart to the jack and ace.

Now you have them, whether the trump return comes at once or after a diamond to East's queen. You win the trump in dummy with the jack, and when you continue with the eight of clubs East buckles at the knees. No matter what he elects to discard, you have your ten tricks and your top score.

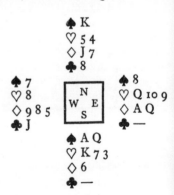

Once again it takes an initial trump lead to defeat four spades on this hand. If West leads a trump, you still have a number of options available. But, no matter what you try, against best defence you cannot quite succeed in squeezing out a tenth trick.

An initial trump lead is not always the right answer in these situations, however, nor is it the only counter-measure available to the defence.

Take the West seat for the next hand and try defending against a similar 4–3 trump fit.

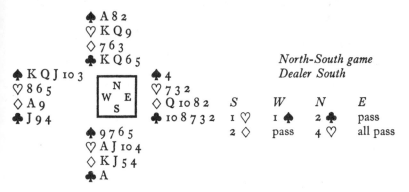

```
              ♠ A 8 2
              ♡ K Q 9
              ◇ 7 6 3
              ♣ K Q 6 5              North-South game
♠ K Q J 10 3        ♠ 4            Dealer South
♡ 8 6 5       N     ♡ 7 3 2
◇ A 9      W     E  ◇ Q 10 8 2    S     W     N     E
♣ J 9 4       S     ♣ 10 8 7 3 2  1 ♡   1 ♠   2 ♣   pass
              ♠ 9 7 6 5           2 ◇   pass  4 ♡   all pass
              ♡ A J 10 4
              ◇ K J 5 4
              ♣ A
```

You are not likely to be tempted to lead a trump this time. That is just as well, for on a trump lead declarer can make his contract. He would win, unblock the ace of clubs, and lead a low diamond to your nine. You would really have to lead a spade at this point, otherwise declarer would simply duck a second diamond to your ace and, after drawing trumps, take the diamond finesse for ten tricks. But South can win the ace of spades, discard two spade losers on the clubs, and exit carefully with a spade. Later he can duck a second diamond to your ace and eventually finesse in diamonds for ten tricks.

You start with the king of spades, however, not because you have thought all this out but because it is your natural lead. Declarer wins with the ace, comes to hand with the ace of clubs, crosses back to the nine of hearts, and discards two spades on dummy's club winners. Now if there is any nonsense about ducking the first diamond to your nine, you can continue with the ace of diamonds and then a low spade for partner to ruff (you know his four was a singleton). A diamond ruff will then give you the setting trick.

Declarer is aware of this danger, and instead of ducking on the first round of diamonds he puts in the jack to force out your ace. It is time to lead trumps, for declarer is threatening to ruff a diamond in dummy, but it may seem harmless enough to cash your spade winner before returning a trump. Harmless? You might as well take a swipe at partner's chin yourself. If you cash your spade, declarer will win your trump continuation in dummy and lead the eight of spades in this position:

You may detect a hint of reproach in partner's eyes before they glaze over.

But you realize in time, of course, that you must not rectify the count for declarer by cashing your spade winner. On winning the ace of diamonds you switch immediately to a trump, and declarer has nowhere to go.

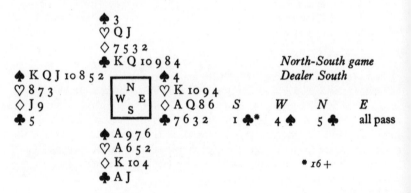

Here is another three-punch knockout – an automatic one this time.

```
                 ♠ 3
                 ♡ Q J
                 ◊ 7 5 3 2
                 ♣ K Q 10 9 8 4          North-South game
  ♠ K Q J 10 8 5 2      ♠ 4                Dealer South
  ♡ 8 7 3       N       ♡ K 10 9 4
  ◊ J 9       W   E     ◊ A Q 8 6     S      W      N      E
  ♣ 5           S       ♣ 7 6 3 2     1 ♣*   4 ♠    5 ♣    all pass
                 ♠ A 9 7 6
                 ♡ A 6 5 2
                 ◊ K 10 4                  * 16 +
                 ♣ A J
```

West leads the king of spades to your ace. Assuming the king of hearts and the ace of diamonds to be right, you still have only ten tricks, and you are short of an entry for a straightforward red-suit squeeze against East. So you decide to see what can be done by reversing the dummy.

You play another spade at trick two and ruff with the king of clubs. *Wham!* East cannot afford to weaken either of his red suits and therefore has to under-ruff. You lead the jack of hearts to the king and ace and continue the treatment by ruffing another spade with the queen of clubs. *Zap!* Again East has to under-ruff, since he can spare neither a heart nor a diamond. Now you lead a diamond to your king and play your fourth spade, ruffing in dummy with the ten of clubs. *Pow!*

The third blow puts East down for the count. If he discards a heart or a diamond, you have no trouble in setting up your eleventh trick in the suit of his discard. And if he parts with yet another club, you end up by ruffing a diamond in your own hand.

Note that in this case the contract is defeated not only by a trump lead but also by a heart or a diamond lead. Yet it seems unnatural for West to lead anything but a spade.

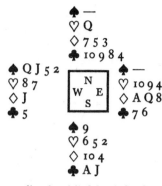

When you are short of an entry to give force to the dummy reversal, you may be able to enlist the aid of the defenders.

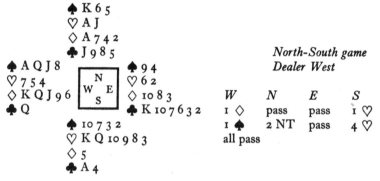

North-South game
Dealer West

W	N	E	S
1 ◇	pass	pass	1 ♡
1 ♠	2 NT	pass	4 ♡
all pass			

On a trump lead you could draw trumps and establish your tenth trick in clubs, but West leads the king of diamonds, inconveniently removing an entry from dummy. Still, you do your best by ruffing a diamond at trick two and then playing the ace and another club. East captures dummy's eight with his ten in this position:

At this point East should consult his booklet, 'Basic Defence Against Knockouts', and return a trump. As the cards lie, even a spade or a diamond return will defeat you. However, East may well consider that his best return is a low club. After all, it kills the potential club winner in dummy and, from

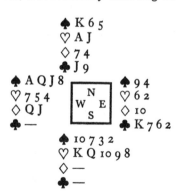

East's point of view, it may even promote a trump in his partner's hand.

What happens now is beyond the expectations of any mortal defender. In forcing you to ruff a club East supplies the missing entry for your dummy reversal, and West is set up for the knockout.

We have already observed that this type of squeeze can function against a defender who holds A x x in trumps. Here is a further example.

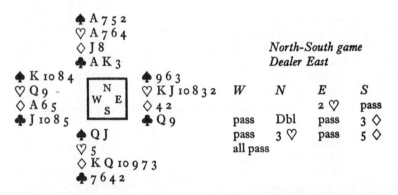

```
          ♠ A 7 5 2
          ♡ A 7 6 4
          ◇ J 8                  North-South game
          ♣ A K 3                Dealer East
♠ K 10 8 4        ♠ 9 6 3
♡ Q 9 -    N      ♡ K J 10 8 3 2   W    N    E    S
◇ A 6 5  W   E    ◇ 4 2                       2♡   pass
♣ J 10 8 5   S    ♣ Q 9          pass  Dbl  pass  3◇
          ♠ Q J                  pass  3♡   pass  5◇
          ♡ 5                     all pass
          ◇ K Q 10 9 7 3
          ♣ 7 6 4 2
```

West leads the queen of hearts to dummy's ace. There are ten tricks in sight, and it is tempting to play on trumps and hope for a simple black-suit squeeze, or perhaps a ruffing squeeze, against West. The trouble with this plan is that it can be defeated by a club switch when West is in with the ace of diamonds and a further club lead when you concede a trick to rectify the count.

So you decide to try for a knockout, leading a heart at trick two and ruffing with the seven of diamonds. You continue with the queen of spades to the king and ace, and ruff another heart with the nine of diamonds. West cannot spare a black card and has therefore to part with a low diamond. Now you cash the jack of spades and lead the three of diamonds.

If West plays low, you will actually be able to complete a material dummy reversal – diamond eight, heart ruff, club to king, spade ruff, club to ace, spade ruff.

If West plays the ace and another trump, you just continue with a third trump to catch him in the ruffing squeeze.

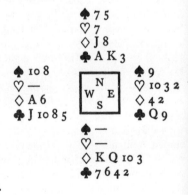

```
          ♠ 7 5
          ♡ 7
          ◇ J 8
          ♣ A K 3
♠ 10 8           ♠ 9
♡ —      N       ♡ 10 3 2
◇ A 6  W   E     ◇ 4 2
♣ J 10 8 5  S    ♣ Q 9
          ♠ —
          ♡ —
          ◇ K Q 10 3
          ♣ 7 6 4 2
```

If West takes the ace of diamonds and returns a spade, you have eleven tricks on a cross-ruff. And finally, if he takes the ace of diamonds and returns a club to dummy's king he is floored when you lead the seven of hearts from dummy and ruff with the queen of diamonds in this position.

The squeeze works automatically because of the extra entry in dummy.

KO technique can also be employed to hammer a defender's hand into shape for an eventual end-play.

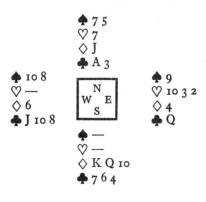

♠ 7 5
♡ 7
◇ J
♣ A 3

♠ 10 8   ♠ 9
♡ —   ♡ 10 3 2
◇ 6   ◇ 4
♣ J 10 8   ♣ Q

♠ —
♡ —
◇ K Q 10
♣ 7 6 4

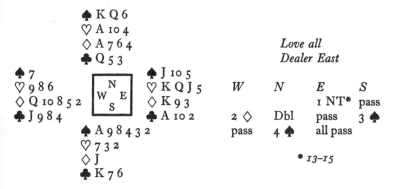

♠ K Q 6
♡ A 10 4
◇ A 7 6 4
♣ Q 5 3

Love all
Dealer East

♠ 7   ♠ J 10 5
♡ 9 8 6   ♡ K Q J 5
◇ Q 10 8 5 2   ◇ K 9 3
♣ J 9 8 4   ♣ A 10 2

♠ A 9 8 4 3 2
♡ 7 3 2
◇ J
♣ K 7 6

W	N	E	S
		1 NT*	pass
2 ◇	Dbl	pass	3 ♠
pass	4 ♠	all pass	

* 13–15

West leads the nine of hearts and is allowed to hold the trick. You win the heart continuation and lead a low club to your king. Now you have nine tricks, assuming there is no trump loser. If the trumps are 2–2 it should be a simple matter to eliminate East's diamonds before throwing him in with the heart to lead away from the ace of clubs. But what if the trumps are 3–1? It is no good hoping to squeeze East by running your trumps. He will discard a club on the last trump, keeping the ace of clubs and two heart winners for the end.

To bring pressure to bear on East you must make him commit himself *before* your last trump is played, and that can be done only by playing on reverse dummy lines. So at trick four you play a diamond to the ace. After a diamond ruff, a spade to the king and another diamond ruff, you

return to dummy with the queen of
spades and lead the fourth diamond in
this position:

What can East do except take it on
the chin? If he throws a heart, you
ruff, draw the last trump and exit
with your heart.

If East throws a club, you ruff and
duck a club at once. After cashing his
heart, East has to yield the last two
tricks in one way or another.

East's remaining option is to play
his trump on the fourth diamond, but
you can over-ruff and exit with your
heart as before.

A similar case:

```
              ♠ 6
              ♡ 10
              ◇ 7
              ♣ Q 5
♠ —                      ♠ J
♡ 6        N             ♡ K Q
◇ Q 10   W   E           ◇ —
♣ J 9      S             ♣ A 10
              ♠ A 9
              ♡ 7
              ◇ —
              ♣ 7 6
```

```
              ♠ A Q 6 5
              ♡ K Q 10
              ◇ 8 6 5
              ♣ J 6 2
♠ K 10 4                 ♠ J 9 8 7 2
♡ 7 6 4       N          ♡ 8
◇ A K 9 3   W   E        ◇ J 10 7 4
♣ K Q 9       S          ♣ 10 8 3
              ♠ 3
              ♡ A J 9 5 3 2
              ◇ Q 2
              ♣ A 7 5 4
```

Game all
Dealer West

W	N	E	S
1 NT*	pass	2 ♡†	Dbl
2 ♠	Dbl	pass	3 ♡
pass	4 ♡	all pass	

* *15–17*   † *transfer to spades*

West cashes the ace and king of diamonds
and switches to a trump. There appear to
be four losers, but by now you know what
to do in these situations. You win with the
ten of hearts, ruff the diamond, finesse the
queen of spades, cash the ace of spades for
a club discard, ruff a spade, cross to the
queen of hearts, and ruff the last spade
with the jack of hearts to administer the
knockout.

If West gives up his exit card in diamonds, you draw the last trump and lead
a low club.

```
              ♠ 6
              ♡ K
              ◇ —
              ♣ J 6 2
♠ —                      ♠ J 9
♡ 7        N             ♡ —
◇ 9      W   E           ◇ J
♣ K Q 9    S             ♣ 10 8
              ♠ —
              ♡ A J
              ◇ —
              ♣ A 7 5
```

[266]

If he throws a club, your answer is to play the ace and another club (or a low club, for that matter) at once.

And if West chooses to under-ruff, a low club again holds him to one trick.

Finally, here is a rather more complex example of a KO strip-squeeze.

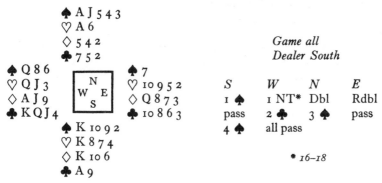

West leads the king of clubs and, when this is allowed to win, continues with the queen of clubs to your ace. A little thought will convince you that the contract is doomed if West has all four trumps. Although you could avoid a trump loser and ruff a club in hand, there would be no conceivable squeeze or end-play for the tenth trick. Fortunately, the bidding seems to mark East with a 1–4–4–4 shape and West with 3–3–3–4. If that is the case, knockout technique may bring about an end-play in diamonds. It should be possible to trim West down to size by ruffing two hearts in dummy.

However, there is a complication. Since it is a *third*-round diamond trick that you hope to establish, you will need to have two trumps left in both hands after the squeeze trick. Otherwise West will be able to slip the punch by throwing a diamond on the fourth heart. So it appears that you can afford to draw only one round of trumps before starting to ruff hearts.

Hang on a moment. Are you sure you can afford even one round of trumps? Clearly it will not do to cash the king, for that card is needed as a later re-entry. Less easy to see, perhaps, is that you cannot afford to play a trump to dummy's jack. If you did that, West would be able to dodge the knockout by ruffing the fourth heart. After over-ruffing with the ace and drawing the outstanding trump with your king, you would be stranded in the wrong hand for the diamond lead. Nor is it much of an improvement to lead the ten or nine of spades at trick three. West can cover with the queen to confront you with the same problem.

You need to be in a position to draw the last trump in *dummy* if West ruffs the fourth heart, and the only way is to start ruffing hearts before touching trumps. So you play off the ace and king of hearts, ruff a heart in dummy, and return to hand with a club ruff (the spade king would do equally well at this stage). Now the play of the fourth heart causes West to lose interest in the proceedings.

If West throws his club, you ruff, draw trumps ending in dummy, and lead a diamond, just covering East's card.

If West parts with a diamond, you ruff, duck a diamond, win the trump return and duck another diamond.

And if West ruffs the heart, you over-ruff, draw his two remaining trumps ending in dummy, and again lose a diamond to West as cheaply as possible.

```
                        ♠ A J 5 4
                        ♡ —
                        ◊ 5 4 2
                        ♣ —
      ♠ Q 8 6                          ♠ 7
      ♡ —          ┌─────────┐         ♡ 10
      ◊ A J 9      │ N       │         ◊ Q 8 7 3
      ♣ 4          │ W   E   │         ♣ 10
                   │   S     │
                   └─────────┘
                        ♠ K 10 9
                        ♡ 8
                        ◊ K 10 6
                        ♣ —
```

You may have noticed that the concontract can be beaten. If West starts with a trump and plays another trump when he regains the lead in clubs, he kills the squeeze simply by taking out too many of your trumps. Well, would you have led a trump from the West hand?

16

The Entry Squeeze Revisited

The sky was as blue as ever but the sun no longer held the same warmth. A certain sharpness in the breeze served as a reminder that the change of seasons could not be held at bay indefinitely. With Alec at the helm, you were beating back across the big lake, heading towards your home port, where you would reluctantly catch a train to the city and Alec would see the *Cormorant* safely berthed at her winter moorings.

The adventures are nearly over and it will soon be time for farewells, but there is still one call to be made. Early in our travels, in Chapter 3, we examined ways of squeezing out cards that were disrupting our entries. Now, on the last leg of our journey, we are returning for a further look at this territory.

Sometimes a squeeze that combines elements of both entry and long-card threats can be used to prepare for a throw-in ending.

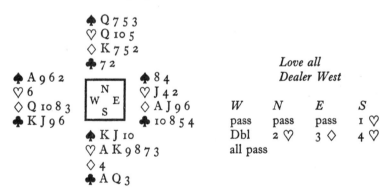

```
              ♠ Q 7 5 3
              ♡ Q 10 5
              ◇ K 7 5 2
              ♣ 7 2
♠ A 9 6 2              ♠ 8 4
♡ 6          ┌─────┐   ♡ J 4 2
◇ Q 10 8 3   │ N   │   ◇ A J 9 6
♣ K J 9 6    │W   E│   ♣ 10 8 5 4
             │  S  │
             └─────┘
              ♠ K J 10
              ♡ A K 9 8 7 3
              ◇ 4
              ♣ A Q 3
```

Love all
Dealer West

W	N	E	S
pass	pass	pass	1 ♡
Dbl	2 ♡	3 ◇	4 ♡
all pass			

West leads the three of diamonds, and you put up the king in order to make a diamond continuation possible. On winning the ace, however, East shifts to the eight of spades, and West allows your king to win the trick. You test the trumps with the ace and queen but, as expected, West shows out on the second round, discarding a club. It looks like another game biting the dust, since West is marked with the club king. If you draw trumps you can't ruff a club in dummy, nor can you score dummy's fourth spade for a discard. Yet if you try to ruff a club in dummy, East will score a spade ruff as the setting trick.

Well, you can't just sit there; you have to do something. What would Uncle Tim do? He'd run his trumps and hope that someone got squeezed. Maybe that's the right way to play hands like this.

When you lead the fifth heart, West comes under a bit of pressure. One possible position:

You know that West started with a 4–1–4–4 pattern and the club king. Let's help him with his discard. Throwing another spade clearly amounts to throwing in the towel. If West throws a club you can – careful, don't rush to set up that club trick or you'll lose control – play the jack of spades, forcing West to gnash his teeth while he executes his hold-up play, *then* set up your queen of clubs for the tenth trick. So West has to part with a diamond. You now play the spade jack. West must duck to deny you

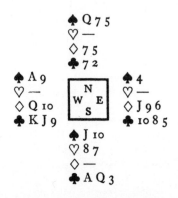

a third-round spade entry, but you overtake with the queen of spades and ruff a diamond to remove West's last exit card. A spade lead then puts him in to lead away from his club king. What fun!

Perhaps you think that West's difficulties stemmed from his failure to keep all his spades – that is what made it necessary for him to hold up in the suit later on. If, instead of keeping 2–0–2–3 as in the diagram, West keeps 3–0–1–3 (3–0–2–2 is obviously bad – with two trumps left you have time to set up a trick in both spades and clubs), what can he throw on the fifth trump? Not a spade – that gets him back into one of the previous variations. Not a club either – you can play the ace and a low club and wind up with a spade trick at the end, since West will run out of diamonds. So it must be a diamond, leaving West with 3–0–0–3. You can now amuse yourself by leading your last trump, and West is helpless.

It would be no more effective for West to play the ace and another spade at tricks two and three. In the six-card ending West would be forced to keep 2–0–1–3, and he would have no good discard when the penultimate trump was led.

Could it be that Uncle Tim knew something we didn't? Well, we know it now.

The next deal shows more clearly a squeeze against 'idle' cards to create a specific entry.

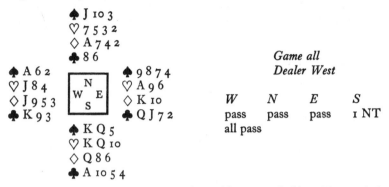

♠ J 10 3
♡ 7 5 3 2
◇ A 7 4 2
♣ 8 6

♠ A 6 2
♡ J 8 4
◇ J 9 5 3
♣ K 9 3

♠ 9 8 7 4
♡ A 9 6
◇ K 10
♣ Q J 7 2

♠ K Q 5
♡ K Q 10
◇ Q 8 6
♣ A 10 5 4

Game all
Dealer West

W	N	E	S
pass	pass	pass	1 NT
all pass			

West leads the three of diamonds to his partner's king. East switches to the two of clubs, and the nine wins the trick when you play low. You duck the continuation of the king of clubs but win the third club with the ace.

The lead from a weak four-card minor suggests not only that West holds 3-3-4-3 distribution but also that he lacked a safe lead in a major suit. Since it is unlikely that West holds both missing aces, you may decide that the position is now:

The lead of the club ten, a losing squeeze card, catches West in an entry squeeze. He must throw a spade, yielding a second entry to dummy which you can use to lead through East's ace of hearts.

However, you must still play with care. East wins the club and returns a spade to your king. West holds off, wins the queen of spades continuation, and leads a diamond. Winning in dummy, you lead a heart to your king. Now you cannot afford to lead a spade to the jack,

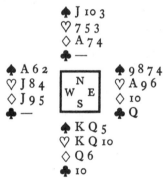

♠ J 10 3
♡ 7 5 3
◇ A 7 4
♣ —

♠ A 6 2
♡ J 8 4
◇ J 9 5
♣ —

♠ 9 8 7 4
♡ A 9 6
◇ 10
♣ Q

♠ K Q 5
♡ K Q 10
◇ Q 6
♣ 10

for that would set up a spade trick for East. First you must cash the queen of diamonds, squeezing East this time in a non-material way and completing a compound invisible squeeze. If East throws a heart, you can set up a heart trick immediately. If East throws a spade, you can safely enter dummy with the jack of spades and lead a heart towards the queen to establish your seventh trick.

Note that on the squeeze trick, after West throws a spade, your discard from dummy must be a diamond, a menace that has served faithfully but can now depart. If a heart is thrown from dummy, the later squeeze against East does not function for East will throw a heart on the queen of diamonds and the defenders will make seven tricks.

As an alternative to giving an extra entry, the squeezee may have the choice of exposing himself to a throw-in. The forced lead then supplies the missing entry. These situations are not hard to recognize in practical play.

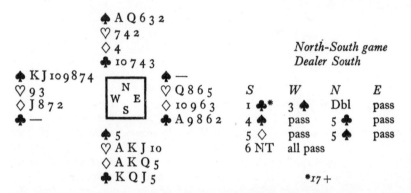

```
                 ♠ A Q 6 3 2
                 ♡ 7 4 2
                 ◇ 4                       North-South game
                 ♣ 10 7 4 3                Dealer South
 ♠ K J 10 9 8 7 4
 ♡ 9 3                ♠ —
 ◇ J 8 7 2            ♡ Q 8 6 5    S      W      N      E
 ♣ —                  ◇ 10 9 6 3   1 ♣*   3 ♠    Dbl    pass
                      ♣ A 9 8 6 2  4 ♠    pass   5 ♣    pass
                 ♠ 5              5 ◇    pass   5 ♠    pass
                 ♡ A K J 10       6 NT   all pass
                 ◇ A K Q 5
                 ♣ K Q J 5                *17 +
```

West leads the jack of spades, and when dummy goes down you see that there is nothing to spare. Six no trumps is not the greatest of contracts, to be sure, but three clubs, three diamonds, four hearts and two spades will see you home. You put in the queen of spades and East discards a club. How should you continue?

The problem is that you may need to lead twice from dummy to pick up the hearts, and East may be able to deny you re-entry to the table in clubs. The club discard, in fact, is a good indication that this is East's five-card suit, and you can be thankful that you avoided playing in six clubs.

If East has an 0–4–4–5 shape, however, there is a simple way of applying pressure. Just continue with the ace of spades at trick two, discarding the small diamond from hand. East is stuck. A heart discard means that you need finesse only once in hearts. A club discard enables you to finesse in hearts, then play high clubs from hand to gain re-entry for a further finesse. So East will probably choose to let a diamond go, but that does not save him. You finesse in hearts and play the king, queen and jack of clubs. When East holds off, you cash your diamond winners and throw him in with the ace of clubs for a heart return.

This may be termed an 'indirect' entry squeeze since all East had to give up was a strategic value – the exit card in diamonds that would have enabled him to avoid the throw-in. In the 'direct' entry squeezes the defender has to choose between conceding the extra entry and suffering immediate material loss.

There are certain situations in which an entry squeeze can act as the first stage of a progressive squeeze. These endings are in a different category because the existence of a two-winner threat is necessary for their success. Here is an example.

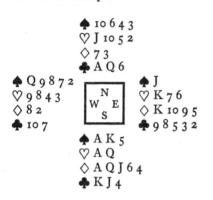

West leads a spade against South's contract of six no trumps.

Declarer wins with the ace and continues with the king and five of spades. West cannot afford to duck, for the ten of spades would provide a third entry for a red-suit finesse and South would lose only a diamond. So West takes his queen and returns a club (as good as anything). South plays the queen *and the jack* of clubs on this trick, then cashes dummy's ten of spades.

At this point East, who has thrown clubs on the second and third spades, is in the grip of an entry squeeze. If he throws a heart, declarer makes four heart tricks (note the two-trick gain) and thus needs only two diamonds. If East throws a diamond, South discards the queen of hearts and makes five diamonds (another two-trick gain) by finessing twice against East.

The position at trick five is shown in this diagram.

East's only remaining option is to give up the entry directly by discarding a third club. This strategic loss is inevitably transformed into a material loss. South discards a diamond, takes a red-suit finesse, re-enters dummy by overtaking the club king with the ace, takes a finesse in the other red suit and cashes the ace of hearts. He then enters dummy for the last time

```
                ♠ 10
                ♡ J 10 5 2
                ◇ 7 3
                ♣ A 6
  ♠ 9 8                      ♠ —
  ♡ 9 8 4 3      N           ♡ K 7 6
  ◇ 8 2       W     E        ◇ K 10 9 5
  ♣ 7            S           ♣ 9 8
                ♠ —
                ♡ A Q
                ◇ A Q J 6 4
                ♣ K 4
```

with the club six, squeezing East in hearts and diamonds in the process. So, on the ten of spades East has to choose between giving up two tricks directly in one of the red suits, and giving up an entry that is worth one trick directly (by allowing declarer to take a third red-suit finesse) plus one trick at the tail-end of the progressive squeeze.

It is only to be expected that squeezes that depend on such delicate mechanism can often be successfully defended. This contract provides opportunities for both standard and non-standard defences. If West leads a diamond at trick one and continues with another diamond when in with the queen of spades, he destroys the entries for any squeeze against East. The diamond leads create one additional trick for declarer, but one trick is not enough.

The non-standard defence, remarkably, is the one that was so effective against the entry-shifting squeezes. Who would have believed that the double one-suit squeeze could have such wide-spread application? Yet here we see it again. If West leads a club, the best that South can do is to win, unblock, and take the heart finesse. (If instead South takes a diamond finesse, West can lead another diamond when in with the spade queen – the standard defence.) Now, three rounds of spades. West wins and leads another club, squeezing the North and South hands in clubs. Declarer is forced to destroy his own entry-creating position prematurely.

Another triple entry squeeze:

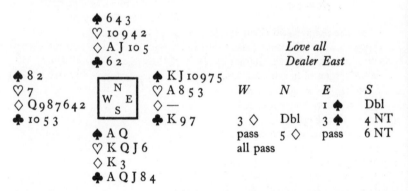

```
              ♠ 6 4 3
              ♡ 10 9 4 2
              ◇ A J 10 5          Love all
              ♣ 6 2               Dealer East
♠ 8 2                   ♠ K J 10 9 7 5
♡ 7            N        ♡ A 8 5 3      W    N    E    S
◇ Q 9 8 7 6 4 2  W  E   ◇ —                      1 ♠  Dbl
♣ 10 5 3          S     ♣ K 9 7        3 ◇  Dbl  3 ♠  4 NT
              ♠ A Q                    pass 5 ◇  pass 6 NT
              ♡ K Q J 6               all pass
              ◇ K 3
              ♣ A Q J 8 4
```

West leads the eight of spades to your queen. You try the king of hearts and then the queen. West discards a diamond on the second round, and East holds up again to deny you an entry to dummy. How should you continue?

You know that East has four hearts and at least six spades. Presumably he is void in diamonds, but you cannot be sure whether his shape is 7–4–0–2 or 6–4–0–3. Fortunately there is a plan that caters for both possibilities. You continue with the jack of hearts, forcing East to hold up again. (If he does not, you will use the heart ten to take a club finesse, then cash the ace of spades. For his last six cards, West will have to keep four diamonds and therefore only two clubs. So, after taking three diamonds, you will be able to run the clubs no matter how they were divided originally.)

After winning the heart jack (on which West throws another diamond) you cash the ace of spades. The purpose of this play is to clarify the spade count. If East turns out to have 7–4–0–2 you will cash the diamond king, finesse the diamond ten, finesse the club jack, cash the club ace (dropping East's king), and continue with the queen and another club, forcing West to lead into the entryless diamond tenace.

In practice West follows to the second spade, and you now presume that East started with 6–4–0–3. Your next move is to lead the three of diamonds. If West plays low, you will steal an extra entry to dummy by finessing the ten. This will enable you to bring in the club suit with the aid of two finesses.

But West is wide awake and plays the queen of diamonds on your three. That's why you couldn't afford to try the entry-stealing play earlier. Now you have a little surprise up your sleeve for West – you allow his queen of diamonds to hold the trick! Since a club return would be fatal, West has to lead another diamond in this position:

You go up with the ace and continue diamonds, East throwing two spades and you a heart. On the last diamond East is progressively squeezed. If he throws a club, the suit will run after one finesse. If he unguards one of the major suits, the play of the new winner from dummy will squeeze him again.

There was no defence on the last

```
                    ♠ 6
                    ♡ 10
                    ◇ A J 10
                    ♣ 6 2
     ♠ —                        ♠ K J 10
     ♡ —          N             ♡ A
     ◇ 9 8 7 6  W   E           ◇ —
     ♣ 10 5 3       S           ♣ K 9 7
                    ♠ —
                    ♡ 6
                    ◇ K
                    ♣ A Q J 8 4
```

hand, for West was caught in a four-suit invisible throw-in and had to help you with his opening lead. Three-suit entry squeezes are tricky things to defend at the best of times. Take the East seat on the next hand and see if you can defeat a cheeky three no trumps.

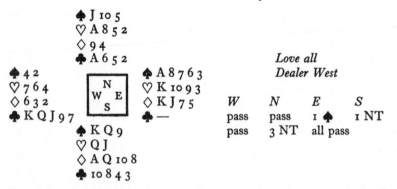

♠ J 10 5
♡ A 8 5 2
◇ 9 4
♣ A 6 5 2

♠ 4 2
♡ 7 6 4
◇ 6 3 2
♣ K Q J 9 7

♠ A 8 7 6 3
♡ K 10 9 3
◇ K J 7 5
♣ —

♠ K Q 9
♡ Q J
◇ A Q 10 8
♣ 10 8 4 3

Love all
Dealer West

W	N	E	S
pass	pass	1 ♠	1 NT
pass	3 NT	all pass	

West leads the king of clubs which is allowed to hold the trick. You discard the three of spades, and West switches to a heart. When dummy plays low, you take the king and return the three of hearts to the queen. Next comes the king of spades. You hold off, and South continues with the queen of spades. What do you do?

It seems reasonable to hold up again to deny South an extra entry to dummy, but, if you do, the menaces against you will extend to three suits. Declarer's next move will be to duck a club, leaving West on lead in this position:

If West returns a heart, South will take the ace, discarding a club from hand, finesse in diamonds, and play the ace of clubs to catch you in a triple squeeze without the count. The same fate is in store for you if West returns a diamond. And on a club return, South will duck again, after which the ace of clubs will inflict an instant triple squeeze.

There is no need to deny South

♠ J
♡ A 8
◇ 9 4
♣ A 6

♠ —
♡ 6
◇ 6 3 2
♣ Q J 9

♠ A
♡ 10 9
◇ K J 7 5
♣ —

♠ 9
♡ —
◇ A Q 10 8
♣ 10 8

a spade entry to dummy, for three diamond tricks are not enough for him. Just take the ace of spades on the second round and return the suit to defeat the contract.

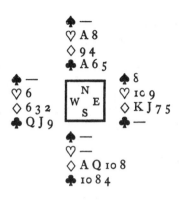

If declarer takes a diamond finesse before ducking a club to West, a diamond return cuts off the closed hand forever.

If South ducks the club before touching diamonds, West will return a club to the ace and you can safely discard a diamond.

These hands are all a matter of timing. Suppose that, instead of switching to hearts at trick two, West leads a diamond, aiming to cut the diamond link between North and South. It looks a promising line of defence, but you have to be very careful. South wins and runs the queen of hearts, playing the five from dummy, and you have to win with the king in this position:

Now if you continue with a second diamond, declarer will change his tack and end-play you. Winning the diamond, he will cash the jack of hearts, unblocking dummy's eight, and lead the king of spades, which you must duck. (If you win and return a spade to the nine and ten, South cashes the club ace to squeeze out your second-last spade. He then discards his queen of spades on the ace of hearts, cashes the spade jack and throws you in with the heart.) When the

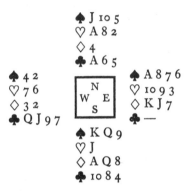

king of spades wins, South continues with a club to the ace to force a spade discard from you. Then comes the jack of spades from the table. If you play the ace, South throws the queen, if you play low South plays the nine, and in either case you are eventually thrown in with the fourth heart to concede two more diamond tricks and the contract.

A second diamond lead would therefore be overdoing things. Just return a heart at trick four and you have an answer to whatever declarer may try.

Let us see if we can find the purest form of entry squeeze.

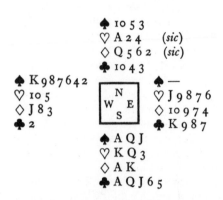

♠ 10 5 3
♡ A 2 4　(*sic*)
◇ Q 5 6 2　(*sic*)
♣ 10 4 3

♠ K 9 8 7 6 4 2
♡ 10 5
◇ J 8 3
♣ 2

♠ —
♡ J 9 8 7 6
◇ 10 9 7 4
♣ K 9 8 7

♠ A Q J
♡ K Q 3
◇ A K
♣ A Q J 6 5

Sitting South, you stagger into six no trumps after West has pre-empted in spades.

West leads the ten of hearts, you mumble 'low', and North picks up the four of hearts from his ill-arranged dummy.

But East is a legal eagle. 'You have to play the deuce,' he tells North firmly. 'Director!'

Fortunately the director is busy. While you await his arrival you have time to reflect. Assuming the club finesse to be right, you will have at least eleven tricks after giving up a trick to the king of spades. And if the clubs are not 3–2 you should be able to squeeze East in the minors for the twelfth trick. Suddenly you see the flaw in this reasoning; your own hand will be squeezed in clubs!

Suppose you play the ace and queen of spades. West wins and plays another heart to your queen. You cash your winners in spades and diamonds, then lead a heart to the ace, squeezing East. But East gives up his diamond guard, leaving:

◇ Q 6
♣ 10 4 3

immaterial

◇ 10
♣ K 9 8 7

◇ —
♣ A Q J 6 5

You now have four diamond tricks instead of three, but you cannot score three club tricks after cashing the diamonds. If you reduce to A Q J in clubs, you cannot retain the lead in dummy with the ten, and if you come down to A Q 6 in clubs East covers the ten.

Is there no way of overcoming this obstruction? Oh, yes. Years ago there was a deal that you bungled. The pain, as always, brings it back.

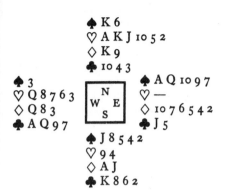

West opened one heart and East responded one spade. North later entered the auction, and you, South, became declarer at three no trumps.

The opening lead was the three of spades. East took two spade tricks (West throwing the three of diamonds) and switched to the club jack, covered by the king and ace. West continued with the queen and seven of clubs, nailing you in dummy.

You were forced to use your only entry at once, so you led the nine of diamonds to your ace and continued with the jack of spades to squeeze West. When he discarded the queen of diamonds you jettisoned the king from dummy, but it didn't help. On the jack of diamonds West gave up his club stopper. Then, when you cashed the good club, he came down to Q 8 7 6 of hearts, and dummy could not discard effectively from A K J 10 5.

At five o'clock the following morning you awakened with the agony of knowing you had missed the winning line. You had to lead the *king* of diamonds to your ace. This sacrifices an immediate trick in diamonds, but it extends the squeeze to a third suit so that the trick comes back with interest.

This is the position when you lead the jack of spades. West cannot throw a heart, for that allows you to discard the diamond and run the nine of hearts. If he throws his club, you discard a heart from dummy and cash your club, repeating the position.

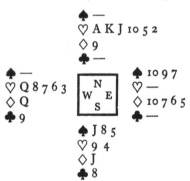

If West ever gives up the queen of diamonds, the jack of diamonds becomes not only a trick but also an entry. And with an extra entry in your hand you can take a preliminary heart finesse, avoiding the one-suit squeeze against dummy. West has no effective defence.

The key to that deal became less mysterious after you had played this one.

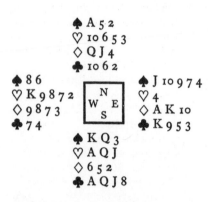

You reached three no trumps after East had opened with one spade.

Spurning his partner's suit, West led the nine of diamonds to the jack and king. East returned his heart to the queen and king, and West played another diamond. East took his diamond winners to make it four tricks for the defence. You were left with nine winners – three spades, three hearts, and three clubs with the aid of the finesse. But the one-suit squeeze threatened. Since dummy had only one entry, you would have to cash the heart ten before playing clubs – and you would be squeezed in clubs on that trick.

Could you do anything about it? You could and did. With the shame of your failure on the previous deal spurring you on, you won East's spade return with the queen and cashed the ace and jack of hearts, forcing East to give up two spades (a club discard would be immediately fatal, since you could then score four club tricks by leading the ten from dummy).

Now the master stroke you missed before – the king of spades to dummy's ace! When you continued with the ten of hearts East was entry-squeezed. If he had thrown a club, you would have discarded your spade and picked up the clubs by running the ten. In practice East threw his spade. You pitched the

```
              ♠ A 5
              ♡ 10
              ◇ —
              ♣ 10 6 2
    ♠ 8               ♠ 10 9
    ♡ 9 8      N      ♡ —
    ◇ 7     W     E   ◇ —
    ♣ 7 4      S      ♣ K 9 5 3
              ♠ K 3
              ♡ —
              ◇ —
              ♣ A Q J 8
```

eight of clubs, finessed in clubs, led the three of spades to dummy's five, and took another club finesse for your contract.

Note that this squeeze does not gain a trick. It gains only an entry, and is therefore a pure entry squeeze.

Meanwhile, back in the tournament. . . .

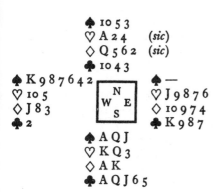

♠ 10 5 3
♡ A 2 4   (*sic*)
◊ Q 5 6 2   (*sic*)
♣ 10 4 3

♠ K 9 8 7 6 4 2
♡ 10 5
◊ J 8 3
♣ 2

♠ —
♡ J 9 8 7 6
◊ 10 9 7 4
♣ K 9 8 7

♠ A Q J
♡ K Q 3
◊ A K
♣ A Q J 6 5

The director has finally arrived and confirms the truth of East's assertion. Dummy must play the two of hearts. Your attention has finally arrived also. You say 'Thank you!' to East and mean it. By now you know that even an attack on the entry suit (usually the best defence in these situations) will not be enough to stop the squeeze if West cannot guard the third round of hearts.

You win the queen of hearts, unblock the diamonds, and play the ace and queen of spades. West cannot afford to hold off (you would simply concede a club), so he wins and continues with the five of hearts.

You play the ace *and* the king on this trick, discard your jack of spades on the queen of diamonds, and lead the spade ten from dummy in this position:

That four of hearts, so nearly squandered at trick one, is the biggest little card East is ever going to see.

Is this overtaking play a Vienna Coup? It is certainly a close relation, using the same unblocking technique to establish a menace against a defender. A normal Vienna Coup, however, does not establish cards that were previously idle. Perhaps this can fairly be called an 'Invisible Vienna Coup Entry Squeeze'.

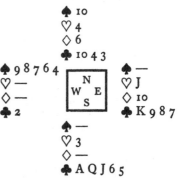

♠ 10
♡ 4
◊ 6
♣ 10 4 3

♠ 9 8 7 6 4
♡ —
◊ —
♣ 2

♠ —
♡ J
◊ 10
♣ K 9 8 7

♠ —
♡ 3
◊ —
♣ A Q J 6 5

In the three no trump contract where dummy had A K J 10 x x in hearts, the entry squeeze was not pure because, having only eight tricks, declarer needed a trick from a squeeze anyway. He needed a trick *plus* an entry. The defenders could have prevailed against that contract in a number of ways – by refusing to rectify the count, for instance, or by attacking the entry suit (diamonds).

Such is not the case on this hand.

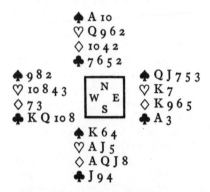

```
            ♠ A 10
            ♡ Q 9 6 2
            ◇ 10 4 2
            ♣ 7 6 5 2
♠ 9 8 2                    ♠ Q J 7 5 3
♡ 10 8 4 3      N          ♡ K 7
◇ 7 3        W   E         ◇ K 9 6 5
♣ K Q 10 8      S          ♣ A 3
            ♠ K 6 4
            ♡ A J 5
            ◇ A Q J 8
            ♣ J 9 4
```

South became declarer at three no trumps after East had opened one spade.

West led the club king, and East overtook with the ace to avoid a blockage. West won the club return and took a third club, but hesitated about cashing the fourth club. Might it not squeeze his partner?

West decided to cash it, and eventually it did squeeze his partner. South threw a spade on the fourth club, and on the spade switch played both dummy's ace and his own king. Then he finessed in hearts and ran four heart tricks, entry-squeezing East in spades and diamonds.

It would not have helped the defence if West had kept his fourth club. The count for the squeeze against East would not have been rectified, but that doesn't matter because a pure entry squeeze gains an entry, not a trick. The only reason an extra entry was needed was because of the threat of a one-suit squeeze in diamonds against South. If West cashes only three clubs, declarer simply takes his nine top tricks.

There is no reason why a pure Vienna Coup entry squeeze should not be executed by the defenders. The opportunity

```
            ♠ 10
            ♡ Q
            ◇ 10 4 2
            ♣ —
♠ 8 2                     ♠ Q
♡ 10          N           ♡ —
◇ 7 3      W   E          ◇ K 9 6 5
♣ —           S          ♣ —
            ♠ 6
            ♡ —
            ◇ A Q J 8
            ♣ —
```

may arise in the most ordinary of contracts. You are East on the next hand.

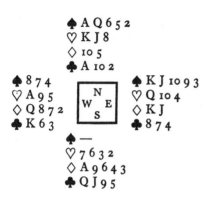

♠ A Q 6 5 2
♡ K J 8
◇ 10 5
♣ A 10 2

♠ 8 7 4
♡ A 9 5
◇ Q 8 7 2
♣ K 6 3

♠ K J 10 9 3
♡ Q 10 4
◇ K J
♣ 8 7 4

♠ —
♡ 7 6 3 2
◇ A 9 6 4 3
♣ Q J 9 5

Game all
Dealer East

In a pairs game, after three passes, North opens one spade. South responds one no trump, which is passed round to you. Needing a top and not fancying your chances without a spade lead, you hazard a double. No-one has any more to say, and partner duly leads the eight of spades.

Declarer does well by going up with the ace of spades, and you counter by unblocking the nine. Discarding a heart from hand, South leads the five of diamonds to the king and ace, then runs the queen of clubs, pitching the ten from dummy. West has to play low again on the next play of the jack of clubs, and declarer switches to hearts in this position:

West plays low, the king is put up in dummy, and your moment of truth has arrived.

If you part with that precious four of hearts, the defence is finished. Declarer will cash the ace of clubs and exit in one of the red suits, and you will have no way of defeating the contract. Although you appear to have seven tricks, that nasty old one-suit squeeze will prevent you from enjoying the queen of diamonds *and* three spade tricks.

There is no chance unless partner

♠ Q 6 5 2
♡ K J 8
◇ 10
♣ A

♠ 7 4
♡ A 9 5
◇ Q 8 7
♣ K

♠ K J 10 3
♡ Q 10 4
◇ J
♣ 8

♠ —
♡ 7 6 3
◇ 9 6 4 3
♣ 9 5

has the nine of hearts, so you jettison the queen of hearts under dummy's king. Now you have an answer to anything declarer may attempt. If, after cashing the ace of clubs, he exits with a diamond to your jack, for instance, you play the ten of hearts to partner's ace and dummy is entry-squeezed when the queen of diamonds is cashed.

Technically, it suffices to play your ten of hearts under dummy's king, but then partner would have to overtake your later lead of the heart queen. No doubt he would do so, magnificent player that he is, but no partner should be subjected to unnecessary pressure of this kind.

A lot of funny things can happen when it is an entry you need rather than a trick. You still remember the quick surge of electric excitement that you experienced as a boy when you first discovered that the term 'favourably placed' could be interpreted in more ways than one.

Great-Aunt Clara, having lectured you on finessing for several weeks on end, at last gave permission for Aunt Alice to tell you about *her* hand.

'Pay attention, boy,' began Alice. 'Suppose you have queen doubleton in dummy and ace, jack doubleton in your own hand. Where do you want the king to be?'

'Why, on my right, of course,' you replied, surprised that she should ask such an obvious question.

'Yet you may be a trick better off if the king is on your left.'

The claim took your breath away for a moment. If it were true, you thought, card players must inhabit a strange topsy-turvy sort of world.

'In China,' hissed Uncle Tim behind his hand, 'where they play their cards anti-clockwise.'

'Not in China.' Aunt Alice's eyes twinkled at your bewilderment. 'Here, I'll show you,' she said, and proceeded to set out her 'Alice-in-Wonderland' deal.

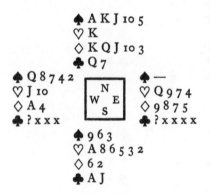

♠ A K J 10 5
♡ K
◇ K Q J 10 3
♣ Q 7

♠ Q 8 7 4 2
♡ J 10
◇ A 4
♣ ? x x x

♠ —
♡ Q 9 7 4
◇ 9 8 7 5
♣ ? x x x x

♠ 9 6 3
♡ A 8 6 5 3 2
◇ 6 2
♣ A J

West leads the jack of hearts against your contract of six no trumps. You win the king, cash the ace of spades, and play a diamond honour. West takes his ace and returns the suit.

Well, where do you want the king of clubs to be? If East holds it, you appear to have twelve tricks – four spades (by leading the nine), four diamonds, two hearts and two clubs. However, you cannot gather those twelve tricks because East will deny you two entries in clubs (not covering if you lead the queen, but putting up the king if you lead the seven). It's that dastardly one-suit squeeze again. No matter what you discard from dummy on the ace of hearts, you will be unable to run three more spade tricks.

So you must change your tack and play for the king of clubs to be 'favourably placed' – with *West*. Finish dummy's diamonds and lead the queen of clubs to your ace, hoping for this ending:

On the play of the ace of hearts West cannot discard a spade, for then you throw dummy's club and lead the nine of spades. And when West discards the king of clubs you throw the small spade, finesse in spades, return to the jack of clubs and finesse again.

And there we have the ultimate paradox – the slam is cold with the king of clubs offside and impossible with it onside.

```
                    ♠ K J 10 5
                    ♡ —
                    ♢ —
                    ♣ 7
♠ Q 8 7 4      ┌─────────┐      ♠ —
♡ —            │   N     │      ♡ Q 9
♢ —            │ W   E   │      ♢ —
♣ K            │   S     │      ♣ 10 9 5
               └─────────┘
                    ♠ 9 6
                    ♡ A 8
                    ♢ —
                    ♣ J
```

We appear to have come full circle. Our course has been erratic at times and our voyage has taken us to many strange shores, but now we are back in familiar waters, heading for home. We only hope that those who have shared our adventures have learned something new about this fascinating game of ours. *We* certainly have.

The *Cormorant* moves steadily towards harbour, the last magnificent sunset fading astern as the lights begin to come on along the waterfront. You sail past the ruined fort, past the old monastery on the hill, past the piers and jetties of the ferry terminal, past villas, casinos, country clubs, where enviable, carefree bridge players are cheerfully mangling their dummies – like Uncle Tim and millions of sensible people around the world, whose wisdom in enjoying the game as a casual, effortless and salutary form of relaxation can safely be praised here, without fear of embarrassment, for they will not have reached this page of the book.